Battling Terrorism
in the
Horn of Africa

See also: Menkhaus, (2002)
The Journal of Conflict Studies
„Quasi-States, Nation-Building,
and Terrorist Safe Havens"
p. 7 - 23

OTHER WORLD PEACE FOUNDATION BOOKS
BY ROBERT I. ROTBERG

State Failure and State Weakness in a Time of Terror
(2003)

Ending Autocracy, Enabling Democracy:
The Tribulations of Southern Africa 1960–2000
(2002)

Peacekeeping and Peace Enforcement in Africa:
Methods of Conflict Prevention
(2000)

Creating Peace in Sri Lanka: Civil War and Reconciliation
(1999)

Burma: Prospects for a Democratic Future
(1998)

War and Peace in Southern Africa: Crimes, Drugs, Armies, Trade
(1998)

Haiti Renewed: Political and Economic Prospects
(1997)

Vigilance and Vengeance:
NGOs Preventing Ethnic Conflict in Divided Societies
(1996)

From Massacres to Genocide:
The Media, Public Policy, and Humanitarian Crises
(1996)

Battling Terrorism
in the Horn of Africa

ROBERT I. ROTBERG

Editor

WORLD PEACE FOUNDATION
Cambridge, Massachusetts

BROOKINGS INSTITUTION PRESS
Washington, D.C.

Copyright © 2005
THE WORLD PEACE FOUNDATION

Battling Terrorism in the Horn of Africa may be ordered from:
Brookings Institution Press, c/o HFS, P.O. Box 50370, Baltimore, MD 21211-4370
Tel.: 800/537-5487   410/516-6956   Fax: 410/516-6998
www.brookings.edu

Library of Congress Cataloging-in-Publication data

Battling terrorism in the Horn of Africa / Robert I. Rotberg, editor.
p. cm.
Summary: "Examines the state of governance in the countries of the greater Horn of Africa
region—Djibouti, Eritrea, Ethiopia, Kenya, Somalia, the Sudan, and Yemen—and discusses
strategies to combat the transnational threat of terrorism, including suggestions for more
effective U.S. engagement in the region"—Provided by publisher.
Includes bibliographical references and index.
ISBN-13: 978-0-8157-7570-6 (cloth : alk. paper)
ISBN-10: 0-8157-7570-9 (cloth : alk. paper)
ISBN-13: 978-0-8157-7571-3 (pbk. : alk. paper)
ISBN-10: 0-8157-7571-7 (pbk. : alk. paper)
1. Terrorism—Africa, Northeast—Prevention. 2. Islam and politics—Africa, Northeast.
I. Rotberg, Robert I. II. World Peace Foundation. III. Brookings Institution.
HV6433.A3553C65 2005
363.32'0963—dc22   2005023711

9 8 7 6 5 4 3 2 1

Typeset in Minion

Composition by OSP, Inc.
Arlington, Virginia

Printed by R. R. Donnelley
Harrisonburg, Virginia

CONTENTS

PREFACE

This book originated in a very lively exchange of views among a collection of seasoned diplomats, scholars, intelligence officials, and military officers at the John F. Kennedy School of Harvard University in late 2004. The papers discussed there, now much revised and supplemented, have become the country chapters that follow. (For a summary of the original meeting and the discussions that took place, as well as a list of participants, see Deborah L. West, "Combating Terrorism in the Horn of Africa and Yemen" [Cambridge, Massachusetts, 2004], www.worldpeacefoundation.org/publications.html.) Deborah West guided the detailed editorial process that helped to transform the early papers into the basis of this book. Elisa Pepe organized the conference in 2004 and has provided administrative support to the enterprise throughout.

For very useful, timely critiques of the first chapter in this volume, I am extremely grateful to Barbara Bodine, Robert Burrowes, Timothy J. Carney, Dan Connell, Lange Schermerhorn, and David Shinn. For their willingness to write well and to tight deadlines, I am, as editor, enormously appreciative of all the contributors, as well as for their collegiality and astuteness. The Board of Trustees of the World Peace Foundation, especially Dean Philip Khoury, its chair, provided strong backing for the meeting and this book; so did Graham T. Allison, the director of the Belfer Center for Science and International Affairs in the Kennedy School, and his staff. The authors and I remain profoundly appreciative of all of their advice and support.

ROBERT I. ROTBERG
July 4, 2005

Battling Terrorism
in the
Horn of Africa

The Greater Horn of Africa and Yemen

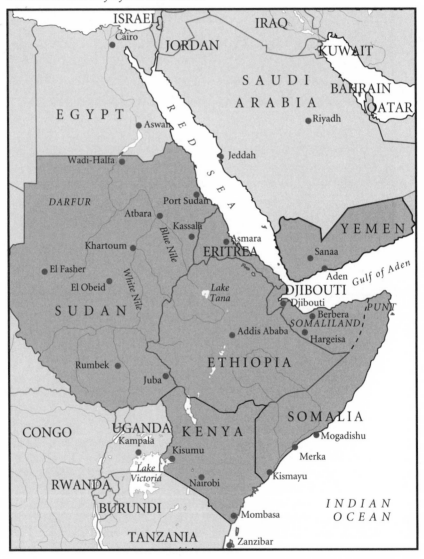

1

THE HORN OF AFRICA AND YEMEN
Diminishing the Threat of Terrorism

ROBERT I. ROTBERG

The greater Horn of Africa thrusts itself toward Yemen and hence the heart of Arabia and the Persian/Arab Gulf. Within the complex region of northeastern Africa that extends from the peaks of Kilimanjaro to the depression of Djibouti and from the deserts of Chad to the Red Sea and on southward, past Cape Guardafui, to the barren coastline of Punt, there are 149 million people, more than half of whom are Muslims.[1]

For geostrategic reasons, especially in an era of terror, Yemen belongs naturally to this greater Horn of Africa region, adding another 20 million people, virtually all Muslims. Although not necessarily cohesive physically, despite the unifying Rift Valley theme (from the Sudan and Djibouti south through Ethiopia and into Kenya), in the global battles for freedom and democracy and against terrorism these seven nation-states (Djibouti, Eritrea, Ethiopia, Kenya, Somalia, the Sudan, and Yemen) astride the Red Sea, the Gulf of Aden, and the Indian Ocean share a common enemy. They also roughly share a paucity of resources and unfulfilled desires for rapid economic advancement.

Al Qaeda can strike anywhere. It has already struck twice in Kenya, at least once in Somalia, and once (with at least two

1

important retaliations) in Yemen. So the greater Horn of Africa and Yemen region is bound together by its recent history as a sometime target, by its geographical proximity to the homeland of Osama bin Laden and the primary regional object of his political anger, by long and continuing interrelationships of licit and illicit trade, by religion, by centuries of Muslim-Christian accommodation and antagonism, by renowned resistances against Western colonizers (in the Horn), and by shared poverty, poor governance, and underdevelopment. This complex web provides a tasting menu for potential terrorists.[2]

Moreover, as the bulk of this book demonstrates, existing instability and potential sources of future conflagration offer added opportunities for infiltration, interference, and backing for extremists. Intensifying repression in Eritrea, unresolved tension between Eritrea and Ethiopia over their disputed border, the genocidal civil war in Darfur, biddable nonstate actors in southern Somalia, Ethiopian attempts to interfere in Somalia, the porous quality of the Somalia-Kenya border, a steady flow of arms and refugees between Yemen and Somalia and Ethiopia, the ease of money laundering (or traceless money transfers), and the widespread availability of inexpensive light weapons and ammunition all provide openings for Al Qaeda infiltration, the effective suborning of local officials, and the coalescence of terrorist surges.

Actual Al Qaeda operatives and sleepers in this region in 2005 are few, but dangerous. Additionally, those with hard knowledge of the region believe that cells linked both loosely and more tightly to Al Qaeda exist, especially in Yemen, Somalia, Kenya, and beyond into Tanzania and the Comoros. Finding and neutralizing those existing and potential pockets of Al Qaeda demands concerted diplomatic, intelligence, law enforcement, and military initiatives. U.S. efforts alone, as the contributors to this book reiterate, are insufficient to deal with the ongoing threats of Al Qaeda and homegrown terror in the region. Only cooperation among component states and security forces in the region, among available international security resources, and among the police and military staffs of the individual nations, the international resources, and the U.S. Central Command's Combined Joint Task Force–Horn of Africa (CJTF-HOA) based in Djibouti (and somewhat parallel operations of the Central Intelligence Agency and the Federal Bureau of Investigation) will diminish the likelihood of further Al Qaeda–sponsored attacks on U.S., allied, or local targets. Without a seamless regional and international response, the greater Horn of Africa and Yemen will remain a reservoir of terror. Such a broad, multinational, and multifactored response has yet to be constructed.

The coastlines of the greater Horn of Africa and Yemen total 5,510 miles. Although these waters are patrolled by British and American naval vessels and a few Kenyan boats and observed from aircraft and satellites and with ground-based radar, dhows and other smaller ships easily can and do slip through such porous defenses, especially the limited maritime ones. Strengthened and more credible coastal patrol capabilities are essential; each of the states of the region needs to build up its own sea and surveillance defenses with U.S. or other assistance. This is an ongoing requirement, best met by jointly developed regional initiatives as well as specially targeted external efforts. CJTF-HOA is a major part of this overall response but it has limited personnel and power, and its earnest efforts are appropriately directed as much to winning local hearts and minds as to military counterterror operations.

Governance and Terrorism

The winning of hearts and minds is about strengthening good governance throughout the region and about making friends for the United States through the projection of soft power and the intelligent exercise of diplomacy. Indeed, each of the chapters that follow contains a substantial section on how best to strengthen the practice of governance in the countries of the region. The optimal path to stability and reduced openings for terror is markedly to improve the manner in which governments in the region serve their citizens, that is, how they deliver governance.[3]

Governance is the effective provision of political goods to citizens. Of those political goods, security is paramount; there can be no economic growth or social elevation without it. To this end, a nation-state's prime functions are to secure the nation and its territory—to prevent cross-border invasions and incursions; to reduce domestic threats to or attacks upon the national order; to bolster human security by lowering crime rates; and to enable citizens to resolve their differences with fellow inhabitants or with the state itself without recourse to arms or physical coercion.

The nation-states that constitute the greater Horn of Africa and Yemen region present a mixed picture with regard to this fundamental criterion of governance. Eritrea and Ethiopia have gone to war over a border, and much else, and neither nation-state can now claim to have eliminated threats to peace between them. Additionally, there are several ongoing civil wars in the Sudan, and most of Somalia remains in a state of collapse, punctuated by assaults and mayhem. Kenya can claim to be secure from external threats, except for outrages perpetrated by Al Qaeda. Yemen has contested Saudi Arabia and Eritrea over territory, has porous borders, and was the scene of two Al Qaeda attacks. Djibouti is the nation-state with the strongest sense of cohesion and, tiny though it is, has the greatest ability, thanks to its defense agreement with France, to protect its frontiers from attack.

Internally, Djibouti may be the regional nation-state with the highest level of human security. Of all the others, Kenya especially endures crime levels at the upper end of the African scale—which adds to its intrinsic domestic insecurity. The other states of the region fall in between, with repressive Eritrea almost as safe (except for political miscreants) as Djibouti, and Ethiopia and the Sudan falling between Eritrea and Kenya. There is little crime in Yemen. Somaliland is reasonably secure domestically, too. But the rest of Somalia, where human security is mediated primarily by those who control the largest number of armaments and irregular militia, is by definition lawless.

The delivery of other desirable political goods becomes feasible only when a reasonable level of security is provided. Good governance next requires a predictable, recognizable, systematized method of adjudicating disputes and regulating both the norms and the prevailing mores of the societies in question. This political good implies codes and procedures that together compose an enforceable body of law, security of property and the enforceability of contracts, an effective judicial system, and a set of norms that legitimate and validate traditional or new values embodied in what is called, in shorthand, the rule of law. Each of the world's nation-states fashions its own rule of law; in the greater Horn of Africa region there are common law and Napoleonic law corpuses, *shari'a* law practices, Coptic church authorities, traditional jurisprudence, and the impositions of non-state actors. Judicial independence and competence are misnomers almost everywhere, so the provision of an articulated and fully practiced modern rule of law remains a work very much in progress. The greater Horn of Africa region and Yemen cannot develop effectively, nor combat terrorism with full vigor, until adherence to the rule of law tradition—not necessarily to any one style of law—is strengthened.

A third political good supplied in greater or lesser degree in the developing world enables citizens to participate freely, openly, and fully in a democratic political process. This good encompasses essential freedoms: the right to participate in politics and compete for office; respect and support for national and provincial political institutions, legislatures, and courts; tolerance of dissent and difference; independent media; and all of the basic civil and human rights. Nowhere in the greater Horn of Africa and Yemen region do citizens enjoy its full possibilities. The inhabitants of Kenya and Djibouti may obtain more of this good than their neighbors in the region, whereas most of those who live within the old borders of Somalia or the new borders of Eritrea arguably receive very little of such a good. Sudanese, amid war and under the rule of an Islamist political culture, also enjoy very little. Ethiopians and Yemenis are somewhat better off in this respect, but only at the margin. How to enable the governments in the greater Horn of Africa region to deliver more of the political good of freedom to their citizens during the next decade without weakening existing frameworks of stability is a question devoid of easy or comfortable answers. Ignoring the issue of freedom entirely, however, provides potential openings for regime opponents to join up with terrorists, especially those allied to Al Qaeda. Even many Kenyans who experienced the important transition from authoritarian single-man rule to democracy in 2002 still await delivery of the full promise of democratic reform.

A fourth critical component of governance is the creation of an enabling environment permissive of and conducive to economic growth and prosperity at both national and personal levels. This political good thus encompasses a prudently run money and banking system, usually guided by a central bank and lubricated by a national currency; a fiscal and institutional context within which citizens may pursue individual entrepreneurial goals and potentially prosper; and a regulatory environment appropriate to the economic aspirations and attributes of the nation-state. Only Kenya, reliant on tourism and agricultural exports, has a fully modern economy. Somalia is the outlier at the other end of the economic continuum, and all of the other nation-states are fragile economically. The Sudan has oil, but little else. (Yemen also has oil, but in diminishing amounts.) Yemen has an excellent port in Aden, Djibouti has a smaller port, and Eritrea has two. Ethiopia has coffee. But the real economic attainments of the nation-states of the greater Horn of Africa and Yemen region have been limited, largely because of scarce natural resources and harsh terrain. Moreover, none of the regimes in the region, except Kenya and Djibouti, is even marginally concerned with providing more than the rudiments of this good of economic growth. Additionally, corruption flourishes everywhere in the region, sapping efficiency, limiting foreign direct investment (except into the petroleum industry), and undermining other political goods like the rule of law and security.[4]

Infrastructure (the physical arteries of commerce), education, and medical treatment are other key political goods, nearly always the responsibilities of governments. Except for Kenya, all of the other countries and areas in the greater region are poor, with underdeveloped road and rail systems, creaking sea and river ports and airports, poor traditional telephone systems and limited teledensity, and low levels of Internet connectivity. Likewise, again except

for Kenya and northern Sudan, health and educational systems are either
nearly nonexistent or primitive (even by African standards). In the medical
services field, for example, in 2001 there was one physician per 35,000 people
in Ethiopia, one per 33,000 people in Eritrea, one per 25,000 people in Somalia, one per 11,000 people in the Sudan, one per 7,500 people in Kenya, one per
7,100 people in Djibouti, and one per 5,000 people in Yemen. In terms of the
number of hospital beds per 1,000 people, Djibouti had more than two, Kenya
and the Sudan more than one, and all the others a few tenths of a bed. Ethiopia
had only 0.24 hospital beds per 1,000. Comparing health expenditures as a
percentage of GDP, Kenya spent the most (nearly 8 percent), Djibouti and
Eritrea followed, and Ethiopia brought up the rear with 1.4 percent.[5] It comes
as no surprise, given these startlingly low numbers for the delivery of health
services, that infant mortality rates per 1,000 live births range from 133 in
Somalia and 114 in Ethiopia down to a comparatively welcome figure of fifty-
nine in Eritrea. Estimated life expectancy at birth thus ranges from a high of
fifty-one years in Eritrea to a low of forty-two in Ethiopia.

Only Kenya has a flourishing civil society. In Somalia, civil society is an oxy-
moron within warlord-controlled fiefdoms. It has been increasingly limited in
Eritrea, as the chapter on that country makes evident. In the Sudan, civil society has been repressed in the North by the military rulers who have run the
nation-state since 1989; elsewhere civil society is a casualty both of the old
North-South war and the new war in Darfur. In Ethiopia, civil society has
been slow to develop amid the tight embrace of authoritarianism and because
of the restraints of traditional cultures of discourse. In Yemen, formal urban
civil society is limited, but there is a long history of discourse and debate
within tribal structures.

The eradication both of existing terrorist cells and potential future terrorist threats and combinations cannot be achieved without careful, considered
attention to uplifting governance in general throughout the region and boost-
ing particular political goods selectively, country by country. Yet, even if the
United States and the European Union (EU) were to expend appropriate sums
to assist the governments of the region with improving aspects of governance,
not all of these nation-states would embrace or welcome such initiatives. Few
are anxious to chance their control or dominance internally. Few are as
desirous as they might be, and fewer are able, to deliver political goods of the
quality and in the quantities that would significantly help to achieve the aspirations of their peoples. The quality of the rule of law or economic
enablement, much less domestic security and political freedom, will not
change for the better without newly created partnerships forged for such ends

between the United States, the EU, and many if not all of the countries in the greater Horn of Africa region. Hence, because the United States desperately wants to reduce the threat of terrorism, Washington must craft new, broad policy initiatives toward the region as a whole and toward the critical nation-states individually. CJTF-HOA, understaffed as it is, cannot be expected to bear the burden of nation building in the Horn of Africa and Yemen.

There are ample opportunities for multinational coordination with regard to improving good governance in the region. France has long had a military and political presence in Djibouti. Italy has an interest, from colonial times, in the region, especially Somalia and Eritrea. Britain has colonial links to Kenya, Somaliland, and the Sudan. Norway played a substantial role in negotiating a peace agreement between the Sudan's North and South. The EU as a whole has a variety of ties to the region and to individual countries. The United States once had an important listening post in Eritrea, enjoys naval rights in Kenya, was alternately allied with Ethiopia and Somalia, and has suffered direct attack in Yemen and Kenya. It also has a military base in Djibouti.

Americans and Europeans should cooperate to increase governmental capabilities in the region. Working together, they can build new and maintain existing infrastructures. They can find ways to create jobs in a region typified by high unemployment. Local educational efforts are few, leading to high rates of underemployment among secondary school leavers and others with less training. Europeans and Americans can direct their attention to such critical needs, can upgrade health facilities in the crucial battles against HIV/AIDS (increasingly a menace to Ethiopia and Somalia), tuberculosis, and malaria, as well as against dangerous epizootic diseases like Rift Valley fever and rinderpest. They should support local efforts to embed the rule of law and expand political freedom. Positive activities in each of these arenas will directly and indirectly strengthen security and counterterrorism capabilities. The battle against terrorism is as much, if not more, a battle for improved governance and, as a consequence, for local hearts and minds.

Although France, Italy, and Britain have a long-standing expert knowledge of portions of the region and high-level staff fluent in local languages, the United States no longer possesses the regional expertise and capable linguists that it once had in the Department of State, the Central Intelligence Agency, and the several military services. Indeed, the greater Horn of Africa region (Yemen excepted) is in too many respects a terra incognita to Washington. Intelligence personnel responsible for overseeing the region may have no direct acquaintance with it. U.S. embassies and consulates are fewer than they were in the 1980s; budget cuts and personnel retrenchments have left U.S. diplomatic, intelligence, and military services impoverished in terms of an intimate knowledge of the region and the countries that it comprises. Although Washington helped to ensure the ultimate delivery of the Sudanese peace pact of early 2005, there was still no permanent American ambassador resident in Khartoum (based elsewhere since 1997) and no equivalent presence in Somalia. Indeed, Washington lacks any coherent vision for integrating and advancing American diplomatic and security initiatives in the region. The struggle against terrorism requires just such a far-ranging vision, directed and coordinated at the highest levels.

The battle against terror in the vulnerable countries along the Red Sea and the Indian Ocean is best prosecuted from a holistic regional perspective. The threat is transnational and respects no boundaries. In any event, none of international land or sea borders presents an effective barrier to infiltrators. Drugs and arms smugglers and cattle and sheep rustlers can cross almost anywhere at will. A history of interpenetration, long decades of evasion, tribal or warrior dominance of frontier areas remote from national capitals, adherence to customary entrepreneurial obligations, and the absence of robust security contingents beyond major cities make regional measures and cooperation necessary, urgent, and probably insufficient. The regional Intergovernmental Authority on Development (IGAD) tries weakly to organize relevant common responses. Bringing Yemen into IGAD would be sensible, and helpful in forging a more vigorous common approach to terror and its eradication. (But Yemen may not wish to be considered "African," and IGAD members might resist the inclusion of a new country.) There is no substitute for greater U.S. involvement in any and all forums for the greater Horn of Africa region and Yemen.

As important as a vastly strengthened regional approach will be, Washington also needs a nuanced new policy crafted for and appropriate to the region and each of its countries.

Somalia and Somaliland

Somalia—the southern and easternmost reaches of what was the Republic of Somalia during the despotic reign of Siad Barre, its last president (1969–1991)—is the least ordered, most volatile, section of the greater Horn of Africa region and the most likely and most obvious locale in which terrorists could gather and from which they could burst forth to spread chaos and devastation. Somalia is a collapsed state—a mere hollow geographical expression—devoid of national government (if not of governance).[6] But that absence alone does not make Somalia a potential bastion of terror. In a number of ways, the implanting of terrorist cells and the free movement of terrorists is always easier when a nation-state emerges from the chaos of collapse and forms a weak central government. It and its leaders become more rather than less susceptible to the blandishments and intimidations, and even to the arguments and ideologies, of terror and terrorists.

In 2005, Somalia's new Transitional Federal Government was attempting to assert its authority over the vast hinterland northward from the international border with Kenya. But its main battle was with the remaining faction leaders controlling Mogadishu, Kismayo, Merka, and other coastal cities and towns. None of these warlords wanted to be deprived of power and privilege within the various domains that each had managed to dominate during the many years of despoliation since Siad Barre's death. None wanted a new, externally supported government to become legitimate, with its own projection of supremacy. Even if the African Union managed to raise a peace-securing force to accompany the Transitional Government's move from Kenya to Somalia, it was not evident that such a force, or the sheer logic of the new government's existence, could or would prevail.

As Kenneth J. Menkhaus writes in his chapter, with or without a legitimate new governmental authority, and with or without the continuation of warlordism, Somalia presents a very plausible safe haven for terrorists and a potential "perfect storm."[7] There are no customs or immigration inspectors; its beaches and borders remain largely unpatrolled. It is a wild, lawless territory of extreme poverty, now ordered by battle-hardened militiamen. Moreover, the territory harbors its own radical Islamist organization, and in the absence of any state-provided social and educational services, local communities have welcomed Islamic charities and schools funded from Saudi Arabia and by the emirates of the Gulf. There is a rising anti-Western feeling among a Muslim population suspicious of Ethiopian and other foreign Christians. Yet, as disordered and ungoverned as Somalia remained, through 2003 Al Qaeda had not established a major presence within its old borders. There was too much danger of betrayal and extortion. Few Somalis had joined the movement. Additionally, over time armed conflict had become more localized and less lethal. Criminality was somewhat reduced. The rule of law existed in the form of local shari'a courts.

By 2005, however, Menkhaus detected a strengthening of Islamist power, especially in Mogadishu. Jihadist attacks were increasing. There were more instances of internal terror. The shari'a courts were extending their jurisdiction and in some areas, like Mogadishu, were being used to further the causes and ambitions of radical Islamists such as Hassan Dahir Aweys. More and more schools, mosques, and charities were expressing an anti-Western agenda.

The passage of terrorists across Somali territory was becoming more frequent. Hard-line Somali Islamists, drawing on inter-clan antagonisms, were gaining agency.

Menkhaus explains how Islamic and clan identity and loyalty have, and have not, hitherto been used to mobilize Somalis for jihadist campaigns. He hints at the disarray that may flow from hostility in some sections of Somalia to the domination of the new Federal Government by the Darood clan, especially among rival Hawiye and the Haber Gedir Ayr subclan (and the Mogadishu business and Islamist elites who belong to it). He also predicts that such a minority-run Federal Government, even if it becomes established inside Somalia with African Union support, might paradoxically create a more (not less) hospitable environment for Al Qaeda.

Somaliland, the northern section of greater Somalia whose (internationally unrecognized) borders are congruent with those of the former British mandated territory of the same name, has a strong government (by local standards) and projects security. It has a legal framework, collects taxes, and provides services that approximate reasonable levels of good governance. Its "stability and economic recovery provide a social context less conducive to radicalism."[8] There is as yet no evidence that Wahhabism or jihadism are active forces. Nor has Al Qaeda established a presence there. Even so, conservative religious practices are growing, along with displays of piety. Recently, too, attacks on foreigners have increased; local radicalism may be intensifying. Geostrategically, Somaliland has a long, easily penetrated flank along the Gulf of Aden. It has few security forces of its own, and must rely on foreign surveillance and assistance.

The recognition of Somaliland as a nation-state in its own right carries many diplomatic perils and would complicate the African and Western desire to see a strong government established in the rest of Somalia. But support of good governance and nation building in Somaliland promises to assist the battle against terrorism now and over the medium term. Given Somaliland's location, and its order amid the continued chaos of greater Somalia, it behooves Washington, London, and Brussels to craft new policies of aid and backing.

Likewise, if the new Federal Government can broaden its limited clan base and avoid being a tool of Ethiopian meddling, Washington should continue to aid Somali efforts to establish a new government. If successful, this partnership could lead to nation building in Somalia as well as Somaliland. Menkhaus is correct to worry that a strengthened central government could provide openings for the penetration of Al Qaeda. But over the medium term better educated Somalis, strong institutions, a refurbished infrastructure, and economic growth are all enemies of Al Qaeda. Somalia cannot remain largely ungoverned forever.

Djibouti

Although a majority Somali-populated nation, Djibouti's colonial heritage is French. It never endured the misrule of a despot like Siad Barre, or Mengistu Haile Meriam in Ethiopia. It has been remarkably stable since gaining its independence in 1977; France has always maintained a large military presence outside the city of Djibouti and for many years advised ("controlled") the country's treasury. Because Djibouti is now an American and French garrison town, but more so because this diminutive nation-state guards the southern entrance to the Red Sea across from Yemen, it plays a key role in contemporary counterterror operations and will influence the manner in which the region and its neighbors respond to the challenges and opportunities of improved governance. Moreover, IGAD is based in Djibouti. If Yemen were to become a member or an associate member of IGAD, that organization could help significantly to knit the region together and strengthen its existing bulwarks against the rise and spread of terror.

In the battle against terror, the government of Djibouti has been more proactive than others in the region. Despite limited resources, it has removed illegal immigrants for other reasons, shut financial institutions with terrorist links, and cooperated with foreign monitoring and collection operations. Most of all, President Ismail Omar Guelleh has moved determinedly to broker peace in Somalia, especially from 1999 to 2003. He continues to seek to exercise a peacemaking and security-bolstering role among his neighbors and regionally. Washington may wish to find ways to enhance Guelleh's mediation authority for the good of the peoples of the greater Horn of Africa region.

But doing so will also mean assisting Djibouti with improving the living standards and economic, political, and social prospects of its own people. Helping to make Djibouti a developmental showcase would not hurt. The country's greatest need is a reliable source of potable water. Its aquifer is rapidly being depleted and massive investments in modern desalination technology may be justified. With water, Djibouti could successfully irrigate its limited arable land and potentially grow more of its own food

But the people of Djibouti also require viable service and industrial employment opportunities. Creating them would help to mobilize jobs. In Djibouti, as in the region, jobs are at a premium. Creating opportunities for gainful employment is one of the more obvious and most likely methods of reducing the attractiveness of Al Qaeda and similar forms of terrorism. Djibouti could be developed as a regional transportation hub: its port and airport facilities (now managed by Dubai) could be expanded and the Addis Ababa railroad could be refurbished and upgraded. Djiboutians also require better educational opportunities in English, as well as in French and Arabic.

From Djibouti's vantage point, writes Lange Schermerhorn in chapter 3 in this volume, everything that happens in the countries of the Horn impacts Djibouti, and conversely, Djibouti's political and economic health and welfare impinges on all of its neighbors. Now, more than ever, Djibouti needs a stable region that is developing in ways that will complement its own potential as a regional services hub. Therefore, policy with regard to Djibouti must be formulated knowing that every action in the region stimulates a reaction. Cooperating and collaborating with other donors to help Djibouti attain its objectives for the delivery of social services, education, and jobs should be an important U.S. policy objective in order to maintain the stability of this major regional entry point.

Washington's stance toward Djibouti should include supporting and advancing the existing UN arms embargo on Somalia, enforced by U.S. and coalition forces; expanding the existing U.S. naval task force that reports to fleet headquarters in Bahrain and operates in the Gulf of Aden; increasing funds and personnel devoted to pursuing the East Africa Counterterrorism Initiative (started in 2003); providing more U.S. Coast Guard assistance to the nations of the region to develop secure ports; strengthening the U.S.- and French-funded De-mining Training Center in Djibouti; and working ever more closely with the French security contingent. Attention to each of these initiatives would acknowledge the linchpin character of Djibouti, an essential ally of the West in the fractured and troubled region of the greater Horn of Africa and Yemen.

Eritrea

In contrast to organized and stable Djibouti, Eritrea, immediately to the north, is tense and greatly endangered despite an autocratic government. Tightened security under the increasingly repressive regime of President Isaias Afwerki simultaneously guards against the spread of terror and encourages frustrated democratic opponents of the administration to forge links with Islamist extremists. The collapse of the new nation-state's once vibrant economy, and the unresolved bitter and losing war with Ethiopia, have also demoralized Eritreans. Although the government actively discriminates against Pentecostalists and other new Christians, it also batters Islam, has tried to regiment leading Muslim preachers, and refuses to accept Arabic as an official language—thus drawing the ire of Islamists and radical mosque preachers. For all of these reasons, Eritrea is no longer a reliable bulwark against the spread of terror. Its growing antidemocratic tendencies indeed invite trouble and troublemakers.

Political parties other than the ruling one are banned, most nongovernmental organizations are prohibited, dissent is forcibly discouraged, the media are shackled, evangelical Christian denominations are banned and their churches closed, and private worship is forbidden. Political prisoners—especially editors, journalists, and students—grow in number. Individuals simply disappear. Torture is prevalent. Urban Eritreans believe that their telephones are tapped, that their public conversations are monitored, and that email is intercepted. The national educational and health services are deteriorating. Pastoralism and traditional grazing rights are threatened by government action and by the migration of Christian Tigrinya speakers from the highlands into the western lowlands. The relatively strong infrastructure is decaying. A middle class economy (by African standards) is becoming poor. As Dan Connell notes in chapter 4 in this volume, tight military control masks the "growing alienation of the population from a central government that continues to operate largely through informal and unaccountable structures of power, behind a façade of ineffectual public institutions."[9]

Once socially and culturally vibrant, Eritrea has regressed toward the mean of African despotisms thanks to the increasingly cranky, personal, heavy-handed rule of Isaias. Opposition groups, nearly all clandestine, are gaining support. Secular groups are active and credible, especially those affiliated with the Eritrean Democratic Alliance, some of whose member organizations are based in Ethiopia. The Alliance is committed to the armed overthrow of the Isaias regime. Armed Islamists are based in neighboring Sudan, where they draw adherents and fighters from the ranks of impoverished Eritreans who have crossed the border. The government in the Sudan backs them in part for ideological reasons, in part because the Eritreans are backing rebels in Darfur. These Eritrean Islamists may also have ties to and receive financing from Al Qaeda. Whether or not Osama bin Laden's associates befriend them, ensuing battles and likely future national instability will offer some cover to terrorist alliances between the enemies of Isaias and Saudi- or Yemen-based fundamentalists. Connell suggests that Eritrea may be plunged into civil war before 2008, thus adding further instability to a volatile neighborhood. He also warns Washington, allied as it is against the spread of terror to the Isaias government, prudently to distance itself from what may soon become a weakened and heavily compromised ally. A proactive, aggressive policy opposing the suppression of liberties and promoting internal democracy would be wise. Connell's twenty-two guidelines for U.S. action promote internal reforms, and if enacted would benefit Eritreans as a whole and measurably harden the shields against terror.

Ethiopia

Ethiopia is under attack from local anti-regime terrorists, as well as from some who are based in Somalia. None of the Ethiopia-based groups has known ties to Al Qaeda or to any other variant of internationally sponsored terror. It is a strong, determined nation-state, too, with distinctive cultures and a long suspicion of foreigners—all positive defensive attributes against the spread of terror from neighbors or from Saudi Arabia. Nevertheless, Ethiopia's many inherent weaknesses may provide convenient openings for the spread of opportunistic terrorism. It has long, porous land borders with five volatile countries, several of whom harbor ongoing internal conflicts or—according to the chapters in this book—are about to be consumed by new warfare. It exists on the periphery of a zone of unquestioned danger. Nearly half of its people are Muslim, many resentful of the tight control of the country by Tigrinya-speaking Christians from the north. Wahhabi preachers and teachers are spreading their faith assiduously throughout eastern Ethiopia, establishing new mosques and madrassas with Saudi Arabian funds. Moreover, Ethiopia is large, very poor, and unlettered. There are severe food deficits, thanks to periodic droughts. Its population is growing rapidly, even though the country has the world's fourth highest number of HIV-positive persons (after South Africa, India, and Nigeria). Its infrastructure is weak and fragmented. There is much, in other words, about which non-Tigrinyans can feel resentful, especially given the results of the 2005 election. (David Shinn's chapter 5 in this volume summarizes the flawed results of that election.) There are growing opportunities for externally sponsored subversion and infiltration.

Although Ethiopian Islam has traditionally been dominated by tolerant Sufi brotherhoods and clerics, and the Christian government has embraced Islamic holy days and generally been evenhanded in its attitude to local Islam, in recent years the clash between intolerant orthodoxy and the heterodox Ethiopian forms of Islam has become sharp. The Wahhabist-influenced preachers and their followers have opposed Sufi practices and the syncretic quality of home-grown Ethiopian Islam. Tombs of Sufi sheikhs, for example, have been desecrated, the Wahhabists claiming that these and similar forms of idolatrous veneration are permeated with pagan sentiment. Backed by wealthy patrons in Saudi Arabia and the states of the Persian Gulf, there has been a steady influx of radical Islamism, largely spread by Wahhabi-controlled charities through mosques and madrassas. Despite such growing animosities, the Ethiopian government has not yet seriously tried to curtail the spread of fundamentalism from Saudi Arabia and elsewhere.

Although Ethiopia is not likely to be the target of an Al Qaeda–sponsored terrorist strike, in the medium term its lamentable inability to deliver meaningful political goods suggests that the battle against terrorism in the country must and will be fought by improving governance and through major efforts of creative nation building. Any initiatives that reduce social inequality and build bridges between mutually hostile ethnic and religious groups will help to limit the appeal of terrorists. So, too, will actions that reduce poverty, increase the number of schools and places of education, enhance the delivery of health services, and provide more phone and Internet availability. New roads are also essential to permit the flow of commerce and reduce the price of goods in outlying areas, both Muslim and Christian. U.S. and European donors should help the regime of President Meles Zenawi to realize such goals for their own sake, as well as to combat terrorism.

Ethnic tensions are likely always to bedevil a country as large as Ethiopia, and they do so despite, or even because of, Meles' willingness to devolve increments of power to the provinces. Ethiopia consists of eighty-five ethnicities, several of which attack each other but do not and would not provide a subversive beachhead for Al Qaeda outposts. However, Somali in the Ogaden and elsewhere have always expressed separatist sentiments. So have Afar (shared with Djibouti and Eritrea) and Oromo, situated as the latter are in the heart of the nation-state. Many nationalist Oromo seek Oromia, a future polity on its own. Many Oromo have joined or covertly support one of several ethnic political parties. One such is based in Eritrea and occasionally attacks Ethiopian forces. The Ethiopians regard these dissidents as terrorists.

Irredentist nationalists, whether Oromo or Somali, might very well seek support from Al Qaeda or forge links to terrorists in one or more of the neighboring countries. The Eritrean and Sudanese governments doubtless fund some of these groups. In any event, both of those regimes and some of the Somali warlords have reason enough to dislike and act by proxy against the Meles administration. In the 1990s, there were a number of attempted assassinations and hotel bombings. In this century, a warehouse on the railroad between Addis Ababa and Djibouti has been bombed. There was an attack on the Dire Dawa railroad station. Bombs have gone off in Addis Ababa and else-where. More of these kinds of acts will occur; Ethiopian security forces are sufficiently strong to suggest that a cascade of such events, leading to pro-nounced instability within the country, is unlikely. Yet, as the waters of tranquility are increasingly being roiled, so externally driven terrorists are able increasingly to take advantage of revealed chinks in the regime's armor.

U.S. and EU counterterror efforts should obviously be directed at helping Ethiopian (and regional) security teams to upgrade their own capabilities, supplying technical forms of assistance, and stepping up existing methods of surveillance and intelligence sharing. The United States and the EU also should encourage the government of Ethiopia to pay closer attention to extremist insinuations into Muslim communities. Most of all, they must develop ingen-ious ways to help the Meles administration govern more effectively, democratize, reduce corruption, and spend ever more generous sums to ame-liorate the lives of urban and rural Ethiopians.

The Sudan

With the signing in early 2005 of a comprehensive peace agreement between the Islamist military government of the Sudan and the southern Sudan Peo-ple's Liberation Movement, the war-ravaged country could focus for the first time in three decades on the spread of peace across the South, the distribution of significant political goods to southerners, and the knitting together of North and South within a context of renewed partnership. At least, those are among the foremost goals of the negotiated compromise that may or may not keep North and South together beyond a six-year grace period; lead to the delivery of enhanced health, education, and human services to southerners; create numerous new jobs; and reduce both warfare and the possibility of terrorism across the vast reaches of the Sudan.

The UN subsequently authorized the recruitment and dispatch of a 10,000 person peacekeeping contingent to monitor the several complicated demobi-lization, disarmament, and reintegration provisions of the peace agreement.[10] The UN resolved, over the protests of the government of the Sudan, to try Sudanese perpetrators in the Darfur conflict before the bar of the International Criminal Court. But the UN, in late 2005, was still leaving almost all direct action to end the Sudan's war in its westernmost province of Darfur to a lim-ited force of weakly mandated African Union monitors and to desultory AU negotiating efforts led by Nigeria and Chad. If the battles in Darfur between rebel groups and marauding camel-borne raiders funded and emboldened by the Khartoum government can also be brought to a peaceful close in 2005, and the main perpetrators punished, then the entire Sudan (including the embattled Beja areas in the east) will be able to focus on economic and social betterment rather than on killing, exploitation, looting, and finding advantage. Such a focus will also prevent potential terrorists, or resumed contacts with Al Qaeda, from gaining traction. Stability is the most effective enemy of terror. So is good governance and economic growth.

The Sudan has long been a failed state, beset by relentless combat and fatally undermined by governments antagonistic to popular participation and to broad social achievements. Since 1989 an intolerant, suspicious military junta has ruled with a heavy hand. Until 1999, its leaders were also thoroughly in thrall to a severe strain of Islamist doctrine. Although those Islamist strictures are now less influential than before, they and the continuing intra-regime tensions over orthodoxy continue to inhibit the Sudanese authorities from providing most of the positive political goods of modern governance to their disparate peoples, and from treating non-Arab Sudanese as beneficently as Arab Sudanese from the dominant North. Once the United States, the European Union, the African Union, and UN end the war in Darfur by cajoling or sanctioning Khartoum, then the United States and the EU may be poised to encourage improved governance.

Such attention to political goods and governance, and to the modern development of the Sudan more generally, would surely provide medium-term barriers to the spread of terrorism. That Al Qaeda was once based in the Sudan does not mean that, as such, it can return. The country is still listed by Washington as a sponsor of terrorists (even though the Sudan has now signed all twelve international conventions against terrorism and seems to have shut the offices of Hamas in Khartoum). However, given the abrasive and authoritarian quality of the current regime, given profound contemporary internal instability, and given the ongoing confrontations with Ethiopia and Eritrea, endless opportunities for outside interference and infiltration remain. And as Timothy Carney notes in chapter 6 in this volume, reducing the internal cohesion and power of the Islamists who now govern the Sudan might offer an opening to even more radical forces within Sudanese Islam. That is a dilemma that can only be managed by fully understanding the several powerful tendencies that compete for hegemony within northern Sudan. For this intricate nest of reasons, the powers of the West need more rather than fewer diplomatic and listening posts in the Sudan. Washington must find means to become more rather than less influential in Khartoum. An effective policy of tough love rather than any new warm embrace of the current Sudanese regime would be appropriate, if difficult to achieve or to calibrate. Without such a new approach to the problems of the Sudan, the battle against terror cannot be won.

Yemen

Of all of the nation-states discussed in this book, Yemen would seem to provide the most propitious setting for infiltration by Al Qaeda and the spread of jihadism. Robert Burrowes suggests in chapter 7 in this book that Yemen could "become a major incubator and exporter" of transnational revolutionary political Islam.[11] Yemen faces both west and south to Africa and east and north into the Arabian kingdoms. Its long, troubled, and contentious border with Saudi Arabia allows for the relatively free movement of persons and weapons. Al Qaeda sympathizers and potential sympathizers are presumably present in the trackless eastern regions of Yemen and the rugged hinterland north of Aden, as well as in cities and towns. Moreover, the country's government, tough and careful though it is, does not fully control all of its distant marches. Nor does it exert unquestioned dominance over its national periphery.

Nevertheless, Yemen has been partially immunized against the rise of revolutionary political Islam and terrorism by a pervasive attitude of traditional conservatism. Islamic fundamentalism was never a pillar of the policies or society of Yemen; the country never embraced Saudi support for Wahhabism and, indeed, Yemen distrusts almost any reactionary and radical impulses that stem from its much wealthier neighbor. Its government has also been careful to monitor the activities of individual Yemenis, radicalized and battle hardened after returning from Afghanistan, Algeria, and elsewhere. Al Qaeda's attacks in Aden and along the coast further aroused official concerns.

Yemen doubtless contains Al Qaeda cells. The southern port of Aden is more cosmopolitan than the capital, Sanaa, and more open to foreigners and foreign influences. Yemeni security forces, supported by and cooperating with U.S. agencies and with CJTF-HOA, follow these cells, intercept some terrorist operatives, and have thwarted possible attacks similar to those on the USS *Cole* and the *Limburg*, a French oil tanker. That battle against Al Qaeda cadres will continue, particularly as Yemeni and U.S. detachments come to work ever more closely with one another and with authorities in Oman and Saudi Arabia.

But, as in all of the countries discussed in this volume, the broader battle against Al Qaeda and the spread of terrorism must be fought largely on the nonmilitary front. Burrowes terms Yemen's economy "not viable"; major reforms are required if the regime's legitimacy, and support for the current ruling political coalition, are to be sustained. Yemenis are desperately poor, with a per capita GDP of $332 and low levels of life expectancy (high levels of infant mortality), few and poor schools, high unemployment (at least 40 percent), and a deficient infrastructure.[12] Most of the country is desperately short of water. The United States should assist Yemen in providing better educational opportunities and new sources of potable water. Yemen has vast need for medical and other social services as well. Most of all, large numbers of new jobs must be created, here and in the other countries discussed, if the aspirations of the youthful majorities are to be satisfied, even appeased.

There is little good governance. Despite a veneer of modernity, Yemen is still a traditional society, especially in terms of institutional capacity, political freedom, and the rule of law. Helping the government to begin to address these problems, and to begin a gradual process of greater adherence to international democratic norms, would strengthen Yemen's ability to counter the appeal of bin Laden and like forces in the medium term. As Burrowes reports, "Yemen is not now a very democratic country, and much of its democracy is more apparent than real . . . with shallow foundations."[13] Only under favorable conditions, and conceivably with nuanced and light-handed foreign guidance, will Yemen evolve into a truly democratic polity.

President Ali Abdullah Salih, who has cooperated with the United States' global and regional counterterrorism endeavors, has run Yemen for twenty-seven years. He heads an oligarchy with strong tribal, commercial, and security connections. It is corrupt and corrupted (Burrowes calls Yemen a kleptocracy) and remains in place thanks to patronage and official licenses to steal. Washington should be aware of the kind of regime to which it is allied, and to some extent dependent upon. If Washington could ease Yemen toward more democratic practices, the medium-term battle for the hearts and minds of Yemenis, and therefore for a marginalization of sympathizers with extreme Islam, would correspondingly be boosted.

Kenya

No country in the greater Horn of Africa and Yemen region is as important to, and has had such a persistent record of strong relations with, the United States as Kenya. A staunch ally during the long presidencies of Jomo Kenyatta and Daniel arap Moi, Kenya has been an equally reliable friend of Washington under the new administration led by President Mwai Kibaki and Vice President Moody Awori. Moreover, Kenya is the economic powerhouse of East Africa and greater Horn of Africa regions, if currently only falteringly, and their air and sea transportation hub. Flawed though its recent performance has been, Kenya also is a beacon of democracy for both regions. The Sudan's peace pact was negotiated over several years in Kenya, and with Kenyan help (on behalf of IGAD). And further testifying to Kenya's critical diplomatic role, so were many of the arrangements connected with the creation of the Transitional Federal Government for Somalia, whose leaders were based in Nairobi.

For those reasons and many others, Kenya has always provided a tempting target to those wanting to attack Western interests and friends of the West. Since the country contains several tourist destinations, American warships visit Mombasa, there is a new U.S. embassy in Nairobi, and Americans, Europeans, and Israelis provide appealing targets, Kenya and the U.S. are joined together in the continuing battle against both externally based and home-grown terrorism.

Because the Muslims and Somali living on Kenya's coast are essentially marginalized politically and economically within the country, because Kenya's economy is growing too slowly to absorb the legions of frustrated job-seeking school leavers, and because of high levels of corruption and crime, radical Islamism and jihadists in general have found Kenya a fertile recruiting ground. Johnnie Carson reports in chapter 8 in this volume that one or two Al Qaeda–affiliated cells have operated within Kenya for more than a decade, with Kenyan nationals and family members being implicated in terrorist attacks. Additionally, several of Al Qaeda's senior leaders have regularly transited Kenya.[14]

The terrorist threat is more palpable in Kenya than in other parts of the greater Horn of Africa region and Yemen. There are more enticing targets. Finding supporters is comparatively easy because of widespread alienation, and resentment by coastal Muslims of their up-country rulers. In order to avoid renewed attacks, the United States and Britain are actively helping to train Kenyan security forces, have strengthened their own local intelligence capabilities, and are training and equipping the Kenyans to watch the Indian Ocean littoral. But much of Kenya's day-to-day preventive capacity will always be contingent on its easily bribable police personnel, and on Kenyan infiltration of clandestine cells. Forestalling terrorist atrocities and physically preventing the growth of an Al Qaeda core in Kenya thus remains a difficult work in progress.

An equally taxing problem is how best to remediate the underlying, long-term social, political, and economic conditions that may predispose some Kenyans to express their frustrations through terrorist acts. Carson writes that opportunities and hope are drying up along the coast of Kenya, especially for politically vulnerable young men. So they have turned to the Middle East for work, for training, for religious education, and for succor. Returning, they have brought Islamist approaches and sympathies, built new mosques and madrassas, and imported new preachers. Improved governance is the obvious answer to the overall problem in the medium term. If the Kenyan government could be persuaded and assisted by the United States to build and staff schools and clinics along the coast, to pay more attention to the other needs of the coastal peoples, and to give a greater political role to their representatives, that could help. So could the steady creation of jobs and more jobs. These same kinds of initiatives are necessary in the Somali and Giriama areas of northeastern Kenya, if much more difficult to achieve. Overall, too, if the Kibaki administration provided more and better political goods for all of its citizens—if it achieved a reputation for good governance and fairness (a robust rule of law would be useful)—Kenya could over the medium term become a less fertile ground for the spread of Al Qaeda–like tendencies.

A Safer and More Secure Region

The countries of the greater Horn of Africa region and Yemen will remain places of intrigue and danger for the foreseeable future. The United States and the European Union will not enjoy the luxury of again neglecting or slighting its peoples and governments. There is too much at stake, no matter what happens in Saudi Arabia, Iraq, and Syria. Indeed, even if Osama bin Laden should be captured and the back of mysterious Al Qaeda broken, the short- and medium-term threats against the region will not vanish.

Each country is fragile, some with weak governments and economies, some with autocratically strong (and thus potentially implosive) governments and poor or stagnant economic prospects. The greater Horn of Africa region and Yemen is typified by poor governance—the insufficient provision of political goods in terms of quality and quantity. Security is largely problematic, rule of law questionable, and political freedom wanting. There is much to be done.

The inhabitants of the region seek lives that are less brutish and more rewarding for themselves and their young people. In the battle to alleviate poverty, provide more education and better health outcomes, and enhance broad political participation, the United States and other donors must redouble their efforts. They can develop imaginative new ways to support and inspire local efforts. They can devise regional as well as country-by-country responses to critical needs. All such endeavors are also a part of the real battle against terrorism.

So will be Washington's own battle for attention to this region. Whereas twenty or so years ago this area commanded more official resources and personnel than it now does, today there are few diplomatic or other listening posts, few knowledgeable analysts, few intelligence specialists, and few persons in government possessing critical language skills. The tiny Combined Joint Task Force, the East Africa Counterterrorism Initiative, naval visits, and other forms of surveillance can only go so far. The United States can and will help the region upgrade its counterterror and security operations, especially at harbors and airports, but its more profound task is to help inoculate the ground against the spread of terrorist sympathizers. That means winning hearts and minds, which—for victory in the ultimate combat against Al Qaeda and terrorism—means helping to strengthen governance and improve the life prospects of all of the inhabitants of this crucial and endangered region.

Notes

1. Fifty-five percent of the people in the region are Muslims, according to the Department of State's *International Religious Freedom Report* (2004) and the latest edition of the *CIA Factbook*. Coptic Catholics in Ethiopia and Eritrea, Roman Catholics in the Sudan and Kenya, followers of traditional religions in the Sudan and Kenya, and Pentecostal and other Protestant groups in all countries, plus Jews in Ethiopia, account for the remaining 45 percent.

2. For valuable essays that complement much of the discussion in this book, see Alex de Waal (ed.), *Islamism and Its Enemies in the Horn of Africa* (Bloomington, 2004). A less profound but nevertheless helpful, largely historical commentary is contained in Shaul Shay (trans. Rachel Liberman), *The Red Sea Triangle: Sudan, Somalia, Yemen and Islamic Terror* (New Brunswick, 2005).

3. This and the ensuing discussion of governance and political goods draws heavily upon Robert I. Rotberg, "The Failure and Collapse of Nation-States: Breakdown, Prevention, and Repair," in Rotberg (ed.), *When States Fail: Causes and Consequences* (Princeton, 2004), 3–5.

4. In 2004, Transparency International's Corruption Perception Index of 145 world nations ranked Eritrea 102, Yemen 112, Ethiopia 114, the Sudan 122, and Kenya 129. Cameroon, Iraq, and Pakistan joined Kenya at the corrupt end of the scale. (Djibouti and Somalia were not ranked, for lack of data.) See www.transparency.org/cpi/2004/cpi2004.en.html.

5. Health statistics are from the World Development Indicators database (World Bank, 2001).

6. See Rotberg, "Failure and Collapse," 9–10.

7. Kenneth J. Menkhaus, "Somalia and Somaliland: Terrorism, Political Islam, and State Collapse," chapter 2 in this volume, p. 38.

8. Menkhaus, "Somalia and Somaliland," p. 38.

9. Dan Connell, "Eritrea: On a Short Fuse," chapter 4 in this volume, p. 66.

10. For details, see Robert I. Rotberg, "Sudan and the War in Darfur," *Great Decisions 2005* (New York, 2005), 57–67.

11. Robert D. Burrowes, "Yemen: Its Political Economy and the Effort against Terrorism," chapter 7 in this volume, p. 141.

12. World Bank, "World Development Indicators" (2003). The figure cited is GDP per capita in constant 1995 U.S. dollars.

13. Burrowes, "Yemen," p. 144. The official U.S. government view of Yemen's democracy is more benign.

14. Johnnie Carson, "Kenya: The Struggle against Terrorism," chapter 8 in this volume.

2

SOMALIA AND SOMALILAND
Terrorism, Political Islam, and State Collapse

KENNETH J. MENKHAUS

O n paper, Somalia appears to be an Islamic radical's "perfect storm." It is a completely collapsed state, where terrorists can presumably operate in a safe haven beyond the reach of rule of law. It possesses a long, unpatrolled coastline and hundreds of unmonitored airstrips, facilitating untracked movement of foreign jihadists and illicit business transactions. It is an Islamic society on the periphery of the Persian Gulf. Many of its people work or study in the Gulf States, so Somalia is in the orbit of Wahhabist preaching. A radical Islamist organization, Al Itihad Al Islamiya (AIAI), provides a potential partner for Al Qaeda. Moreover, Somalia's extreme poverty could be expected to spawn unemployment, desperation, and resentment, and hence make the country an ideal site for recruitment into terrorist cells. Sixteen years of armed conflict and lawlessness have provided a ready corps of battle-hardened militiamen. The rapid expansion of Islamic charities and schools, mostly funded from the Gulf, wins over hearts and minds and provides a convenient structure for recruitment of young Somali to the cause. And rising anti-Western sentiment among Somali, fueled in part by a sense of abandonment, in part by anger at American counterterrorism policies, and in part by opposition to the war in Iraq, is easily exploited by radical Islamists.

Yet, to date Somalia's role in the global terror network has been relatively modest. Al Qaeda has not established a major presence there. No Somali figure prominently in Al Qaeda leadership. Somalia does not appear to be a very fruitful recruitment site for terrorist foot soldiers. Few acts of terrorism have occurred within Somalia's borders. And Somalia's Islamist movements have not had nearly as much success as have those in the neighboring states of Yemen, Ethiopia, Kenya, the Sudan, and Tanzania. What has been surprising in Somalia is not that political Islam is ascendant—it is—or that Islamic (and other) terrorists have exploited Somalia's state collapse—they have—but that these movements have not been as active as one might have expected.

The puzzle of why Somalia has not yet become a bastion of terror may, however, increasingly be moot. Since late 2003, numerous jihadist attacks have been launched against international aid personnel in Somalia, leading Somali civic leaders, and pro-Western or pro-Ethiopian Somali political figures. This pattern of assassinations is linked to a small but extremely dangerous jihadi cell based in Mogadishu. On the political level, hard-line Somali Islamists formerly associated with AIAI have built a robust political base in Mogadishu and have successfully mobilized portions of the public. The jihadist assassinations and the revival of hard-line political Islamism are not necessarily linked and may in fact constitute rival Islamist movements. But they have occurred at the same time as a national peace process has produced an accord on a new Transitional Federal Government (TFG), led by pro-Ethiopian (and fiercely anti-Islamist) President Abdullahi Yusuf. How the TFG state-building project, increasing jihadist violence, rising hard-line Islamism, and Western counterterrorism policies interact in Somalia will be a major theme during the next several years.

Any assessment of terrorism in Somalia must confront the fact that evidence about local terrorist activity and radical Islamist movements is very sparse and fragmentary. As a result, existing analyses of long-term trends of radicalism and terrorism in Somalia vary wildly. On the alarmist side of the spectrum, analysts such as Medhane Tadesse claim that Somali businessmen, the Mogadishu political elite, the progressive Islamist group Al Islah, and AIAI are all closely linked to one another and to Al Qaeda.[1] On the more sanguine side of the spectrum, analysts such as de Waal claim that political Islam's influence in Somalia and the Horn peaked in the late 1990s and that the current American insistence on a terrorist threat in the region is an overreaction that paradoxically is fueling anti-Western, Islamist sentiments, creating a self-fulfilling prophecy.[2] Some of these differences reflect honest disagreements over interpretation of available evidence; in other cases, however, actors with political or ideological agendas exploit the uncertainty surrounding the question to advance their own cause. Consumers of analyses of the terrorist threat in Somalia must approach this topic with appropriate caution.

With that caveat in mind, in this analysis of state collapse, Islamism, and terrorism in Somalia, I advance the following set of arguments. First, despite the complete collapse of the state, Somalia has not been a major safe haven for foreign terrorists, due to a variety of factors, not least of which is the chronic insecurity and risk of betrayal and extortion that foreign terrorists encounter in Somalia. Its principal role in the terrorist portfolio has been as a transshipment point, allowing easy movement of men, money, and materiel into East Africa for operations of short duration. Nonetheless, an eventual increase in terrorist activity in Somalia was predictable and now appears to be occurring, though executed mainly by Somali jihadists rather than foreigners. American counterterrorism policy in Somalia since 2001, which has relied on local militia leaders to help monitor and apprehend suspects, has had only limited success, may be producing a public backlash, and now is on a collision course with local state-building initiatives. Some of the American allies are warlords who oppose a revived government. The United States faces the challenge of reconciling its counterterrorism policy with its stated desire to revive a central government. Ironically, efforts to revive a central government in Somalia may in the short run actually provide a more conducive environment for terrorists, who seem to prefer working within weak, quasi-states rather than collapsed ones.

Second, the gradual increase in presence and power that Islamist movements are enjoying in Somalia appears to be an enduring trend—Islamism is the ascendant ideology, and Islamic institutions, including schools, hospitals, charities, and local *shari'a* courts, are among the most functional and effective sources of services and security in Somalia. But in Somalia Islamism comprises a very diverse set of movements, ranging from progressive to conservative to radical; the dominant reformist movement today subscribes to nonviolence and relatively progressive Islamist thinking. Policies that engage progressive Islamists and marginalize radicals, that assist Somali in efforts to build a viable economy, and that support state building where it appears to be legitimate and sustainable, will go a long way toward defusing the threat of Islamist extremism. The alternative—focusing exclusively on counterterrorism surveillance, containment, and "snatch-and-grab" operations—runs the risk of creating a far more hostile environment in Somalia than currently prevails.[3]

I further consider the emerging confluence of interests between hard-line Islamists and one particular subclan in Somalia, the Haber Gedir Ayr. I argue that unless steps are taken to persuade the Ayr sub-clan that its long-term interests will be damaged by association with Islamic radicals and jihadists, this phenomenon could produce something akin to the Taliban-Pashtun linkage in Afghanistan or the jihadist–Sunni Arab linkage in Iraq, in which hard-line Islamists enjoy a "force multiplier" effect by successfully conflating their agenda with the interests of a broader ethnic group.

Background

Islam and Clan in Somalia

Traditionally, the practice of Islam in Somalia has been described as moderate—a "veil lightly worn."[4] Islam was and remains integrated into local customs. The strict, conservative Wahhabist practice of Islam in the Gulf States was largely unknown in Somalia until recently and considered foreign to Somali culture.

Somalia is a lineage-based society, with virtually every individual identified as a member of a clan family. Somali clannism is fluid, complex, and frequently misunderstood, but at the risk of oversimplification one can make the case that—especially since the collapse of the state in 1991—it forms the basis for most of the core social institutions and norms of traditional Somali society, including personal identity, rights of access to local resources, customary law (*xeer*), blood payment (*diya*) groups, and support systems. Islamic identity is one of several "horizontal identities" that cut across clan lines but tend to be subordinate to or complement rather than challenge the primacy of clannism. Religious leaders are often influential, but their authority is generally limited to their own clans. Beyond their clans, they act as ambassadors or negotiators representing their clans' interests. Likewise, shari'a law historically has never been a primary source of law, but aspects of shari'a were assimilated within xeer. Somali sheikhs and religious leaders have traditionally controlled limited judicial functions. Typically these encompass family law, including divorce and inheritance disputes, and respected sheikhs are called upon as arbitrators or peacemakers (*nabadoon*).[5] Despite the ascendance of a political Islamic movement in contemporary Somalia, clannism remains the dominant political logic within which Islamists and shari'a courts are generally constrained.

Sufist brotherhoods are the oldest and most widespread Islamic organizations in Somalia, and also cut across clan affiliations. These religious orders are moderate and embrace peaceful coexistence with secular political authorities. The Qadiriya, Salihiya, and Ahmadiya sects—found worldwide—are the most influential in Somalia today. Of these, only the Salihiya is distinguished by involvement in modern politics—it was the sect of Said Mohamed Abdullah Hassan (the "Mad Mullah"), who waged a twenty-year war of resistance against British and Italian colonial rule in northern Somalia, beginning in 1899. It is noteworthy that the two examples in Somalia's history of Islamic identity being successfully mobilized for jihad were both anti-foreign, anti-Christian liberation movements: the Said's anticolonial resistance and a sixteenth-century jihad against Abyssinian conquest, led by Imam Ahmed Gurey.

The Context of State Collapse

Somalia has been without a functional central government since early 1991, making it the longest-running instance of complete state collapse in post-colonial history. This unique context has been an important factor in the evolution of both nonviolent and jihadist Islamic movements in the country.

Over a dozen national peace initiatives have been launched unsuccessfully over a fourteen-year period, including the sustained efforts of a large UN peacekeeping mission in 1993–1995 (UNOSOM). This lengthy period of state collapse may soon end, however, if the Transitional Federal Government—declared in October 2004 as the culmination of a two-year peace process in Kenya—succeeds in reviving the central state. Whether the TFG will succeed or fail remains to be seen. But even in a best-case scenario it will possess only modest and loose control over the country; for the next several years, Somalia will remain de facto a collapsed state.

Importantly, the prolonged collapse of central government has not led to complete anarchy.[6] Critical changes have occurred since the early 1990s in the nature of armed conflict, governance, and lawlessness, rendering the country less anarchic than before. Contemporary Somalia is, in other words, without government but not without governance. Armed conflict is now more localized, less lethal, and of much shorter duration. Criminality, though still a serious problem, is much better contained than in the early 1990s, when egregious crimes could be committed with impunity. A variety of local forms of governance have emerged to provide Somali communities with at least minimal levels of public order. Informal rule of law has emerged via local shari'a courts, neighborhood watch groups, the reassertion of customary law and blood compensation payments, and the robust growth of private security forces that protect business assets. More formal administrative structures have been established at the municipal, regional, and transregional levels as well.

Somaliland is by far the most developed of these polities, and, since the late 1990s, it has made important gains in consolidating rule of law, multiparty democracy, functional ministries, and public security. Other substate administrations have tended to be vulnerable to spoilers and internal division, or have had only a weak capacity to project authority and deliver core services. Collectively, these informal and formal systems of governance fall well short of delivering the basic public security and services expected of a central government, but they provide a certain level of predictability and security to local communities.

This phenomenon of governance without government has been driven by gradual shifts in the interests of key local actors, and in the manner in which they seek to protect and advance those interests. The general trend is toward greater interests in improved security, rule of law, and predictability. This can be traced to an inadvertent impact of the UNOSOM presence in Mogadishu in 1993–1994. Though the intervention itself was a failure, the large UN operation poured an enormous amount of money, employment, and contract opportunities into the country, which helped to stimulate and strengthen legitimate business, shifting activity away from a war economy and toward construction, telecommunications, trade, and services. In the process, it helped to reshape local interests in security and rule of law, and eventually local power relations as well. It also helped to give rise to a business community in Mogadishu, which by 1999 broke free of local warlords and bought militiamen out from beneath them. The result is that today the private security forces of businessmen are the largest and best-armed militias in the city. Warlords, though still potential spoilers, are not nearly so powerful as they once were.

The evolving interest in rule of law and predictability is also actively promoted by neighborhood groups, who have formed local security watches to patrol their streets; professionals, especially in the education and health sectors, who are at the forefront of Somalia's nascent civil society; clan elders, who are seeking to recoup their traditional role as peacemakers; and even many militiamen, who over time prefer the stability of a paid job in a private security force to the dangers of banditry. In many instances, these sentiments constitute potential opportunities for reconciliation and state-building. The prominent role that civil society groups played in implementing the Mogadishu Stabilization and Security Plan in May–June 2005—an initiative that attempted to canton militias and remove militia roadblocks in the city— underscores the rising importance of public mobilization (*kadoon,* in Somali) in promoting and advancing public security.

Both progressive and hard-line Islamic movements have benefited from this complex state of governance without government in Somalia. The complete collapse of government social services, for instance, has provided Islamic charities with the opportunity to become the primary provider of education and health care services. The absence of a formal judiciary has enabled shari'a courts to step into the vacuum; they are now one of the most important forms of local rule of law. For hard-line Islamists, the continued collapse of the central government has provided a useful political environment—an opportunity to call for Islamic government as the cure for Somalia's crisis, an easily exploited cauldron of social frustration and resentment with which to rally radical anti-Western sentiment, and a safe haven from a state that, if revived, might be tempted to crack down on hard-line Islamist groups.

Recent Developments

Several major developments—the establishment of the Transitional National Government (TNG) beginning in August 2000, the ascendance of counterterrorism policies in the aftermath of the 9/11 attacks in 2001, and the formation in late 2004 of the Transitional Federal Government, the successor government to the failed TNG—have altered the Somali political landscape in ways which have had an impact on both the threat of terrorism and the fortunes of hard-line Islamists in Somalia.

The establishment of the TNG in 2000 did not yield a functional central government as most had hoped. It was never able to project its authority beyond portions of the Mogadishu area and was rejected by a large set of Somali regional states (such as Puntland and Somaliland) and factions. It did, however, affect Somali politics in other ways. The TNG's financial dependence on the Arab Gulf States, its anti-Ethiopian nationalist rhetoric, and its perceived ties to Islamist organizations such as AIAI alarmed Ethiopia, which responded by supporting Somali coalitions opposing the TNG. The TNG's failure to become operational during its three-year mandate exposed the facts that much of the Somali political elite continued to view the state as a source of personal gain, not a tool of administration, and that some key Somali constituencies maintain an interest in continuing state collapse. The Arta conference of 2000 established a template for power sharing based on fixed proportional representation by clan, the so-called 4.5 formula, which was adopted again in the 2002–2004 talks to establish a successor to the TNG. Finally, the TNG experience revealed much about the intentions of Islamist figures in Somalia, many of whom sought to parlay their leadership of shari'a courts into constituency-representative or cabinet positions in the government.

By acting like just another faction, the Mogadishu-based Islamists lost some of their legitimacy in the eyes of Somali citizens.

The terrorist attacks of 9/11 partially transformed the security context in which regional and global actors viewed Somalia. Throughout the 1990s, its state of collapse posed numerous security threats both regionally and globally, and the country attracted attention as a site of transnational criminality, Al Qaeda transit operations into Kenya, and arms flows and spillover of armed criminality into neighboring states. The 9/11 attacks dramatically increased concerns that Somalia was being exploited in some manner by Al Qaeda and other radical Islamist groups. In partnership with regional states, Western states engaged in much more vigilant monitoring of Somali businesses, money transfers, shipping, and cross-border movements, including freezing the assets of several Islamic charities and one remittance company suspected of having links to Al Qaeda. Some local authorities in Somalia have partnered with the United States in its efforts to monitor the terrorist threat.

The most important recent development in Somalia has been the declaration of a successor government to the TNG. The Transitional Federal Government was the result of two years of difficult negotiations under the auspices of the Intergovernmental Authority on Development (IGAD) in Nairobi, Kenya, starting in 2002. In late 2004, the peace talks produced a government composed of 275 members of parliament (selected along the lines of the 4.5 formula of clan proportional representation) and an eighty-nine-person cabinet led by President Abdullahi Yusuf and Prime Minister Ali Mohamed. The accord that produced the TFG was not in any sense a national reconciliation—it was instead a power-sharing agreement among Somalia's quarreling faction leaders and clans. It left most of the serious conflict issues unaddressed. This power-sharing accord would probably not have been achieved had it not been for concerted external pressure from Kenya, Ethiopia, Djibouti, IGAD, and the European Union.

The government that emerged from the talks has a number of key features. First, it is dominated by a pro-Ethiopian coalition and remains very close to the Ethiopian government. This feature has given opponents of the TFG, including hard-line Islamists, an easy rallying point, allowing them to paint the government as a tool of the Ethiopians. Second, though ostensibly a government of national unity, its top positions have remained in the hands of members of Yusuf's own clan (Mijerteen/Darood) or have been awarded to figures from other clans who are closely controlled by either Yusuf or the Ethiopians. This outcome has raised suspicions among some Hawiye (another prominent clan) that the TFG is dominated by the Darood. Third, the TFG includes few of the former leadership of the TNG, who have largely been shut out of the process.

Because the TNG was dominated by the powerful Haber Gedir Ayr subclan, which includes both some of the top businessmen in Mogadishu and some of the most prominent Islamist leaders, its virtual exclusion meant that a very important clan constituency in Mogadishu was less than enthusiastic about the outcome. Fourth, the TFG leadership is staunchly opposed to political Islamists of all kinds, even the more progressive movements like Al Islah (discussed below). This appeared to place the TFG on an early collision course with Islamists. Inevitably, Mogadishu became the epicenter of collective opposition to the TFG. That posed a major problem for the TFG, which insisted on a temporary capital outside of Mogadishu in the small agricultural town of Jowhar. Disputes over the site of the capital worsened the rift between the two rival wings of the TFG, known as the Mogadishu Group and Yusuf Group.

President Yusuf's solution to this crisis was to turn to the African Union (AU) and to IGAD countries for what he hoped would be a robust international peacekeeping force that would impose security in Mogadishu. IGAD seized the initiative and proposed a peacekeeping force for Somalia, and Ethiopia declared its intent to provide a contingent of peacekeepers. But the prospect of foreign peacekeepers—especially Ethiopians—was extremely unpopular in Mogadishu and among the Hawiye. This issue, and the general politics of relocation, created major fissures within the TFG. Hard-line Islamists in Mogadishu exploited these tensions, loudly rejecting the proposal for foreign peacekeepers and threatening to oppose them with force.

At the time of its establishment, the TFG faced several possible scenarios, all of which have implications both for terrorist threats and for radical Islam in Somalia. In a best-case scenario, the TFG would gradually build up its capacity to govern inside Somalia and maintain a government of national unity. The TFG would receive an adequate amount of external assistance in a timely fashion; exercise adequate stewardship of those funds; minimize and contain defections and rejectionists; make a pact with Hawiye business leaders in Mogadishu to allow the TFG to operate in the capital; manage relations with Somaliland peacefully; and begin rebuilding a modest state structure. In this successful scenario, the TFG would need to bring progressive and moderate political Islamists into the government, while marginalizing the hard-liners. Seven months into its existence, the TFG had achieved none of these benchmarks, raising real doubts about its viability. The unwillingness of the rival wings of the TFG to meet and reconcile raised additional doubts about the TFG's prospects.

A second possibility is a stillborn state scenario, in which disputes over issues such as relocation and foreign peacekeepers would cause the TFG to remain divided and dysfunctional, much as was the case with the ill-fated

TNG in 2000–2001. Though the TFG would continue to insist on its juridical sovereignty over the country for the duration of its five-year mandate, in reality Somalia would revert to a state of collapse. War would not break out between rival wings of the TFG because the TFG would be too weak to pose a threat to rejectionists, and because both sides appear reluctant to risk international sanctions and blame for provoking a war. For rejectionists, this outcome is optimal, and hence encourages them to "play for a stalemate" by blocking TFG progress. Islamic charities and shari'a courts would benefit from this outcome, filling the vacuum left by the collapsed state. Reversion to a collapsed state would unquestionably serve the interests of local jihadists and foreign terrorists as well. The Somali political landscape would in this scenario be dominated by the rise of multiple regional states, along the lines of Puntland.

In a worst-case scenario, the relocation of the TFG to Somalia and the introduction of IGAD peacekeeping forces would trigger war. The "Yusuf wing" of the TFG and Ethiopian forces would face armed resistance from the "Mogadishu Group," a loose coalition of Hawiye political and militia leaders, businesses, and shari'a court militias. Islamist hardliners would exploit this radicalized atmosphere to recruit and to establish themselves as the principal guardians of Somali nationalism (expressed as anti-Ethiopianism).

For the northern secessionist state of Somaliland, the period since 2000 has been marked both by political consolidation and by growing crisis. Politically, Somaliland has enjoyed impressive consolidation of its democracy and constitutional rule. It has made the transition to multiparty democracy, held local and presidential elections, resolved a disputed and extremely close presidential election without violence, and executed a peaceful constitutional transfer of power upon the death of President Muhammed Ibrahim Egal in 2002. At the same time, internal political divisions are increasingly acute; numerous assassinations of foreign aid workers during 2004, some apparently conducted by Islamic radicals, have damaged Somaliland's reputation for security; a military standoff with Puntland over control of parts of the Sool region remains unresolved and has resulted in several serious armed clashes; and the formation of the TFG has created deep uncertainty over Somaliland's future. Somaliland was preparing to hold a parliamentary election as this book went to press.

Contemporary Islamism in Somalia and Somaliland

The threat of terrorism in contemporary Somalia springs almost exclusively from radical Islamic movements and jihadi cells, so an assessment of terrorist threats there must begin with a close examination of general trends in political Islam.[7] Islam unquestionably plays a much more visible role in Somali society today than prior to the civil war. This heightened role manifests itself in different ways—in shifts in political rhetoric, the rise of shari'a courts, the ascendance of Islamic charities and Islamic schools, attitudes regarding women and matters of public morality, and views of the West. Somalia cannot at this time be depicted as a hotbed of Islamic radicalism. It is, however, a hotbed of competition and debate among Islamist movements for legitimacy and public support. That competition can broadly be defined as a struggle between the traditional Sufi religious leadership, the modernist or reformist Al Islah movement, highly conservative but nonviolent Salafists, and the radical Al Itihad Al Islamiya movement. Of these, only one—Al Itihad Al Islamiya—is designated as having links to terrorist organizations. However, in recent years a number of assassinations and attacks by small jihadist cells in Somalia point to a new, decentralized, terrorist threat whose linkages to established Islamic movements are as yet unclear.

Traditionalists

The majority of sheikhs, clerics, and Islamic scholars in Somalia fall into the category of Sufi traditionalists. Many of these clerics are organized in one of several Sufi brotherhoods. They tend to be apolitical and moderate in their interpretation of Islam. Most of the communal centers of learning and production (*jamaaca*) associated with the brotherhoods were destroyed or dispersed during the civil war, and most observers concur that the brotherhoods have lost some social authority and credibility in Somali society. In 1991, the traditionalists were organized in an umbrella group, the Ahlu Sunna wal Jama'a (ASWJ), by General Mohamed Aideed. He hoped to use them as a counterweight against rising fundamentalism. ASWJ preaches a message of social harmony and nonviolence and fiercely opposes Salafists and the AIAI. Its greatest strength is its cultural nationalism; it criticizes new Islamist movements as Wahhabism, arguing that they represent a "non-Somali," foreign imposition of Islamic practices.[8]

Progressive Reformists

Al Islah is the most important and visible of the modernist Islamic movements in Somalia. Its presence is concentrated in Mogadishu; it is not a significant factor in the rest of the country. It is associated ideologically with the Muslim Brotherhood, or Ikhwan Muslimiin, subscribing to progressive, nonviolent ideals. It seeks to establish a modern Islamic state compatible with democracy, civil liberties, and women's rights. Al Islah began as a charity in postwar Somalia but evolved into what Bryden describes as a "sophisticated political movement with a strong base of support among Mogadishu's youth, professionals, and business community."[9] To date, it has not sought a direct political role in Somalia, but it exercises considerable informal influence as a network and interest group. It initially threw its support behind the Arta peace process and the TNG before becoming disillusioned, and it has been able to promote large street demonstrations against warlord violence in Mogadishu. Its principal claim to fame, however, has been its role in establishing the University of Mogadishu and supporting educational associations, including the Formal Private Education Network (FPEN), which provides schooling at the primary and secondary levels to 100,000 children, mainly in Mogadishu.[10]

Nonviolent Salafists

Salafists—a worldwide group of "fundamentalist" Islamists who seek to purify the practice of Islam by correcting what they view as centuries of corrupting influences and misinterpretations—have made significant headway in Somalia through extensive missionary, educational, and charity work. Unlike Al Islah, Somalia's Salafist movements have made inroads throughout the country, with especially active bases in Mogadishu, the lower Shabelle region, Kismayo, Burao, and Puntland. Worldwide, Salafists have for years been split over doctrine, with some advocating jihadist violence to establish Islamic states and others claiming that most Islamic societies first need a generation or more of education, socialization, and purification of Islamic practices before jihad can be sanctioned and the goal of Islamic governance achieved.[11] In Somalia, this split is reflected in the division between the Salafist missionary movements such as Al Tabliq and the violent AIAI.

Al Tabliq and Majuma Ulema are two highly conservative Salafist movements in Somalia. Tabliq, a global movement originating in Pakistan, has quickly grown into the largest fundamentalist Islamist movement in the country, drawing on foreign funding to establish schools across the country. Elsewhere it has been accused of using *madrassas* to recruit for Al Qaeda, but in Somalia its leadership insists that it subscribes to a doctrine of nonviolence that distinguishes it from AIAI. In reality, it is difficult to ascertain the extent to which a doctrinal "firewall" really separates Tabliq from AIAI.

For its part, Majuma Ulema, based in Mogadishu, consists of a group of Islamic clerics who claim to be the "highest scholars of Islam in Somalia"; they periodically issue political statements reflecting a highly conservative, fundamentalist vision. In recent times, they have issued statements on "un-Islamic" practices, condemned Somali collaboration with Western counterterrorism efforts, and rejected the IGAD peace talks. Though ostensibly distinct from AIAI, Majuma's willingness to point a finger at "un-Islamic" practices, essentially leveling a charge of *takfir* (or apostasy) at implicated Somali leaders, is dangerous, as that charge is a central justification for jihadi Salafists to use violence against Muslim rulers. (Jihadi Salafists are proscribed by Islam from taking such action without a charge of takfir.) The Majuma leadership's penchant for making such charges runs the risk of what Wiktorowicz calls "decentralized takfir," in which takfir "becomes a blanket weapon selectively wielded to legitimize attacks against those deemed obstacles to Salafi thought and activism."[12] Moreover, it throws into doubt the group's claims that it is nonviolent; by declaring apostasy, it justifies the killing of Somali leaders by jihadists and is arguably complicit in the violence.

Al Itihad Al Islamiya

AIAI first arose in Mogadishu in the late 1980s as a movement composed mainly of educated young men who had studied or worked in the Middle East.[13] They came to the conclusion that the only way to rid Somalia of the corruption, repression, and tribalism that prevailed under the regime of President Siad Barre was through political Islam. In this sense, it mirrored many other Islamic movements in the Middle East. With the collapse of the state in early 1991, AIAI made several attempts to hold strategic real estate, including seaports (it failed to hold Bosaaso in the north, but temporarily ran seaports at Kismayo and Merka) and the commercial crossroads town of Luuq in southern Somalia, near the Ethiopian border. Some observers claim that AIAI's influence and organizational capacity peaked as early as 1993. AIAI managed to govern Luuq from 1991 to 1996, imposing shari'a law on the community. In other towns, it developed cells that exercised varying levels of political influence locally. In 1996, the Ethiopian branch of AIAI engaged in several acts of terrorism inside Ethiopia, including two hotel bombings and an assassination attempt. Those acts prompted the U.S. State Department to label AIAI a terrorist organization. They also led the Ethiopian government to crack down on the organization. Ethiopia launched military attacks against Luuq, which had been suspected of hosting non-Somali Islamists from the Sudan. AIAI was driven out of the town and scattered. It is not clear that all branches of AIAI in Somalia (which were generally clan based) supported acts of terrorism in Ethiopia. But AIAI has also been implicated in a number of attacks inside Somalia, including the 1999 murder of an American aid worker near the Kenyan-Somali border.

Since 1996, Al Itihad has embraced a new strategy. First, it has decided not to try to hold towns or territory, as that only makes it an easy fixed target for Ethiopia and other enemies.[14] Instead, it now integrates into local Somali communities. AIAI has also forsaken short-term political goals and adopted a long-term strategy to bring Islamic rule to Somalia, making the organization increasingly difficult to distinguish from nonviolent Salafists such as Tabliq. It focuses on key sectors of society—education, local judiciaries, the media, non-profit organizations, and commerce—to build constituencies, place members, socialize Somali, and construct a power base. As an organization, AIAI has essentially disbanded, existing only as a loose network of "alumni," in part to attract less attention from counterterrorism surveillance.

However, some ex-AIAI leaders, such as Hassan Dahir Aweys, remain politically active. Aweys has successfully co-opted local Somali shari'a court structures as a platform for political influence; as deputy chairman of the Joint Shari'a Courts, Aweys made headlines in October 2004 by vowing to order shari'a militia to attack any foreign peacekeeping troops deployed in Somalia to assist the TFG. He claimed that it was Somali's "religious duty" to fight peacekeepers, arguing that clan fighters might earn God's forgiveness for past crimes if they "cleansed themselves with the blood of the foreign invaders."[15] Aweys and the residual network of AIAI alumni remain potentially dangerous, but they have carefully avoided direct association with or responsibility for recent jihadist assassinations in Mogadishu, making it more difficult for the United States and its counterterrorist partners to build a case against them. Aweys has in fact enjoyed considerable success in placing himself more in the mainstream of Mogadishu's politics, perhaps in order to make a bid for political leadership in the future.

Shari'a Courts

Since the early 1990s, political Islam has been propagated in Somalia through the establishment of shari'a courts in a number of different cities and towns, but particularly in Mogadishu and the Shabelle river valley. A variety of motives lay behind the establishment of these courts, which manage some of the country's best-equipped militia forces. First, the courts can be considered a response by local communities to improve security conditions in the absence of state police forces. Second, the courts provide a secure environment for Somali businessmen who profit from local and regional trade. The businessmen are protected from attacks by uncontrolled militia and bandits—thus reducing the need to pay high overheads for private security forces. Third, they have in some cases served as institutional vehicles for a small number of Islamic radicals to promote political agendas.

Although popular with local communities for reestablishing a semblance of law and order, the shari'a courts face substantial challenges and limitations. First, they are strongly opposed by some of Somalia's strongest warlords, who view the shari'a leaders as potential rivals for power. Second, the courts are invested with authority by the clan elders. Unless they are able to develop political, military, and financial autonomy, this fact limits their ability to reach decisions that go against the interests of the clan. Third, the jurisdiction of these courts rarely extends beyond the subclan operating them, limiting their ability to handle most crimes. Finally, many Somali—although pleased with the short-term improvements in security that the courts provide—are wary of the longer term consequences if the courts bring Islamic fundamentalism into the political mainstream.

Since the beginning of 2004, the shari'a courts in Mogadishu have returned to prominence. By mid-2004, eleven different shari'a courts had been established in the capital city, and their leadership and militia were pooled into a single Joint Islamic Courts administration. Members of the Joint Courts include a number of former AIAI leaders, including Aweys, the courts' deputy chairman. This use of the shari'a courts as a political base by a hard-line Islamist leader marks a departure from the past. Recently, Aweys has sought to expand the role of sharia militias from their narrow policing function to enforcers of public morality, sending them to close down mixed-gender parties and shops selling alcohol.

Until recently, the militias employed by shari'a courts were simply paid gunmen with no particular allegiance to Islamism. Even when AIAI administered the district of Luuq from 1991 to 1996, its militia was frequently unruly, accused of theft and other "non-Islamic" behavior. Most shari'a court militiamen will work for whoever pays them—they in no way resemble a committed corps of young mujahideen. This is an important but often poorly understood dimension of the shari'a militias. And it may limit the ability of a hard-liner like Aweys to mobilize them in combat, should he choose to call them to arms.

Islamic Charities

Islamic charities are a relatively new phenomenon in Somalia. They focus on key social sectors of education and health, earning legitimacy by exploiting the failure of local government to provide these services. They rely heavily on *zakat*, or tithing, from foreign sources, but enjoy significant success in building a sense of local ownership of and responsibility for the schools and health centers that they support, as reflected in effective cost-recovery via user fees. Somalia's Islamic charities struggle with new demands for transparency and accountability in their operations. They use aid strategically to pursue an Islamist vision of social order. All of these features mirror broader trends in Islamic charities worldwide.

Most important, evidence from Somalia's Islamic charities reveals a divergence between two competing schools of thought. The mainstream school embraces a relatively progressive vision of a future Islamic order that is intended to replace the destructive, clannish, and corrupt factions and militias currently dominating the Somali political scene. A much smaller group of radical Islamists operates charities supporting mosques and schools with a sharp anti-Western agenda. The mainstream charity groups have to date enjoyed much greater success and support, as their agenda resonates with the immediate concerns of local communities—namely, access to needed services and an alternative vision of a political order to the clannism, violence, and state collapse that have plagued Somalia for fourteen years.[16]

Islamism in Somaliland

Islamic charities, Salafist missionary movements, and radicals all have a presence in Somaliland as well as Somalia, but their activities and influence are considerably lesser in Hargeisa than in Mogadishu. Somaliland's stability and economic recovery provide a social context less conducive to radicalism; its government is relatively effective at monitoring radicalism within most of its borders (though less so in the town of Burao, which is the Islamist stronghold in Somaliland); strained relations with Arab Gulf States have increased the sentiment in Somaliland that Salafist Islam is an "un-Somali" form of Saudi Wahhabist cultural imperialism; and its partnership with Ethiopia and the West in the war on terror increases Somaliland's strategic importance and is a vital element of its bid for international recognition. Still, even in Somaliland, long-time observers see a clear trend toward the increased expression of more conservative Islamic practices and displays of piety (such as a notable increase in the number of women wearing the chador) than in the past.

The Terrorist Threat in Somalia

Concern that Somalia's Islamist movements might constitute a broader threat to international security first arose in the aftermath of the Al Qaeda–sponsored terrorist attack on the U.S. embassies in Nairobi and Dar es Salaam in

1998.[17] No Somali were implicated in the attacks themselves, but evidence suggested that Somalia had been used as a preparation site.[18] It was then that analysts began to reconsider the claims made years earlier by Osama bin Laden that Al Qaeda had directly supported the Somali militia in attacks on American peacekeeping forces. "Bin Laden, we now believe, provided training and equipment in the early 1990s to the factional fighters that killed Americans in Mogadishu," claimed former Assistant Secretary of State for Africa Susan Rice.[19] But most observers did not take the claim at face value and instead saw it as an attempt by bin Laden to earn credit for events in which Al Qaeda had played no substantial role.[20]

In the aftermath of the 9/11 terrorist attacks on New York and Washington, concerns about terrorist links inside Somalia rose dramatically. As Al Qaeda was attacked and driven from Afghanistan, Somalia quickly earned a spot on the shortlist of countries that might be targeted in an expanded war on terrorism. U.S. naval interdiction and patrolling of the Somali coast was initiated, aerial surveillance was conducted over the country, and increased American intelligence assets were devoted to monitoring a country that had been given little attention since 1994. In 2001, the U.S. Treasury Department froze the assets of Al Barakaat, the largest Somali remittance and telecommunications company, claiming that it was part of Al Qaeda's global financial empire. The department never provided information to clarify the specific charges against Al Barakaat. Among Somalia analysts, the move is widely seen as questionable.[21]

Some of the most alarmist fears—that Al Qaeda had training camps and bases in Somalia or that AIAI was operating as a subsidiary of Al Qaeda—were eventually dispelled as the United States stepped up monitoring and intelligence gathering. That effort produced no evidence of Al Qaeda bases in Somalia. The U.S. Department of Defense, which had initially relied uncritically on Ethiopian military intelligence, discovered that the Ethiopians and some of their Somali allies had vested interests in exaggerating the threat of radical Islam in Somalia.

In reality, Somalia has turned out to be less than ideal as a safe haven for Al Qaeda, particularly in comparison with other options. First, terrorist cells and bases are much more exposed to international counterterrorist action in zones of state collapse. Violations of state sovereignty by a U.S. Special Forces operation are less problematic (or might even go undetected) where a central government either does not exist or is unable to extend its authority to large sections of the country. The establishment of an 1,800 man base at Camp Lemonier in neighboring Djibouti, designed to provide the U.S. military with what one spokesperson termed the capacity to "go into an ungoverned area in pursuit of Al Qaeda," serves as a reminder of U.S. capacity to launch such counterterrorist missions.[22] Likewise, in a zone of state collapse, the United States and its allies can subcontract the hunt for terrorist suspects to local militias and warlords with fewer political complications, as the United States is currently doing in Somalia through several warlords. Similar bounty hunting within the territory of a sovereign state would raise fierce objections.

Second, areas of state collapse tend to be inhospitable and dangerous, so few if any foreigners choose to reside there. The fewer the foreigners, the more difficult it is for foreign terrorists to blend in unnoticed. At present, the number of foreigners resident in Somalia is probably only in the hundreds. Those who do are mainly international aid workers, businessmen, teachers in Islamic schools, and spouses of these individuals and of Somali. Unless exceptional measures are taken to hide in a safe house, a non-Somali's presence is known to all, and his or her agenda becomes a matter of great interest to the local community. To the extent that secrecy matters to a terrorist cell—presumably, a great deal—a collapsed state is not an ideal location. There, terrorists may be beyond the rule of law but not beyond the purview of curious and suspicious locals. The case of Suleiman Abdulla (discussed below) suggests that a non-Somali terrorist can pose as a legitimate businessman and operate freely for a period of time, but his eventual identification and apprehension also demonstrate how risky that tactic is in a context like Somalia. Likewise, it is entirely possible that a cell of Somali Islamists could provide shelter for a foreign Al Qaeda member—and rumors circulate in Mogadishu that such safe houses do exist—but to remain undetected that individual would have to be virtually housebound.

Third, the lawlessness of collapsed states such as Somalia is a double-edged sword for terrorists. On the one hand, it reduces the risk of apprehension by law enforcement agencies, but on the other, it exponentially increases vulnerability to the most common crimes of chaos—kidnapping, extortion, blackmail, and assassination. The same security threats that plague international aid agencies in these areas would also afflict foreign terrorist groups. Ironically, it appears that lawlessness can inhibit rather than facilitate certain types of lawless behavior.

Fourth, foreign terrorists would be susceptible to betrayal by Somali eager to reap the rewards of handing over a terrorist suspect to the United States. Somali leaders have seized upon the war on terror as an opportunity to demonstrate their value to the West, in the expectation that doing so might translate into tangible benefits: foreign and military aid. In reality, this approach has not been as effective a deterrent to terrorist operations as Western governments had hoped, mainly because of the very high risks associated with betraying a terrorist cell and the subclan protecting it. Some would-be local allies in the war on terror have been reluctant to pursue suspects on behalf of the West.

Fifth, external actors find zones of endemic state collapse and armed conflict difficult environments in which to maintain neutrality. Somalia has been exceptionally challenging on this score. Local contacts and supporters are invariably partisan in local disputes, and the external actor—whether an aid agency or terrorist cell—can quickly become embroiled in those disputes and be seen as choosing sides simply by making hiring, rental, and contract decisions. Once viewed as being "owned" by a particular clan, the external actor becomes a legitimate target for reprisals by rival clans.

Finally, Somalia's state of collapse and poor security have virtually emptied the country of Western embassies and other "soft targets," making it far less interesting as an operational base than neighboring Kenya. For all of these reasons, the terrorist threat has turned out to be somewhat less significant in Somalia than was initially feared.

Using Somalia for Terrorism

Nonetheless, the general concern that Al Qaeda could use Somalia in some manner is not unwarranted. From 2001 to 2003 evidence began to emerge that terrorist activities inside Somalia were in fact in a state of evolution.

In 1998, Al Qaeda operatives bombed the U.S. embassies in Nairobi and Dar es Salaam. These attacks represented a new level of involvement by Somalia in terrorism. Though no Somali were directly involved, Somalia was used as a transit point for bomb materiel, and after the attacks at least two of the bombing suspects, including the mastermind, Comoros citizen Fazul Abdullah Mohammed, came from and went through Somalia. Its use as a transshipment point for terrorist weapons and as a temporary safe haven for foreign terrorists conducting attacks against Western targets constituted a significant evolution in Somalia's role in terrorism.

This role resurfaced in December 2002, when terrorists bombed a hotel in Mombasa and attempted to bring down an Israeli charter plane at the Mombasa airport. Evidence later emerged that foreign suspects had acquired surface-to-air missiles and other explosive materiel for the attack in Mogadishu, had trained there for a month, and fled into Somalia after the attack.[23] Concerns that Somalia was becoming a safe haven for terrorists grew in May 2003, when Suleiman Abdulla Salim Hemed, a Yemeni terrorist suspect who had lived and worked in Mogadishu for four years, was apprehended by the Somali militia of strongman Mohamed Dheere, working in cooperation with American and Kenyan authorities. That same month the U.S. government persuaded Saudi Arabia to close the quasi-government charity Al Haramein in Somalia on grounds that it was being used as a front for terrorists.

A foiled terrorist operation in Kenya in June 2003 revealed a new level of Somali involvement in Al Qaeda. The attack on the U.S. embassy in Nairobi, by light aircraft and truck, had not only been planned inside Somalia but directly involved Somali and Somali Kenyans associated with Al Qaeda. Until then, Somali individuals had had little to no direct involvement in terrorist attacks against Western targets.

Since October 2003 there have been a series of assassinations of Western and international aid workers and journalists in Somalia and Somaliland. As of mid-2005, these attacks have claimed the lives of six people and injured several others, and have forced international aid agencies to take stringent security precautions. In almost every case, Somali Islamists appeared to have been implicated. The assassinations were well planned. The fact that most of these attacks occurred in Somaliland, which previously had a reputation as a very secure environment, is especially troubling, suggesting a possible fusion of interests between southern Somali seeking to discredit and destabilize Somaliland and jihadists looking for soft Western targets.

This series of attacks hints at a new and worrisome threat emanating not from a well-defined group like AIAI, but rather from a small decentralized jihadist cell composed of Somali committed to killing Westerners. Whether these cells operate entirely independent of Al Qaeda or take cues from Islamist figures like Aweys is unknown. Likewise, it is as yet unclear whether the assassinations are being executed by a new group of highly committed terrorists or are merely the work of paid gunmen. What little is publicly known about the jihadi cell in Mogadishu was revealed in a July 2005 Crisis Group report. That report documented that the jihadi cell is small and is led by a young militia named Aden Hashi 'Ayro, who himself has little schooling in Islamist thought but who may be using jihadism as a pretext for political violence. Whatever the depth of their knowledge and commitment to Islamic radicalism, the 'Ayro cell has introduced a new dimension of terrorism into Somalia since 2002 and demonstrates the destabilization and fear that a small jihadi cell can produce in the absence of effective government policing. In any case, they have introduced a new dimension of terrorism to Somalia.[24]

This security threat will present a real problem to the UN, aid agencies, and foreign embassies if the TFG succeeds in reviving the central government and the international community begins to reestablish a larger presence inside Somalia. The explosion of a car bomb in Mogadishu in February 2005, apparently intended to hit an AU delegation visiting the city, was an ominous sign both of the willingness of jihadists to strike international targets and of a new familiarity with more sophisticated tactics, probably imported from Iraq.

Finally, since 2004 jihadists have assassinated a number of Somali civic and political figures in Mogadishu. The assassination of leading peace activist and civic leader Abdulqadir Yahya in July 2005 was especially troubling. In addition, a number of former military commanders who have openly supported the call for international peacekeepers or who have cooperated with U.S. counterterrorism efforts have been killed.[25] The explosion that occurred during Prime Minister Ghedi's speech at Mogadishu Stadium in May 2005 may also have been a jihadi assassination attempt, though the case remains unsolved. This, too, represents a dangerous escalation of jihadist activity. It runs the risk of embroiling Mogadishu in cycles of revenge killings and generalized inter-clan warfare.

One of the most worrisome aspects about the recent ascendance of both jihadist violence and hard-line Islamist leadership in Mogadishu is the possibility that their narrow agenda will be increasingly—and intentionally—conflated with the political interests of some Mogadishu-based clans, which have produced much of the top Islamist leadership and business elite. This tactic of conflating a narrow Islamist agenda with the interests of a broader ethnic group has been a complicating factor in places such as Afghanistan (the Taliban-Pashtun linkage) and more recently in Iraq (the jihadist–Sunni Arab linkage). To date, Aweys and his associates have exploited a number of grievances that resonate closely with some Hawiye clans through their opposition to the proposal to introduce foreign peacekeepers in Somalia, Ethiopian influence over and patronage of the TFG, Abdullahi Yusuf, the Darood clan's dominance of the TFG, and calls for political decentralization and federalism. By seizing the role of principal spokesperson on these matters, and by wrapping these essentially clannish grievances in the mantle of Islam, Aweys has succeeded in linking the fate of the hard-line Islamists to the fate of an entire clan. This tactic could provide Aweys and his group with what amounts to a force multiplier effect in the struggle against the TFG.

For the West, however, the overriding concern in Somalia remains the possibility that foreign terrorists will exploit Somalia in some manner. This concern was underscored in the summer of 2005 by a high-ranking U.S. military officer in Central Command, Major-General Douglas Lute, who publicly predicted that top Al Qaeda figures in Iraq are likely relocate to "vast ungoverned spaces" of East Africa and specifically named Somalia as a possible spot.[26] There are five roles that terrorists have assigned or might assign to Somalia:

Safe haven. Somalia can be exploited by foreign terrorists seeking to evade detection and apprehension by residing beyond the rule of law. Though to date it has proven to be relatively inhospitable to foreigners seeking safe haven, the complete lack of customs and immigration control at landing strips, sea ports, and borders makes this prospect worrisome.

Transshipment. Unpatrolled beaches and borders mean that men, money, and materiel can be easily moved through Somalia into neighboring countries for use in attacks against soft international targets.

Base for attacks on international targets inside the country. Since 2003, six international aid workers and journalists in Somalia have been killed in what appear to have been targeted assassinations implicating Somali jihadists. This constitutes a new and very dangerous development for the aid community, diplomats, and other foreigners who need to have a physical presence in Somalia.

Misuse of businesses and charities. The absence of government oversight and law enforcement in Somalia makes it difficult to monitor the activities of businesses and charities, at present accountable to no one. The vast majority of these entities are legitimate, but a few, such as the company Al Barakaat and the charity Al Haramein, have been accused of serving as fronts for terrorist groups.

Recruitment site. To date, Somalia has not been a significant source of recruitment for Al Qaeda or other terrorist organizations, but Somalia's ongoing crisis constitutes an ideal environment for such recruitment, especially among uneducated, unemployed young men who currently face a bleak future, as well as the large number of Somali migrants and students residing in Gulf States, where they are exposed to Wahhabist Islam. That factor, coupled with rising anti-Western sentiments and anger at the relatively low level of international engagement in Somalia, could turn some Somali toward Al Qaeda or its affiliates. The arrest of a Somali refugee as an accomplice in the failed copy-cat underground bombing in London in late July 2005 raised fears that the Somali diaspora in the West, previously an unimportant source of recruitment into terrorist cells, may be becoming more receptive to Al Qaeda.

State Building and Terrorism

The conventional wisdom, expressed in countless papers and reports in the past several years, is that failed states constitute a national security threat to the United States as safe havens for Al Qaeda and other terrorists. Nation building, only a few years ago reviled as a fool's errand by most national security analysts, is once again on the front burner.

In terms of Somalia, the case for reviving the central government as part of the war on terror is clear. A functional government will serve as a vital law enforcement partner to monitor terrorist movement and activities inside Somalia. As the TFG attempts to establish an administration within the country, this rationale is likely to figure prominently among its advocates.

Yet, evidence from Somalia and neighboring states suggests that the relationship between state building and terrorism is more complex. Specifically, an argument can be made that the initial phase of reviving the state in Somalia—a period of at least a decade—will produce conditions that may actually be more, not less, conducive for terrorism.[27] A fully functional and effective state can deter terrorist activity, but a "quasi-state"—one in which the central government enjoys juridical sovereignty but is largely unable to exercise it within its borders—constitutes an ideal operating environment for terrorists, who can exploit corrupt or ineffective police and border patrols, hide from unilateral U.S. counterterrorism operations behind the banner of Somali sovereignty, infiltrate the new government, and target a growing set of soft Western targets that would reestablish a physical presence in Somalia. The relationship between state building and counterterrorism is thus complicated by a crisis of transition from collapsed state to fully functional state—a period when the TFG is weak, vulnerable, but sovereign. Hence the security paradox of nation building: the very success of post-conflict reconstruction in a collapsed state will produce a temporary political situation in which terrorist networks could thrive.

Moreover, the reality is that, at least up to now, transnational criminals and terrorists have found zones of state collapse like Somalia to be relatively inhospitable territory in which to operate. In general, terrorist networks have instead found safety in weak, corrupted states—Pakistan, Yemen, Kenya, the Philippines, Guinea, and Indonesia. Terrorist networks, like mafias, appear to flourish where states are governed badly rather than not at all.

At the heart of this security dilemma lie two propositions, both of which are disquieting. The first proposition correctly identifies the collapsed Somali state as a major security threat in the war on terrorism. The second proposition, offered by critics of nation building, correctly argues that nation building as currently conceived is an enterprise with a high rate of failure.

There are several potential policy responses to this dilemma. One is quietly to abandon the nation-building enterprise in Somalia and accept that the war on terrorism there will continue to be reactive, not preventive, executed as a protracted military and counterterrorist operation against threats that thrive in a swamp the U.S. has opted not to try to drain. There are obvious costs and shortcomings with this approach, but it has attractions, too. It has the simplicity of a duck hunt, and because it calls for responses for which the United States is well equipped, it is entirely plausible that this approach will win favor.

Indeed, this option may be especially attractive to some because it allows the United States to avoid changing its current counterterrorism policy. That policy relies on local militia leaders to assist in monitoring and occasionally apprehending suspects. Many of those militia leaders do not support the idea of a revived central government, and would stand to lose the counterterrorist "contract" with the United States. As the TFG leadership attempts to establish its presence inside Somalia, the United States may be compelled to reconcile its support for state building with its operational reliance on warlords who stand against the state-building process.[28]

The alternative is to devise some new security architecture that would simultaneously allow the United States and its allies to revive a central government while retaining a transitional caretaker role in monitoring and pursuing terrorists inside Somalia. This result would provide some means of reducing the likelihood that terrorists would exploit Somalia during its long transition from collapse to full functionality.

Notes

1. Medhane Tadesse, *Al Ittihad: Political Islam and Black Economy in Somalia* (Addis Ababa, 2002).

2. Alex de Waal (ed.), *Islamism and Its Enemies in the Horn of Africa* (Bloomington, 2004), 231–239.

3. This finding mirrors the conclusion reached by International Crisis Group regarding U.S. counterterrorism strategy in the Sahel. See ICG, "Islamic Terrorism in the Sahel: Fact or Fiction?" Africa Report 92 (Dakar/Brussels, March 31, 2005), 2–3.

4. Portions of this section are adapted from a recent study in which the author was lead consultant. He acknowledges the contributions, in both writing and analysis, of co-authors Mark Bradbury, Matt Bryden, and Andre Le Sage. See Development Alternatives, Inc., "Somalia Programming and Policy Assessment" (Washington, D.C., January 2005), 10–17.

5. Andre Le Sage, *Stateless Justice in Somalia: Formal and Informal Rule of Law Initiatives* (Nairobi, 2005), 29–38.

6. This section is derived from chapter 1 in Menkhaus, *Somalia: State Collapse and the Threat of Terrorism*, Adelphi Paper 364 (Oxford, 2004), 15–36.

7. One possible exception is the sporadic use of Somalia as a base of operations or transit by secular Ethiopian insurgencies such as the Oromo Liberation Front and the Ogaden National Liberation Front. Both groups view themselves as liberation movements, not terrorist organizations; the Ethiopian government disagrees.

8. Typically, the practice of referring to Salafist beliefs as Wahhabism is intended to be derogatory, implying that the belief system is distinct to Saudi Arabia, where Wahhabism is practiced.

9. Matt Bryden, "No Quick Fixes: Coming to Terms with Terrorism, Islam, and Statelessness in Somalia," *Journal of Conflict Studies,* XXIII (2003), 39.

10. Andre Le Sage with Menkhaus, "The Rise of Islamic Charities in Somalia: An Assessment of Impact and Agendas," unpub. paper presented at the International Studies Association annual conference, Montreal (March 17–20, 2004), 17–18.

11. Quintan Wiktorowicz, "The New Global Threat: Transnational Salafis and Jihad," *Middle East Policy*, VIII (2001), 22.

12. Ibid., 27.

13. An in-depth assessment of AIAI can be found in International Crisis Group, "Somalia: Combating Terrorism in a Failed State" (Washington, D.C., May 2002). See also Roland Marchal, "Islamic Political Dynamics in the Somali Civil War," in de Waal (ed.), *Islamism and Its Enemies*, 114–145.

14. For several years, AIAI maintained a remote base in the coastal settlement of Ras Kamboni near the Kenyan border, but the size and significance of that settlement was greatly exaggerated in the aftermath of 9/11. Claims that Ras Kamboni serves as a terrorist training camp, made by writers such as Shaul Shay (in *The Red Sea Terror Triangle* [New York, 2005]) are based on information that is both outdated and inaccurate.

15. Quoted in "Holy War Threatened if Peacekeeper Force Is Sent to Somalia," *Toronto Star* (March 26, 2005), A11.

16. Le Sage with Menkhaus, "Rise of Islamic Charities." See also Andre Le Sage, "Somalia and the War on Terrorism: Political Islamic Movements and U.S. Counterterrorism Efforts," unpub. Ph.D. dissertation (University of Cambridge, June 2004), 185–227.

17. Portions of this analysis are derived from chapter 3 of Menkhaus, *Somalia: State Collapse*, 49–76.

18. Thomas Ricks, "Allies Step up Somalia Watch; U.S. Aims to Keep Al Qaeda at Bay," *Washington Post* (January 4, 2002).

19. Quoted in "Somalia 'Most Likely to Be Next Base' for Al Qaeda," *The Straits Times* (Singapore) (December 1, 2001).

20. Nonetheless, linkage of Al Qaeda to the deaths of eighteen U.S. soldiers in the Black Hawk Down incident in Somalia has now become conventional wisdom.

21. Menkhaus, "Remittance Companies and Money Transfers in Somalia," unpub. paper (October 2001); Roland Marchal, "The Outcome of U.S. Decision on al-Barakaat," unpub. paper for the European Commission (January 2002); Mark Bradbury, "Somalia: The Aftermath of September 11th and the War on Terrorism," unpublished report for Oxfam Great Britain (February 2002), 19–30.

22. "More Troops Sent to Horn of Africa," *New York Times* (August 11, 2002).

23. United Nations Security Council, "Report of the Panel of Experts on Somalia Pursuant to Security Council Resolution 1474 (2003)," S/2003/1035 (November 4, 2003), 27–32.

24. International Crisis Group, "Counter-Terrorism in Somalia: Losing Hearts and Minds?" (Brussels, July 11, 2005), www.crisisgroup.org/home/index.cfm?l=1&id=3555.

25. Ibid.

26. "US Predicts Zarqawi Africa Flight," BBC News (August 25, 2005), http://news.bbc.co.uk/2/hi/africa/4185596.stm.

27. This argument is adopted from Menkhaus, "Quasi-States, Nation-Building, and Terrorist Safe Havens," *Journal of Conflict Studies*, XXIII (2003), 3–21.

28. Menkhaus, "Calibrating Counterterrorism Strategy with U.S. Regional Interests in East Africa," paper presented at the workshop, "Terrorism's New Front Lines: Adapting U.S. Counterterrorism Strategy to Regions of Concern," National Defense University (Washington, D.C., May 8–9, 2003).

3

DJIBOUTI

A Special Role in
the War on Terrorism

LANGE SCHERMERHORN

Historically better known as a transit point than a destination, the Republic of Djibouti has not been perceived as a hospitable location for permanent operations by terrorist groups or observers of the terrorist landscape. Prior to 9/11, most observers discounted the possibility that international terrorist activity might be based in Djibouti, although a novel published in the early 1980s told of a German terrorist trained in Yemen, arriving clandestinely in Djibouti and smuggled out on a cargo ship departing for Europe.[1] Djibouti is more desirable and plausible as a transit point because it has a relatively homogeneous local population, with a long commitment to following daily events and comings and goings; most residents and observers believe that its security forces are well informed and well positioned to take necessary counterterrorist measures.

That said, the calculus now may have changed. The advent of various military forces in addition to the long-standing French presence has increased the number of potential foreign targets. These targets include Dutch forces attached to the UN monitoring mission for the Eritrea-Ethiopia border conflict in 2001 (now departed), a small command element of the German forces participating in that mission, and U.S. personnel at Camp

Lemonier in Djibouti City. Djibouti's support for the war on terrorism, its hosting of a significant U.S. military presence, and persistent economic hardships throughout the Horn, one of the most poverty-stricken parts of the world, provide grounds for increased activity and interest by external groups.

The Aftermath of 9/11

Djibouti has achieved prominence as a center of U.S. counterterrorism efforts in the wake of 9/11. Renewed recognition of the role Djibouti can play in U.S. military planning and operations has implications extending beyond the United States' immediate focus on the Horn of Africa into other areas of the U.S. Central Command's jurisdiction and for the adjacent U.S. European and Pacific Commands.[2]

A former French overseas territory, Djibouti came late to independence. Although dwarfed by its heftier neighbors, this mini-state plays a strategic role in the Horn of Africa as a result of its location at the entrance to the Red Sea—the crossroads of Africa and the Middle East—its physical geography, its ethnic and religious composition, its French colonial legacy, and the interest of a new Djiboutian president in asserting regional leadership.

How Djibouti plays that role is a function of its style of government, its size, its resources, and its mutable relationships within the framework of the Inter-governmental Authority on Development (IGAD), a seven-member regional organization composed of Djibouti, Eritrea, Ethiopia, Kenya, Somalia, the Sudan, and Uganda. Djibouti is one of the fifty-six members of the Organization of the Islamic Conference, one of the five sub-Saharan member countries of the Arab League, and one of the fifty members of the Organisation Internationale de la Francophonie.[3]

After launching operations in Afghanistan in late 2001, the United States solicited Djibouti as a host for American forces (codified by an agreement signed in late 2001) and welcomed the country as a partner in the "Global War on Terrorism."[4] This is not the first time that the United States has profited from Djibouti's geographic relevance and accessibility; U.S. forces transited frequently under an informal understanding during the Gulf War and the UNOSOM/UNITAF peacekeeping exercises in Somalia, hospitality that was largely forgotten by the United States, although keenly remembered by Djibouti (which took away some lessons about the value of quid pro quos).

The U.S. government describes the government of Djibouti as

> a staunch supporter in the global war on terrorism [that] . . . has taken a strong stand against international terrorist organizations and

individuals. . . . The Government took extraordinary measures from its limited resources to try and ensure the safety and security of Westerners posted in Djibouti. The Government also began an aggressive immigration campaign to remove illegal [Ethiopian] aliens from Djibouti in an attempt to weed out potential terrorists. The Government also has closed down terrorist-linked financial institutions and shared security information on possible terrorist activity in the region. The counterterrorism committee under President [Ismail Omar]Guelleh moved to enhance coordination and action on information concerning terrorist organizations.[5]

Guelleh earned this accolade because of his public support for counterterrorism efforts. Reinvigorated bilateral relations were celebrated by U.S. Defense Secretary Donald Rumsfeld's stop in Djibouti in late 2002 and a White House meeting between Guelleh and President Bush in early 2003, an event that resulted in promises of significant increases in U.S. aid.[6]

Resources

Yemen and the Horn of Africa countries constitute an area approximately one-third the size of the United States, with approximately 5,500 miles of coastline. Djibouti is small in area (approximately the size of Massachusetts), sharing borders with Eritrea, Ethiopia, and Somalia. The city of Djibouti is the major port of entry for East Africa between Port Sudan on the Red Sea and Mombasa, Kenya, with particular relevance for the northern and central regions of land-locked Ethiopia. Abutting the Bab al-Mandeb Strait, the southern entrance to the Red Sea, Djibouti's port provides easy access to major shipping lanes through the Gulf of Aden and the Indian Ocean. Population estimates for the country range from 600,000 to 750,000 (underlining the need for a formal census).[7] Current estimates show an ethnic distribution of approximately 60 percent Somali—the majority are Issa, with the Mamassan subclan prominent, some Isaaks and a scattering of other clans—and 35 percent Afar, with the remaining 5 percent Arab, French, Ethiopian, or other. Djibouti's indigenous population is virtually 100 percent Sunni Muslim.

Like its fellow countries of the Horn and East Africa, Djibouti ranks in the bottom 30 percent of the 177 countries on the United Nations Development Program's Human Development Index (HDI).[8] Djibouti ranks 154, slightly higher than Eritrea (156) and Ethiopia (170) and slightly below other IGAD members: the Sudan (139), Uganda (146), and Yemen (149). Life expectancy is 43.12 years, and approximately 43 percent of the population is under 15 years old. HIV/AIDS prevalence is estimated at 2.9 percent of the population, with approximately 9,000 active cases. This number may well be higher, as the Addis Ababa–Djibouti road is a major transit route for HIV/AIDS, as well as for drugs, illegal aliens, currency, etc.

Djibouti has virtually no manufacturing industry. With only 0.04 percent of its land arable, it must import almost all of its food, other than meat from nomadic goat, sheep, and camel populations. Water is at a premium, and the main aquifer is rapidly being depleted. Of the few potential resources that Djibouti possesses, one is energy from geothermal, solar, and wind power sources. Situated at the northern end of the Great Rift Valley, Djibouti is allegedly the most earthquake-prone country in the world. Since the quakes generally fall below 3.5 on the Richter scale, however, they are not a perceptible feature of daily life. A seismic station at Arta is part of a global geophysical monitoring network. Djibouti's Scientific Research Center is the site of a demonstration solar project established in the 1980s by USAID. The center concentrates on water and energy research in partnership with various donors, among which France, Japan, and Germany are prominent.

Lack of jobs for the burgeoning numbers of young people is as critical for Djibouti as it is for the other countries of the Horn of Africa. Economic development and job creation will depend on Djibouti's ability to attract investment and develop its potential as a transportation hub, a monumental task for a small country with virtually no resources except human capital. Success in achieving this growth depends on maintaining political stability, making the climate attractive to potential investors, and creating an educated workforce capable of providing support for service industries ancillary to operating a regional center of transportation and communications. One important component is acquiring English, which, added to French, Arabic, and Somali language skills, will enable Djiboutians to capitalize on their potential to develop a local service industry.

Governance

President Guelleh, on taking office in 1999, vowed "to formulate reforms that are most appropriate for the development of my country . . . to defend liberty, equality and peace," and "never to compromise on security."[9] He has had some degree of success in the economic and security areas, less so in his commitment to political and civil rights. Freedom House (on a scale from a high of 1 to a low of 7) gives Djibouti a 4 for political rights and a 5 for civil rights, earning it the designation "partly free," shared by Ethiopia, while Kenya is designated "free" (4/4), and Eritrea, the Sudan, Somalia, and Yemen, "not free."[10]

Independence came late to Djibouti; the inhabitants of what was then the French Overseas Territory of the Afars and the Issas voted "no" twice, fearing that when the growing ethnic Somali community attained a majority, the Afar would lose the status that they enjoyed under French administration and be excluded from the political process. A third referendum in 1977 was successful, and Djibouti was granted independence that year. Hassan Gouled Aptidon, one of two Djiboutian deputies in France's Assemblée Nationale, became president under a constitution that provided for only one political party. In the early 1990s, Afari dissidents staged an armed rebellion protesting their exclusion from the political process and seeking constitutional changes. Some of these changes were granted in 1992 in a constitutional revision that allowed for four legal parties.

One element of the Afar-led FRUD party (Front for the Restoration of Unity and Democracy) ceased hostilities in 1994 and signed a peace accord that granted it, among other things, two cabinet seats; another element under Ahmed Dini Ahmed continued to harass government troops. Legislative elections in 1997—considered more credible than the 1992 elections, which were widely viewed as fraudulent—easily returned the ruling Rally for Progress (RPP) Party to power. A coalition of RPP and the legalized arm of the FRUD won all sixty-five national assembly seats.

Having served continuously since independence, in 1999 Goulaid stood down in favor of Ismail Omar Guelleh, his chief of cabinet (and nephew), a former police and security officer thirty years younger. The election was contested by Moussa Ahmed Idriss, who ran for the Unified Opposition Party, an amalgam of seven opposition leaders representing five parties. The party's formation six weeks before the election reflected the recognition that a cohesive opposition would carry more weight than the efforts of seven independent individuals. Although Idriss did not prevail, the unity of the opposition stimulated greater transparency: Guelleh vowed to run an "American style campaign," offering to debate Idriss (who declined), granting coverage by the government-owned media, publishing his platform as a "Vision for Djibouti," and generally adopting the paraphernalia of a modern Western election. Guelleh won with 74.1 percent of the vote to 25.9 for Idriss. As a result of this approach, international observers from the Arab League, la Francophonie, and the Organization of African Unity (OAU) declared that the election was "generally free, fair, and transparent" and an improvement over previous efforts.[11]

The advent of a new president in 1999 brought the remaining FRUD Afar dissidents in from the cold. In 2000, Ahmed Dini Ahmed returned from exile in Paris to Djibouti amid great acclaim and some hopes to negotiate with the government. He sought more power for the districts as a means of sharing resources with the entire Afar community. Negotiations culminated in an agreement, signed in 2001, that provided for electoral transparency through an independent electoral commission, expanded the numbers of legal political parties, and decentralized various judicial, administrative, and social services functions to five "autonomous" regions. The nomination of Dileita Mohamed Dileita, a former Djiboutian ambassador to Ethiopia and protégé of Ahmed Dini, as prime minister (a position traditionally reserved for an Afar and appointed by the president) was considered a good omen. At the signing, the president asserted that he was "convinced that the sincere application of this agreement [would] consolidate the national cohesion and unity and prevent the repetition of the causes which were the origin of our conflict."[12]

Guelleh launched his presidency with a blitz of public relations exercises designed to motivate Djiboutians while convincing the donor community that reform was under way. These efforts included the appointment of a *mediateur* (ombudsman) for the republic; the appointment of the first woman to the new portfolio of junior minister of women's and family affairs; a country-wide roundtable in 1999 for teachers, parents, and students on the future direction of education in Djibouti; a national colloquium on the justice system; revitalization of the health and agriculture ministries; and public discussion of sectoral reforms in the economy.[13] However, the new president's boldest initiatives were in the domains of economic privatization and regional security. These steps dramatically altered Djibouti's relationship with Ethiopia. They also served notice to the region that the president intended to pursue his view of Djibouti's national interests aggressively, while also staking a claim that Djibouti, and he personally, was a force for reconciliation.

In 2005, Guelleh, the sole candidate, was re-elected president for his second and final term. The opposition boycotted the election but about 79 percent of registered voters cast ballots.

The president has described his people as "African at heart, Arabist in culture, and universalist in thought," explaining that these three pillars are sensibilities innate in Djiboutian society. The president's eclecticism and pragmatism are evidenced in his foreign affairs priorities: support for Palestine; encouragement of increased Chinese investment in Djibouti; support for the U.S. counterterrorism agenda; revitalization of Djibouti's relationship with

France; strengthening of ties to the United States; and improvement of relations with Libya and its Investment Fund.[14]

The relative transparency of the electoral process is seriously flawed by a winner-take-all system. Opposition candidates won approximately 45 percent of the vote in Djibouti City districts in the 2003 legislative elections. However, overall, the incumbent coalition won a majority and thus no opposition candidates entered the legislature. Unless this system is altered, opposition parties and candidates other than those representing the current ruling coalition will be excluded permanently from participation within the national assembly as a loyal opposition.

The lack of inclusiveness in Djiboutian governance, as demonstrated by the results of the 2003 legislative elections, is a recipe for continued frustration not only for the Afar but for Somali who are not members of the Issa Mamassan subclan, which has kept a firm grip on the levers of power (president, chef de cabinet, and chief of security, among others) since independence. As power is concentrated particularly in these three functions, actions and decision-making are not unduly bureaucratic and can be reached with dispatch. Government-owned media (a single newspaper, radio, and television) exacerbate the problem of political participation. The only other outlets are broadsheets, produced erratically by opposition parties, which are from time to time shut down by the government. A small print-reading public, attributable to a low literacy rate, and the lack of a commercial advertising base militate against the creation of independent print outlets. The BBC Somali Service is listened to avidly. Radio-Television Djibouti (RTD) produces local programs and rebroadcasts programs from French and Arabic radio and television stations. The Voice of America operates an Arabic-language station from Djibouti.

Economic Security

Under an agreement signed with the government of Djibouti, the Ports Authority of Dubai will manage the Port of Djibouti for twenty years (from 2000), as one of the six ports currently in its portfolio. Previously operated by the government as a parastatal (a semi-autonomous, quasi-governmental, state-owned enterprise), the port is the country's greatest economic asset and its sole source of revenue. The deal was brokered by Abdulrahman Boreh, a close confidant of the president and one of the premier businessmen of Djibouti, with extensive shipping and other business interests throughout East Africa, the Gulf, and beyond.

The agreement was presented as a fait accompli, since its authors knew well that prior consultation with the interested parties (government ministers who depended on port revenue for operational funds, the government of Ethiopia as the port's principal user, and employees of the port) would only lead to endless wrangling. Reinvesting in the port, fencing off revenue, and making operations more efficient would be virtually impossible if the port remained a parastatal. The Ethiopian government took umbrage at what it considered high-handed treatment, the more so because Assab was no longer available as a port for Ethiopia because of its war with Eritrea. The Ethiopians initially attempted to gain greater control over Djibouti's port, including stationing their own security and customs staff, measures that were construed as challenges to Djiboutian sovereignty.

The privatization has been a great success, so much so that in 2002 the Ports Authority of Dubai began managing Djibouti's international airport. Ethiopia has become reconciled to the seaport's new status as it has gained assurance that its short-term economic interests have not been damaged and has begun to understand that its medium- and long-term interests would be better served by a modernized port with an enhanced capacity to run efficiently. The success of both privatizations has been a catalyst for infrastructure development: a new container holding area has been built near the existing port; a bulk port with an oil terminal and possibly a refinery is under construction at Dorale, approximately eight miles along the coast from the old port. Several new regional airlines are flying into Djibouti. The centerpiece of the development of light manufacturing or assembly operations and for in-bond transit cargo is the creation of a "free zone" in the port area, a project conceived more than seven years ago and now fully realized. Another larger free zone is contemplated for Dorale port.

One very important piece of the economic puzzle is to adopt and implement a telecommunications strategy that would encourage the development of a regional service hub. Djiboutians understand the importance of this issue and are moving in a measured manner to ensure that they get it right.

The minister of education, building on the results of the 1999 roundtable, has garnered donor support for a variety of initiatives at the primary and secondary levels, in addition to opening Djibouti's first university in 2000. Diplomas can be earned long-distance, in conjunction with selected universities in France and the Arab world. An important focus of the university is computer literacy, as preparation for the kind of jobs that Djibouti hopes to attract. Formerly, graduates of the local lycée had to go abroad for university training, which was expensive and inefficient, as few found places in foreign universities and graduates generally did not return to Djibouti.

Regional Security

President Guelleh devoted the principal part of his maiden speech to the UN General Assembly in 1999 to launching a renewed initiative for reconciliation in Somalia.[15] Although Guelleh's words received tepid support in New York, they immediately galvanized elements of the Somali community around the world and launched eleven months of intensive consultation, discussion, and negotiation in the small town of Arta, thirty miles from Djibouti City. These talks culminated in the establishment of a Transitional National Government (TNG) for Somalia in 2000. The TNG moved from Djibouti to Mogadishu later in 2000, but was unable to function effectively before its three-year mandate expired.[16]

Djibouti has continued to play a key role as a "frontline" state, with Kenya and Ethiopia, in reconciliation efforts under IGAD's auspices. The achievement of some measure of equilibrium in Somalia continues to be viewed by Guelleh both as an overriding goal for regional stability and as a means of wielding his own influence. Much of the motivation for his political activism derives from prominent businessmen in Djibouti, Dubai, and Mogadishu, who realize that Somalia's business potential cannot be exploited fully and positively amid instability.

From Djibouti's vantage point, everything that happens in the countries of the Horn has an impact on Djibouti; and conversely, the state of Djibouti's political and economic health and welfare impinges on all of its neighbors. Now more than ever, Djibouti needs a stable region that is developing in ways in which its own services hub can play a role. Therefore, U.S. policy with regard to Djibouti must be considered and formulated, recognizing that every action in the region stimulates a reaction.

U.S. Counterterrorism Policy

Two counterterrorism measures initiated in the region by the United States have given renewed emphasis to the importance of helping Somalia attain a viable and durable solution to their governance problems. At the same time, the measures as implemented have skirted around the centrality of Somalia to the issue of counterterrorism in Yemen and the Horn. The establishment of the Combined Joint Task Force–Horn of Africa (CJTF-HOA) at Camp

Lemonier in 2003, under the jurisdiction of the U.S. Central Command (CENTCOM), acknowledged the potential for terrorism both within and infiltrating into the area, demonstrated a commitment to deal with it aggressively, and provided a focus around which the efforts of nations in the region could coalesce on a regional and cooperative basis, rather than on a bilateral basis. CJTF-HOA had to develop a model for working with six sovereign governments, six U.S. embassy country teams, and other military representatives of the Department of Defense who were working with the individual countries on a bilateral basis.

U.S. military engagement in the Horn of Africa is not new; its techniques (military-to-military training, joint exercises, security assistance procurement, and civil and humanitarian engagement) have been CENTCOM's stock in trade in the region since the inception of regional military commands in 1985. However, the value of expanding the pace, number, and focus of the humanitarian and civil affairs projects, as is being done, has already been amply demonstrated in terms of increased access to areas of interest and creation of goodwill in local communities. More important, the greater intensity of such activities and a conscious effort to engage host nation forces more directly in their planning and execution provide useful programs for host nation military and civilian officials engaging constructively with their local communities.

Prior to the establishment of the CJTF-HOA, CENTCOM sent small teams to the Horn of Africa for short periods. Moving the base of operations within the region to Djibouti provided a cautionary message to actual and potential terrorists, allowed for continuity, and now leaves a positive footprint. (Although CJTF-HOA nominally covers Somalia and the Sudan, it has no engagement in either territory.)

The United States also participates in the Combined (Coalition) Naval Task Force (CTF-150) operating out of Bahrain. It was established "to monitor, inspect, board, and stop suspect shipping" and to pursue the war on terrorism in support of Operation Iraqi Freedom.[17] Countries that are now or have previously contributed naval vessels to CTF-150 include Australia, Britain, Canada, France, Germany, Italy, New Zealand, Pakistan, Spain, and the United States.[18]

Second, the East Africa Counterterrorism Initiative (EACTI) of 2003 allocated $100 million over fifteen months to U.S. initiatives in the Horn of Africa. Its creation acknowledged that remedial attention was needed so that host nations could help themselves to develop their own capacities to counter terrorism. However, three factors hobble the EACTI: lack of stimulus for regional cooperation because funds are allocated and administered on a bilateral basis;

incomplete current funding and lack of future commitment; and, most important, the specific exclusion of the Sudan, still on the list of states sponsoring terrorism, and Somalia, the black hole. The absence of a pro-active, constructive stance on Somalia is the major limiting factor to achieving success in counterterrorism efforts in East Africa, when success is defined as "stabilizing the region."

There is no agreement on what constitutes a constructive Somalia policy, but neither has there been any great impetus to do the hard work of arriving at a consensus and acting upon it. Some experts believe that laissez-faire is the best policy, a point of view that has played perfectly into the hands of policy-makers who wish to ignore the difficulty of committing scarce resources to Somali reconstruction. One can argue that in the absence of an established, recognized government in Somalia with which to cooperate, counterterrorism efforts undertaken with dubious partners and focused on short-term results may prove inimical to longer term U.S. interests.

The longer that Somalia remains without governing institutions, the more difficult it will be to create a stable environment where people respond to accepted social norms of behavior and do not fall prey to the lethargy and despair which opens the door to the very result that counterterrorism initiatives are designed to prevent. Failing to invest greater attention and coordination in the Horn of Africa at a relatively low cost—before another crisis—would be foolish.

Conclusion

Djibouti is not a bastion *of* terror but a bastion *against* terrorism. To maintain its ability to be an effective partner in counterterrorism efforts, it will need ongoing training and technical and financial assistance for initiatives under the EACTI rubric. For it to continue on the path of economic reform and educational innovation in support of its plan to become a services hub will require development, and possibly additional budgetary, assistance from a variety of donors.

Despite rhetorical acknowledgment of the need to ameliorate conditions in countries that may provide fertile ground for international terrorists and the commitment to a "regional approach" explicit in the EACTI, the creation of the CJTF-HOA, and the regional USAID office for East Africa in Nairobi, the United States continues to implement programs under the well-worn bilateral model, with long pipelines, extensive bureaucracy, and little attempt to coordinate planning and procurement with neighboring country programs or to pursue greater coordination among all donors. The Millennium Challenge Account and HIV/AIDS initiative, for example, are administered bilaterally, not comprehensively by region.[19]

Both the Clinton and the current Bush administration encouraged African countries to develop regional organizations and exhorted them to use such structures to foster political, social, economic, and scientific cooperation, as appropriate to the charter of the individual organization. IGAD has been used to good effect as an umbrella for the peace processes for two of its member states, the Sudan and Somalia. Other assistance to the Horn of Africa comes from many host countries, donor countries, international organizations, international and local nongovernmental organizations, charitable foundations, and private businesses. Scarce resources need to be leveraged by closer cooperation to ensure maximum impact. The reenergized African Union is taking a more pro-active stance. President Jacques Chirac announced in 2003 that France would "revitalize" its relations with Africa, reversing previous policies. On the ground in Djibouti, the French remain the senior and most influential foreign influence; French military and civilian officials are cooperative and hospitable to American personnel.

The salient point in discussion of counterterrorism measures is the extent of the coastlines of the countries of the Horn. Maritime cooperation is essential for effective surveillance and interdiction of terrorists and weaponry. UN Security Council Resolution 733 of January 23, 1992, decided "that all states shall, for the purposes of establishing peace and stability in Somalia, immediately implement a general and complete embargo on all deliveries of weapons and military equipment to Somalia until the Council decides otherwise." This resolution has been reaffirmed more than ten times. Resolution 1474-03 of 2003 noted "with regret that the arms embargo has been continuously violated since 1992" and recommended "exploring the establishment of a monitoring mechanism for the implementation of the arms embargo." The Sanctions Committee of the Security Council subsequently mandated a four-person Panel of Experts, which issued an initial six-month comprehensive report in 2003.[20]

The Panel of Experts was extended for a further six months in 2004, and again in 2005. Although the original resolution reflected concern for the flow of small arms into Somalia during the early 1990s, that problem continues to plague the countries of the Horn and includes the flourishing arms trade of Central Africa. Putting into place an effective embargo is virtually impossible, but evincing UN interest in monitoring the situation has had a salutary effect. In addition, U.S. Coast Guard assistance to host nations in satisfying International

Systems for Port Security Code regulations would increase their ability to meet counterterrorism objectives and standards.

Has the investment by the U.S. government in Djibouti to date been worthwhile?[21] One school of thought claims that if Djibouti did not exist, it would have to be created. Djibouti functions not only as a lifeline for Ethiopia but, given the volatility and unpredictability of its larger neighbors, both as a safety valve for the region and an insurance policy. The "premiums" we have paid to keep that policy in force have constituted a worthwhile investment, giving the United States a base from which to pursue its counterterrorism agenda but, more importantly, a platform on which to demonstrate that the U.S. wants to help others to develop their own counterterrorism capabilities.

There are a number of actions and initiatives that the United States should take to leverage existing resources:

1. Acknowledge and remedy the need for better intelligence on and cultural awareness of the Horn of Africa by American civilian and military personnel.

2. Continue the relationship with Djibouti on a mutually beneficial basis with regard to leases, assistance, terms and conditions, etc.; maintain CJTF-HOA, while evaluating regularly the form and shape it should take to maintain its relevance and importance to U.S. counterterrorism objectives.

3. Acknowledge that it is time to engage constructively with Somalia and develop a policy accordingly; with other IGAD Partners' Forum members assist the new Transitional Federal Government in the difficult task of setting set up governance institutions in Somalia.

4. Acknowledge the primary importance of the maritime factor in the Horn in countering terrorism and in Somalia policy:

a. Support the activities of the Panel of Experts of the UN Security Council's Sanctions Committee with respect to monitoring the arms embargo on Somalia (in place since 1992—an estimated 30 million small arms are already in private hands in the region);

b. Support the expansion of and contribute to enforcement actions undertaken by the coalition members of CTF-150, a naval task force operating in the Gulf of Aden and reporting to the United States Naval Forces Central Command (NAVCENT) Bahrain.

c. Direct and expand EACTI efforts on a priority basis so as to develop greater host nation capabilities individually *and cooperatively* for maritime surveillance and interdiction.

d. Immediately provide U.S. Coast Guard assistance to meet International Systems for Port Security Code regulations.

5. Stimulate greater use of IGAD as a regional cooperative entity by member states and donors:

a. Cooperate with existing partners and solicit World Bank participation in funding the major infrastructure projects for which the design mandated by the Partners' Forum in IGAD's 1996 revitalization has now been completed; develop transportation and communications infrastructure in the countries of the Horn to create a viable economic base for the region.

b. Design a follow-on to the Greater Horn of Africa Initiative (GHAI) in collaboration with USAID and the U.S. Congress. Learn from the implementation problems of the first GHAI in the late 1990s better to coordinate U.S. development assistance on a regional basis.

6. In support of the stated goal in the Bush administration's "National Strategy for Combating Terrorism" of "defeating terrorist organizations of global reach through the direct or indirect use of diplomatic economic, information, law enforcement, military, financial, intelligence, and other instruments of power," continue and expand the work of embassy country teams in host countries and of the CJTF-HOA to coordinate and integrate U.S. government resources and other donor activities. The newly established Office of Post-Conflict Reconstruction in the Department of State or some other organization should be designated as the focal point of these efforts.[22]

a. Develop the concept of regional "centers of excellence" for technical training for military, police, and customs personnel, shared by host nation personnel and utilizing and coordinating experience from existing multilateral efforts by other donors and host nations, such as joint military training for Kenyan, Tanzanian, and Ugandan military personnel in collaboration with Britain.

b. Begin by expanding the U.S.-funded Djibouti De-mining Training Center into a regional center, noting the successful methodology outlined in "Tailoring Partnerships for Success: Experiences from the Djiboutian Humanitarian De-mining Program."[23]

c. Inventory and develop a database of the numerous multilateral initiatives emanating from the UN and its agencies, the African Union, the European Union, the United States, host nations, among others—such as the East African Standby Brigade, the African Police Training Center, and various HIV/AIDS initiatives—the better to avoid redundancy and overlap. Reinventing the wheel is a favorite pastime and institutional memory increasingly is short or nonexistent.

7. Capitalize on the French military's presence in Djibouti to cultivate deeper operational cooperation and consultation between the United States and France.

Notes

1. Helen McInnes, *Cloak of Darkness* (New York, 1982).

2. During the Gulf War and the UN peacekeeping missions in Somalia in the early 1990s, U.S. personnel transited Djibouti regularly, although there was no Status of Forces Agreement or permanent stationing. The operational jurisdiction of U.S. Central Command, headquartered at McDill Air Force Base, Tampa, Florida, covers twenty-seven countries: seven in Africa (six in the Horn plus Egypt) and the remainder in the Middle East and South and Central Asia. All other countries in Africa come under the operational jurisdiction of the European Command, based in Stuttgart, Germany. The Pacific Command based in Honolulu has operational responsibility for four countries adjacent to the Horn of Africa littoral: the Comoros, Madagascar, Maldives, and Mauritius.

3. Also known as la Francophonie, the French-sponsored intergovernmental organization was developed "for cooperation in the areas of education, culture, media, economy, and good governance among fifty states for whom French is a major language" (see www.francophonie.org/).

4. For the "Global War on Terrorism," see www.whitehouse.gov/homeland/progress/. Djibouti is not listed among the African countries in the "Coalition of the Willing," as are neighboring Eritrea and Ethiopia.

5. U.S. Department of State, "Patterns of Global Terrorism Report 2003" (Washington, D.C., 2004), www.state.gov/s/ct.

6. The USAID Mission in Djibouti closed in 1994. Military assistance in the period 1994–2001 consisted of a small amount of International Military Education and Training funds to cover tuition and expenses in the United States for two students per year, and a few civil/humanitarian affairs projects. Together, these programs cost approximately $350,000 per year. A de-mining training program also was funded by the United States from 2000.

7. The UN underwrote a census in the early 1990s but the results were not published, reportedly due to problems in data collection and to ethnic sensitivities during a period of strain between the Afar and Somali communities.

8. UN Statistical Service, *The Human Development Index* (New York, 2003).

9. Author's translations from *La Nation*, May 1999. *La Nation* is Djibouti's triweekly French language government newspaper, available at www.republique.com.

10. Freedom House, "The Annual Survey of Political Rights and Civil Liberties—2003" (New York, 2003), www.freedomhouse.org.

11. Informal translation, communiqué issued in Djibouti on April 11, 1999, by the Joint Election Observer Mission.

12. Author's translation from French articles in issues of *La Nation*, May 2001.

13. Author's translation from French articles in issues of *La Nation*, November 1999, and February, April, June, October 2000.

14. Author's translation of the president's manifesto (in which this quote appears), outlining the achievements to date of his tenure as president (from www.republique.com).

15. President Omar Ismail Guelleh, speech delivered on September 22, 1999, in New York; text issued by Djibouti's Mission to the UN.

16. See also Kenneth J. Menkhaus, "Somalia and Somaliland: Terrorism, Political Islam, and State Collapse," chapter 2 in this volume.

17. Information on CTF-150 is available at www.newsnavy.mil.list.

18. Not all of the countries listed have ships in CTF-150 all of the time. Commanding admirals rotate every two months.

19. Given the porosity of national borders, treating countries on a bilateral basis, particularly in the health and infectious disease arena, is dysfunctional. For example, Djibouti's HIV/AIDS problem stems directly from traffic on the truck route between Addis Ababa and the Port of Djibouti. The presence of a USAID HIV/AIDS program in Ethiopia without one in Djibouti cannot address adequately or effectively the problem in the region.

20. Sanctions Committee, UN Security Council, "Report of the Panel of Experts in Somalia pursuant to Security Council Resolution 1474 (2003)" (New York, November 2003).

21. Precise figures are difficult to calculate. Development assistance over two years for education and health (perhaps in the neighborhood of $25 million) has been allocated to Djibouti, and USAID opened an office in Djibouti in late 2003 to administer it. There are other smaller amounts, such as the funds under EACTI. A news story in 2003 claimed that Djibouti received the most U.S. assistance per capita, citing a total approximate figure of $100 million divided among Djibouti's small population. This figure is probably vastly overstated, as it may include estimated start-up and operating costs for Camp Lemonier. Moreover, other than lease payments, very few of these funds percolate into the Djiboutian economy.

22. "National Security Strategy: Challenges and Opportunities of the Twenty-First Century," chapter 3, The White House, Washington, D.C. (September 17, 2002), www.whitehouse.gov/nsc/nss.

23. Alan Childress and Matt Zajac, "Tailoring Partnerships for Success: Experiences from the Djiboutian Humanitarian De-mining Program," *Journal of Mine Action*, VI (2003), 8–11.

4

ERITREA
On a Slow Fuse

DAN CONNELL

Eritrea's diverse society—half Christian, half Muslim, from nine distinct linguistic and cultural groups—has long rendered it vulnerable to centrifugal political forces, while its strategic location at the southern end of the Red Sea has made it the target of regional and global powers, from the Ottoman Empire half a millennium ago to the United States and the Soviet Union at the peak of the cold war. The former Italian colony's first political parties were organized along confessional lines in the 1940s. The liberation movement divided along religious and regional lines in the 1960s and 1970s. Today, as Eritrea struggles to establish itself as a viable state, these fault lines threaten to reassert themselves, opening the country to increased ethnic and religious extremism that could spill over Eritrea's borders, even as it draws inspiration and resources from the hostile states that ring it.

Introduction

Africa's newest nation got off to a promising start. Upon winning de facto independence from Ethiopia in 1991 and affirming its sovereignty through a United Nations–monitored referendum two years later, Eritrea set out to construct the institutions of a law-based state with a high degree of popular participation. At the outset, the country boasted low levels of crime and corruption, a strong work ethic, high levels of volunteerism, little evident tension among ethnic or confessional groups, relatively good relations with its neighbors, and no international debt. But in recent years its trajectory has been downhill.

During its first decade as a recognized state, Eritrea careened from one armed conflict with its neighbors to another, while sliding ever deeper into political repression and economic malaise. One by one—and at times simultaneously—Eritrea trained its guns on the Sudan, Yemen, Djibouti, and Ethiopia to resolve outstanding disputes. In the last instance, unresolved border questions, together with festering economic and political issues, triggered three rounds of all-out war between Eritrea and Ethiopia that left tens of thousands dead, hundreds of thousands displaced, and both countries' economies in tatters, just as drought intensified throughout the region, adding to their economic woes. In Eritrea's case, another casualty was the prospect of democratic development, as the beleaguered president circled his political wagons against mounting criticism from within and without the ruling party over his intransigent approach to peace negotiations, his conduct of the war, and his resistance to democratization.

Today, all political parties are banned, all but a handful of nongovernmental organizations (NGOs) are prohibited, a constitution—ratified in 1997—has not yet been implemented, national elections have repeatedly been postponed, public criticism has been silenced, independent media are shut down, churches have been forcibly closed, and dissidents indefinitely detained. While these measures put a temporary lid on public expressions of protest, they set the stage for escalating instability in which political violence is almost certain to increase in scope and intensity.

The aftereffects of the Border War, coupled with the regime's deepening repression, have reopened fissures within the fragile society and harrowed the ground for the rise of old and new opposition groups, many of which draw support from border states. Among them are armed Islamists based in the Sudan and loosely affiliated with Osama bin Laden and a gaggle of secular splinters from the original independence movement, many of which, like the Islamists, are committed to the armed overthrow of the present Eritrean government.

Although it is unlikely that global terror networks can implant their own cells in Eritrea, the reverse scenario—that indigenous armed groups, Islamist and secular, will seek affiliation or assistance from such networks to further local agendas—is a strong possibility. Should Eritrea descend into civil war, as it could do within the next two to three years, it will add further to the instability of an already explosive neighborhood. Meanwhile, under the present regime's policies of providing support for armed opposition groups operating in nearby states, Eritrea is already a center of regional instability.

The problem Eritrea poses is not one of state weakness (or failure), in which external terrorist organizations can establish stopover points or find safe havens. Rather, it is one where conditions of conflict and repression mask the growing alienation of the population from a central government that continues to operate largely through informal and unaccountable structures of power, behind a façade of ineffectual public institutions. This alienation shows itself mainly through acts of passive resistance and noncooperation with the state, but such postures could change suddenly in the event that the growing but yet fragmented underground opposition finds enough common ground among its many competing factions to constitute a threat to public order.

The United States has embraced Eritrea as a key ally in the global war on terrorism, both for its strategic location and for its military prowess in the face of local terrorist threats. However, Eritrea's uncertain political trajectory could make this a risky investment. Conflicted—and at times contentious—relations with the United States, deriving from both current events and a legacy of mistrust, could place Washington in the crosshairs of those contesting for power in Eritrea.

U.S.-Eritrean Relations

The relationship between the United States and Eritrea was shaped from the outset by regional considerations, principally involving Ethiopia. In the 1940s, the United States was plunged into World War II and was beginning to project its power globally. When postwar decolonization got under way, Ethiopia provided an entry point for influence over emergent African states and a base for pursuing strategic interests in the region. It was the first African state to which the United States turned. U.S. relations with Eritrea were subsumed under this relationship.

Weeks after British-led forces defeated Italy in 1941 and took charge of Eritrea, the American firm of Johnson Drake & Piper began implementing military projects there that were taken over by the U.S. Army when Washington joined the Allied war effort. An aircraft-assembly plant was constructed at Gura; workshops in Asmara, the Eritrean capital, were converted to a repair base; naval facilities were established in Massawa, and communications facilities were set up in Asmara. Eritrea's strategic coastline, facing Saudi Arabia and Yemen and stretching to the narrow mouth of the Red Sea at Bab el-Mandab, also gave the former Italian colony a special geostrategic importance. Keeping open the vital sea lanes that connected Europe and North America with East Africa, the Persian Gulf, and Asia through the Suez Canal was essential.[1]

In the late 1940s, Washington was the main champion of landlocked Ethiopia's claim to Eritrea, with its 600-mile Red Sea coast, as the newly established United Nations debated its status. In 1950, a U.S-backed plan was adopted to link both territories in a federation under Ethiopia's control. It went into effect on September 15, 1952. The arrangement gave Eritrea authority over the police, control of other domestic affairs, and the right to levy taxes and adopt its own budget, but Ethiopia controlled defense, foreign affairs, currency and finance, and international commerce and communications. Eritrea had a constitution with a U.S.-style bill of rights, a separate parliament, a national flag, and two official languages—Tigrinya and Arabic—but it lacked the power to defend those attributes.

Meanwhile, the United States and Ethiopia signed agreements that gave Washington a twenty-five-year lease on military bases in Eritrea, including a spy facility in Asmara at Kagnew Station, in return for which it pledged to provide military aid and training to Ethiopia. Between 1953 and 1960, U.S. military advisors built black Africa's first modern army, with three divisions of 6,000 men each, equipped largely with surplus weapons and equipment from World War II and the Korean War (to which Ethiopia contributed an army battalion).

During the 1950s, Ethiopia systematically dismantled the federation. Emperor Haile Selassie first decreed a preventive detention law, then arrested newspaper editors, shut down independent publications, drove prominent nationalists into exile, banned trade unions and political parties, forbade the use of indigenous languages in official transactions, and seized Eritrea's share of the lucrative customs duties. Whole industries were relocated from Asmara to Addis Ababa. Finally, the emperor ordered Eritrea's flag replaced by that of Ethiopia and forcibly dissolved its parliament.

In 1957 Eritrean students mounted demonstrations against Ethiopian rule, and in 1958 Eritrean trade unions called a general strike. Both were violently put down. With all avenues for peaceful protest closed, Eritrean exiles in 1960 founded the Eritrean Liberation Front (ELF) to fight for independence. As the revolt gained momentum, the United States stepped up military aid to Ethiopia. In 1964, President Lyndon Johnson sent fifty-five counterinsurgency specialists. He also approved the transfer of twelve F-5As to Addis Ababa, the first supersonic jet fighters in black Africa. The next year, 164 anti-guerrilla experts arrived under Plan Delta to teach the new "civic action" techniques being introduced in Vietnam. U.S. military aid to Ethiopia from 1946 to 1975 totaled $286.1 million in grants and loans, two-thirds of Washington's annual military assistance to all of Africa. From 1946 to 1975, Washington also provided Ethiopia with over $350 million in economic assistance, and the United States was Ethiopia's largest trading partner, taking 40 percent of its exports (mainly coffee).

By the mid-1970s, however, the importance to the United States of both Eritrea and Ethiopia declined. Other African states had more modern infrastructures, were more deeply integrated into the world market, and held more promising opportunities for American investors. Kagnew Station, whose eavesdropping facilities were being replaced by satellite systems, was phased out when the twenty-five-year treaty with Ethiopia expired in 1978.

Against this backdrop, and with the war in Eritrea going badly, a self-described "socialist" military committee overthrew Ethiopia's aging emperor in 1974, ousted the United States two years later, and then aligned Ethiopia with the Soviet Union, which pumped billions of dollars in new arms into the country, prolonging Eritrea's independence war another fifteen years. Throughout the next phase of this protracted conflict, however, the United States declined to support the Eritreans—out of a deep distrust of the left-leaning nationalist movement, now led by the breakaway Eritrean People's Liberation Front (EPLF), and with a view to wooing Ethiopia away from the Soviets once the Eritreans were defeated.

The independence war was a long-drawn-out affair due both to the nationalist movement's lack of external support and because it was divided into rival armies that fought each other—principally, but not only, the EPLF and the ELF. The EPLF decimated the ELF in a bitter civil war in the early 1980s. It then went on to defeat the Ethiopian army in 1991 and set up a provisional government based almost exclusively on its own membership, but it left numerous, intensely hostile political fragments in its wake and it did nothing to bring them in from the cold once the independence war was over—setting the stage for internal instability and conflict later.

Two years after the fighting ended, the EPLF-led government, acting with the approval of a new Ethiopian regime, held a UN-monitored referendum on the territory's political status. It produced an overwhelming vote for independent sovereignty (98.5 percent), which the Eritreans declared in May 1993. However, even with such a mandate, the victorious liberation movement did not see fit to provide space for its former rivals, whose supporters continued to be harassed—even arrested—through the 1990s.

The United States became one of the first countries to recognize the new state, and bilateral relations grew stronger through the decade as Washington provided relief and development aid and military training. With its apparent success at transcending ethnic and religious divisions, its extremely low levels of corruption and crime, and its dedication to self-reliant development, Eritrea was an attractive partner in post–cold war Africa. President Bill Clinton characterized it, together with Ethiopia, Uganda, and Rwanda, as emblematic of the "African renaissance." Clinton met several times with Isaias Afwerki, Eritrea's president and the former EPLF commander. Hillary Rodham Clinton visited the country in 1998, arriving to a banner at the Asmara airport proclaiming "Yes, it takes a village," a homage to her then-recently published book.

The emergence of a Sudan-based terrorist threat to Eritrea in the form of Eritrean Islamic Jihad (EIJ)—at the top of President Isaias's agenda when he visited Washington in 1995—heightened the urgency of aiding Eritrea. Numerous high-ranking military officials, including Gen. Tommy Franks, then the head of CENTCOM, visited the country in the 1990s, and Gen. Sebhat Ephrem, then Eritrea's chief of staff—later defense minister—made frequent visits to the United States to confer with Pentagon officials about regional security. Between 1994 and 2001, Eritrea received $6 million in Foreign Military Financing (FMF) and $2 million in International Military Education and Training (IMET) assistance.[2]

This evolving relationship was hindered, however, by growing concerns that the Eritrean leadership was still operating as if it were a band of bunkered guerrillas running a liberated zone, rather than officials governing a modern state. Each time a dispute arose with one of its neighbors, Eritrea rolled out the artillery—first against the Sudan (1994), then Yemen (1995), Djibouti (1996), and finally Ethiopia (1998). Doing so helped to cement Eritrea's reputation as a volatile warrior-state and made the United States wary of getting too close, especially after Eritrea resumed the war with Ethiopia.

Relations between Eritrea and Ethiopia had appeared to be friendly after the former's independence, allowing the United States to pursue ties with both, but a legacy of petty rivalry and tension remained close to the surface. After several disputes over economic policy in the mid-1990s and following a year-long series of armed incidents along the two countries' as-yet-undemarcated border, war broke out in May 1998. Early American efforts to mediate the conflict collapsed amid Eritrean charges that the United States was tilting toward Ethiopia.

There were three rounds of fighting before a cease-fire was reached: May–June 1998, February–March 1999, and May–June 2000. Once the combat began, long-buried resentments and unresolved grievances erupted with a depth and intensity never before experienced in this volatile region. First Ethiopia, then Eritrea deported people whose ethnic origins—sometimes going back two generations—identified them with their foe, regardless of whether they were legally citizens of the country from which they were being ousted. This tactic helped to poison the atmosphere for future reconciliation.[3]

A temporary truce went into effect between the warring states in June 2000 and a formal agreement to end hostilities and turn the dispute over to an international commission was signed in Algiers in December. United Nations peacekeepers were deployed the following February and have remained in place ever since, their mandate routinely renewed by the UN Security Council every six months. On April 13, 2002, the Boundary Commission issued a binding verdict that made adjustments to the boundary in each country's favor and placed the village of Badme, where the first shots of the war had been fired, within Eritrea. Both states at first accepted the verdict, but Ethiopia subsequently rejected key parts of it—notably, but not only, the placement of Badme—and the commission's decision has yet to be implemented in mid-2005. As a result, hundreds of thousands of soldiers remain deployed along the disputed frontier.

When leading members of the Eritrean president's party criticized the conduct of the war, the failed negotiations, and the slow pace of democratization, Isaias had them arrested, shut down the private press, refused to implement a newly ratified constitution, and postponed national elections. These measures, coupled with the detention of two Eritreans employed at the American embassy, led to a cooling of U.S.-Eritrean relations. Relations took another turn for the worse in 2002, as the Asmara government blamed Washington for coddling Addis Ababa rather than pressuring it to follow through on its commitment to abide by the results of the arbitration. Nevertheless, in 2003, the United States provided Eritrea with $71.6 million in humanitarian aid, including $65 million in food assistance and $3.36 million in refugee support. It also gave Eritrea $10.16 million in development assistance.[4]

Eritrea's importance to the United States in the 1990s had been in part influenced by the Clinton administration's hostility to the Islamist government in the Sudan, which supported Iraq in the first Gulf War and provided bases to Osama bin Laden and other terrorist groups during the first half of the decade. Because Eritrea provided bases for the Sudanese opposition forces, the United States designated it a frontline state in this confrontation and gave military and other aid on that basis. However, under the administration of President George W. Bush, which invested heavily in a peace process to end the Sudan's long-running North-South civil war, Eritrea's importance declined, despite the fact that it supported the American-led intervention in Iraq and offered military facilities to combat regional terrorism.

Relations continue to be uneven, due to American unease with Eritrea's poor human rights record and perceptions that the new nation is unstable, as well as Eritrean perceptions that the United States continues to favor Ethiopia. For their part, many Eritreans—in and out of government—argue that it is hypocritical to criticize their new nation for human rights abuses when the United States has behaved similarly in Afghanistan and Iraq. This resentment has fed efforts by the authoritarian government to weaken support for civil liberties and multiparty politics, which it derogates as Western imports unsuited to Eritrean culture or current conditions.

The Postindependence Eritrean State

Eritrea's contemporary political culture has long been authoritarian, predicated upon secrecy and the arbitrary exercise of absolute power. Throughout the 1970s and 1980s, the EPLF was organized and led from within by a clandestine Marxist core chaired by Isaias: the Eritrean People's Revolutionary Party. The EPRP met in secret to draft the EPLF's program prior to its three general congresses (1977, 1987, 1994); to select slates for leadership prior to elections; and, unbeknown to non–party members, to manage its affairs on a day-to-day basis. EPRP and EPLF members who broke the rules were punished mercilessly and then suddenly rehabilitated, as was the practice in Maoist China, where Isaias had received military and political training in 1968–1969. This pattern of behavior, established in the liberation movement in the 1970s and 1980s, held true for the government in the 1990s, obtains today, and will define the practices for future elections convened under this leadership—if and when they occur.

Isaias took formal control of the EPLF in 1987 at its second congress, though as party head he had always been the key figure within the EPLF, controlling the secret party and pulling the strings for the liberation front. In 1989, he froze the operations of the EPRP (known by then as the Eritrean Socialist Party) but continued to meet secretly with its leadership to plan the postwar transition. This positioned him both to assume the postwar presidency and to make the state the dominant institutional apparatus in an independent Eritrea, subordinating both the Front and what remained of the party to it.[5]

Prior to the EPLF's third congress in 1994, when it changed its name to the People's Front for Democracy and Justice (PFDJ), Isaias convinced many veterans to step aside from the leadership in order to bring what he called "new blood" into the political movement. Afterward, however, he rarely used the Front's newly elected bodies to decide issues. Instead, the PFDJ's nineteen-member executive committee spent most of its time discussing how to implement policies determined elsewhere. In this respect, the newly christened organization mimicked the EPLF's operational forms during the liberation struggle—but with a singular difference. There was no constituted party providing the guidance; no collective body, however secret, was operating behind the scenes. There was only the president and his personally selected advisors.

The same was true of the state. Though there appeared to be a separation of powers in the new government—an executive office with a cabinet of ministers, an interim parliament (pending the first national elections), and a nominally independent judiciary—it was an illusion. The cabinet did not provide a forum for debate or decision-making. It, too, served mainly as a clearinghouse to determine how policies hammered out elsewhere would be put into practice. Even the military remained under the president's personal control, as Isaias leapfrogged his own Defense Ministry to exercise direct command through four theater-operation generals whom he had brought with him from the EPRP.

Throughout the 1990s, Isaias expanded and strengthened the president's office with specialized departments for economic and political policy that duplicated (and effectively outranked) equivalent ministries. He staffed these departments with loyal individuals who reported to no one but him. Ministerial portfolios were frequently shuffled to keep rivals from developing power bases of their own. High-ranking officers and government officials who questioned the president's judgment found themselves subjected to the Chinese practice of *midiskal* (freezing), in which they were removed from their posts, kept on salary but not permitted to work, and then abruptly brought back into the fold when they were perceived to be rehabilitated. After the Border War, these practices turned uglier, as dissatisfaction with Isaias's rule became widespread.

Meanwhile, individual members of oppositional groups like the Eritrean Liberation Front were allowed to return to the country. A few were even awarded top positions in the ruling party and government or on special commissions, such as the one that drew up the constitution in the mid-1990s—but only if they renounced their former organizations. Even so, most of these ex-ELF fighters—including Ibrahim Totil, former head of the ELF's Political Department, who served as governor of the Northern Red Sea *zoba* (province)—

were stripped of their posts in 2004, as the regime bolstered its defenses and purged those considered potentially disloyal to the beleaguered president. This action left no legal, institutional base for contesting Isaias's leadership.

Up to 2001, however, the president's authority and judgment had been vigorously tested behind the scenes within the PFDJ, and measures to draw a widening circle of the general population into the country's political life had encouraged many to hope for a more open future. The two-year mobilization for the 1993 referendum on Eritrea's political status brought thousands of people into the political process for the first time. A three-year, highly participatory, constitution-making process produced a legal foundation for the articulation, exercise, and future contestation of basic civil and human rights. Despite its flaws, the manner in which it was produced—involving tens of thousands of Eritreans at home and abroad in discussions on what rights they held dear and what they wanted from their newly created state—added value beyond the constitutional document itself. It fed the dream held by many liberation-era veterans that Eritrea was on the road, however rocky, toward a popular democracy that would come to operate transparently within a defined legal framework—once it passed the transitional stage.

Up against this dream was the apparent conviction at the center of power that the people could not be trusted to rule themselves, especially in an unsettled regional environment where enemies and spies might manipulate them against their own interests. What was needed under these conditions, those close to Isaias argued, was "guided democracy," in which an enlightened few would make the key decisions about Eritrea's future and involve the general population (and the rest of the movement) largely by mobilizing people after the fact.

Throughout the 1990s, the country followed two paths at once—one toward shared participation in the very definition of the "New Eritrea," as well as in its reconstruction, development, and rule; the other toward increasingly centralized executive power that stripped the population of any agency in the process, providing them material benefits but only as objects, not subjects, of their collective destiny—in a word, patronage. Renewed war brought these contradictions to a head, and decisively resolved them in favor of the latter path.

The Crackdown on Dissent

The continuing hostilities between Ethiopia and Eritrea provided the government of Eritrea with a rationale for suspending moves toward democratization and for suppressing public criticism of the regime. The limited dissent that had been tolerated after the independence war—a period that saw the appearance of a vigorous and critical private press, heated debates among government and party officials, the convening of an international Eritrean Studies Association conference with papers raising questions about democracy and development, and more—was sharply curtailed in the summer and fall of 2001. Indeed, the stage had already been set, with the failure to implement the new constitution after it was ratified in 1997.[6]

In August 2000, several high-ranking PFDJ officials privately criticized Isaias's conduct of the Border War at a closed-door session of the PFDJ leadership. Among them were top military and political leaders who had been at the forefront of the liberation movement for thirty years. They also questioned the president's resistance to diplomatic solutions to the Ethiopian conflict before Eritrean defenses collapsed in May 2000, and they called for rapid progress toward multiparty democracy in Eritrea. These criticisms were repeated in September at a closed-door session of the National Assembly (a majority of whose members are on the PFDJ's Central Council). This was the last time Isaias permitted the body to meet until it was purged of his critics.

Over the next four to five months, Isaias's critics continued to question his leadership within the EPLF/PFDJ. When he refused to convene a meeting to take up their charges, they went public. Known as the Group of 15 (or G-15), they first published their critique on the Internet. Later, several gave lengthy interviews to Eritrea's private press. Their arguments kicked off a vigorous public debate about the country's political future.

Isaias's crackdown on dissent gathered momentum in mid-2001 with the arrest of Semere Kesete, a student leader at the University of Asmara, after he criticized the government for underpaying students for enforced "national service" during the summer months—echoing protests raised by liberation army fighters in 1993 (the only prior mass public protest in Eritrea's modern history). Hundreds of university students were rounded up and sent on a work project to contain the rising protest on the campus. Parents who objected to the treatment of their children—several of whom died—were also arrested. Semere remained in prison for months without being charged before making his escape with the help of sympathetic guards.[7]

On September 18–19, 2001, the Eritrean government initiated a sweeping crackdown on its high-level critics, arresting eleven of the fifteen who had signed the open letter to the president (one recanted and three others were not in Eritrea at the time of the arrests). Shortly after this crackdown, the government closed all the private newspapers in the country and began arresting others associated with the G-15 or with expressions of dissent during the previous year. Their justification was that those arrested, and the press, had constituted an Ethiopian fifth column, though no formal charges were brought, no evidence presented, no trials conducted, and no explanations ever offered.[8]

In the years since, there have been numerous, less publicized arrests—of elders who sought to mediate on behalf of the detainees, more journalists, mid-level officials, merchants, businessmen, young people resisting conscription, and church leaders and parishioners associated with minority Christian denominations, among others. Some were held for short periods and discharged. Others, like the G-15 and the journalists, have been held indefinitely, with no charges leveled and no visitors allowed. Some of those who were released claim that they were tortured, but no executions have been reported.

In 2002, the government banned all religious denominations but Islam, the Eritrean Orthodox Church, the Roman Catholic Church, and the Evangelical Church of Eritrea (Lutheran). Members of prohibited denominations were forbidden from worshipping anywhere in Eritrea, even in private homes. Dozens of members of Pentecostal and other independent evangelical groups and Jehovah's Witnesses have since been arrested for flouting these restrictions.[9]

Eritrean public opinion on political issues has been extremely difficult to gauge since the crackdown began, as there is no legal outlet for expressing perspectives at odds with official policy. This repression has produced a climate of fear in the urban centers, where citizens believe that telephones are tapped, public conversations are monitored, and email is routinely intercepted. These anxieties have been enhanced by the manner in which arrested dissidents are treated: People disappear, after which no one has access to them, including their families. The lack of clarity on where the red lines are—what will get one arrested—has engendered a pervasive terror of the authorities and a growing mistrust of friends, neighbors, co-workers, and others in the general population.

Amnesty International reported that fourteen journalists remained in prison without charge in December 2004, including Aklilu Solomon, a reporter for Voice of America, who was detained in July 2003 after reporting adverse public reaction to the government's announcement that soldiers had been killed in the Border War with Ethiopia.[10] In December 2004, one former detainee claimed in an email message that he had seen the VOA reporter in a secret prison near Abi Abieto in the Eritrean highlands, where he was held without charge in a shipping container. Aklilu was released at the end of that month in poor physical condition.[11]

By the middle of 2004, visitors reported that residents of Asmara—long noted for their outspoken character—spoke of politics only in hushed tones and clipped utterances. Most had become deeply pessimistic and were preoccupied with the declining economy, as prices had doubled or tripled and fuel was extremely scarce. More disturbing, the Eritrean people, known for their generosity and openness to outsiders but fed on a steady diet of anti-foreign propaganda since 2001, had begun to turn aggressively xenophobic, blaming outsiders for their increasingly desperate plight. All foreigners were required to get special permission from the Ministry of Foreign Affairs to travel in Eritrea outside Asmara. Few did so, leaving most of the country cut off from the outside world and informed about it only by party cadres and government-controlled print and broadcast media.

External Threats

Armed threats to the Eritrean government come from two directions: Islamist and secular. Nearly all opposition groups, regardless of ideology, derive from splits or spin-offs from the original independence movement, the Eritrean Liberation Front, and draw strength from those constituencies that have either run afoul of or feel shorted by the ruling EPLF/PFDJ since it came to dominate the nationalist movement. Separately, none constitutes an imminent threat to the regime in the sense of having the capacity to seize power—or even to render the country ungovernable—but taken together they signal a gathering drift toward instability whose cumulative effect will be to weaken the central state, accelerate political polarization, and contribute to conditions in which a sudden rupture could occur. That such a danger exists was underlined by the government itself in early 2005, when it charged the Sudan with harboring terrorists who plotted Isaias's assassination.[12]

The principal Islamist threat comes from Eritrean Islamic Jihad, which was slow to garner support within Eritrea in the first flush of postindependence euphoria, in part because political Islam lacks historical roots in Eritrea. However, it has lately found fertile soil in which to grow by capitalizing on Muslim dissatisfaction with the secular regime in Asmara while linking its critiques of the Isaias government to Eritrea's relations with the United States and Israel.

For their part, the secular groups have begun to accelerate efforts to form a coherent opposition alliance, though so far with little notable success beyond the production of fresh polemics. What remains is for them to set aside their parochial organizational interests and personal rivalries to mobilize around a credible program of democratic development—and to demonstrate that there is more to such a formulation than mere words. Should they do so, they would almost certainly find support, both active and passive, among the repressed and increasingly restive population inside the country, allowing them to operate clandestinely in the densely populated highlands and large urban areas, where EIJ has failed to establish a foothold. This development would abruptly alter the security situation across the country.

Eritrean Islamic Jihad

In 1989, the newly installed National Islamic Front (NIF) government in the Sudan opened its coffers to armed opposition groups from countries in Africa, the Middle East, and beyond. In Eritrea's case, those given support included both Islamist and secular guerrilla groups. Chief among them were the Eritrean Islamic Jihad Movement (EIJM, often shortened to EIJ) and factions of the Eritrean Liberation Front, which had split into numerous rival groups in the 1980s. By 1993, Eritrean organizations operating from bases in the northeastern Sudan and drawing on the large impoverished Eritrean refugee population there, were carrying out sporadic terrorist attacks inside Eritrea. Once war broke out between Eritrea and Ethiopia in 1998, many of these groups found sanctuary in Ethiopia as well, operating radio stations beamed into Eritrea as well as mounting military and political actions.

The EIJ received support from both the NIF and Osama bin Laden's emerging Islamist coalition, headquartered in the Sudan through the first half of the 1990s. It also resonated with simmering discontent in Eritrea's long-marginalized Muslim communities, and it drew recruits from the large population of war-displaced Eritreans living in the Sudan, some for decades. While it initially failed to generate large-scale popular backing, a series of missteps by the Eritrean government, the clumsy implementation of reconstruction and development programs, and then the outbreak of the Border War with Ethiopia (with all its economic, social, and political repercussions) prepared the ground for the EIJ to expand its influence and to step up its clandestine operations. With no outlet for political protest in Eritrea, the Islamist resistance became by default the channel for rising popular dissatisfaction among Eritrean Muslims. The help that it received from outside facilitated its growth, but was not causal.

Harakat al-Jihad al-Ertrrya al-Islammiya, as the EIJ was called in Arabic, had its roots in Eritrea's labyrinthine political past. In its early years, the Eritrean Liberation Front was dominated by Muslims from the western lowlands and coastal plains. After the ELF split over internal differences in 1970, the two main trends that emerged from it—the ELF and the EPLF—adopted strongly secular orientations. This drove some with Islamist politics to quit both Fronts. When the two rivals fought a civil war in 1980–1981 and the ELF split into weakened, contending factions, Islamic radicals among the refugees and former fighters in the Sudan formed their own organization: the Eritrean Muslim Pioneers Organization (Munezemet Arrewad al-Muslimeen al-Ertrrya). Two years later, a second group in the Sudan formed the Eritrean National Islamic Liberation Front (Jebhat al-Tahrir al-Ertrrya al-Islammiya al-Wetenniya).

The EIJ was launched at a conference in Khartoum in late 1988, when these two Islamist organizations merged with several smaller ones that also drew from disaffected guerrilla fighters and the refugee community in the Sudan. Among them were Islamic Uprising, the Movement of Oppressed Eritreans, and the Islamic Defense Committee. The founding conference's final communiqué denounced the EPLF and "vowed to liberate the country and raise the banner of Islam over it," though there was little evidence of the EIJ's military activity until after independence.[13]

The first EIJ combatants entered Eritrean territory in 1989, nearly two years before the end of the independence war and shortly after the NIF seized power in the Sudan, but the EIJ's first offensive military operations did not take place until January 1992. In the interim, the movement had already experienced one minor split. More were to occur over the next decade, as the more extreme wing came to dominate and as the organization deepened its affiliation with bin Laden and his emerging global terror network. By the mid-1990s, the EIJ fielded an estimated 500 fighters.[14]

Throughout these years, bin Laden and his operatives schooled guerrillas from the EIJ and other Islamist guerrilla groups in the use of explosives, forgery, coding, and other such skills, according to a former noncommissioned officer who defected from the Sudan in 1996 and with whom I spoke in western Eritrea while researching the arms trade for Human Rights Watch. Weapons for the guerrillas were imported mainly from Iran and China through Port Sudan, and then trucked to Khartoum, where the Ministry of Defense turned them over to bin Laden's representatives. Officers who carried out successful operations were rewarded with money and arms.[15]

Another defector who acted as a liaison between the NIF and bin Laden's Islamist coalition said that the EIJ held a seat on the new international network's coordinating council, the Majlis al Fatwa. This body, a precursor of Al Qaeda, had forty-three members, who served on sub-councils responsible for security, military affairs, economics, media and information, and policy. They included representatives from such far-flung armed groups as the Egyptian

Islamic Group, the Oromo Islamic Front in Ethiopia, the Islamic forces of Sheikh Abdullah in Uganda, Algeria's Islamic Salvation Front, and the Moro Liberation Front from the Philippines.

By 1993, the EIJ was carrying out occasional raids and ambushes. As reports of its clandestine activities filtered into Asmara, representatives of foreign NGOs operating in western Eritrea also began to speak off the record about pressure being put on rural residents not to participate in government-sponsored rehabilitation and development projects. None of this talk reached the domestic or international media, however, as Eritrean officials sought to play down the threat. Meanwhile, informal discussions between Eritrea and the Sudan carried out through a regional forum, the Intergovernmental Authority for Drought and Development (IGADD, the earlier incarnation of IGAD, the Intergovernmental Authority on Development), failed to reach an agreement to end these raids. The relationship between the two states began to sour, especially after 1993, when Eritrean forces captured EIJ operatives who said they had been trained at camps in the Sudan.

At the EIJ's second general conference in Khartoum in late 1994, the organization pledged to expand and continue its jihad "until achieving victory or martyrdom." Shortly afterward, EIJ units launched a cross-border attack, during which Eritrean forces reportedly killed a half-dozen guerrillas, including at least two from other countries. This thrust underlined EIJ's growing participation in bin Laden's terror network, and it led to a rupture in diplomatic relations between Eritrea and the Sudan in early 1995, when Asmara publicly called for the overthrow of the NIF government. Soon after, Eritrea opened its doors to the Sudanese opposition, hosting two conferences by the National Democratic Alliance (NDA), an emerging political and military coalition, and giving it the shuttered Sudanese embassy for a headquarters.

The Sudan People's Liberation Army (SPLA), which the Eritreans had directly assisted with troops and training in the south in the early 1990s, provided the core of the NDA's military capacity, and SPLA leader John Garang was initially appointed the new coalition's military leader, though he was rarely in the field. By the end of the decade, veteran SPLA commander Pagan Amum had taken over the post and was personally responsible for conducting some of the NDA's most daring military actions into the northeastern Sudan, including a twenty-four-hour takeover of the important border city of Kassala in late 2000. The rebels claimed to have captured thirteen government tanks and a large quantity of artillery and light weapons before withdrawing to their desert base area.[16]

The opposition alliance's largest political components, apart from the SPLA, were the traditional northern parties—the Umma Party and the

Democratic Unionist Party—that had dominated the Sudan's politics since independence, but neither one initially fielded military forces. The newly formed Sudan Alliance Forces (SAF)—led primarily by northern, Arab dissidents, many of them former military officers—developed a military arm that operated from bases in Eritrea and Ethiopia. It later merged with the SPLA and then experienced a series of debilitating leadership splits, but its units continued to engage in battles with government forces. The Beja Congress, whose base was among peoples living along the Eritrean-Sudanese border and whose origins date to the 1950s, also received Eritrean support and fielded a small militia that operated in the northeastern Sudan. It has since grown to be one of the largest armed opposition movements operating there.

The launch of an armed northern opposition, first from bases in or adjacent to Eritrea and later from western Ethiopia, posed a different kind of threat to the Sudan's central government from that in the chronically conflicted south. At various points, these groups launched attacks that threatened such key economic targets as the Roseires Dam near Damazin in the Blue Nile region and the highway linking Port Sudan with Khartoum in the northeast. The government responded to these armed incursions with calls for a national mobilization and a renewed quest for arms from its global suppliers, while charging its neighbors with invading its territory. It also stepped up support for Eritrean opposition groups, particularly the EIJ.

In an interview in early 1998, Abul Bara' Hassan Salman, the second-in-command, characterized the EIJ's objectives as liberating the region from Christian-Jewish control through armed struggle and regional diplomacy and replacing the Isaias Afwerki regime with an Islamic government. In defining the enemy, he pointedly linked Eritrea with the United States and Israel:

> As for the latest Christian onslaught, which is being led by America, its scenario is being executed by the puppet regimes in the region. This onslaught is also an attempt to impose the sovereignty of the Christian minorities in the region in order to ascertain the strategic security and economic needs of the imperialists. . . .
>
> [T]he Afourgy [Afwerki] regime is regarded as one of the elements of the Christian strategy in the African Horn. This is evident in its employment of Eritrea and its people to destabilise the security of the region. The behaviour of the regime, its enmity to neighbouring countries such as the Sudan and Yemen, and its complete denial of the role of the Arab countries and the Muslims (during the war for liberation from Ethiopia), and its alliance with the Jews are amongst the biggest indicators of this.[17]

At its third general conference in 1998, shortly after the outbreak of war between Eritrea and Ethiopia and after Al Qaeda's attacks on the American embassies in Kenya and Tanzania had focused the global spotlight on the Sudan, the EIJ changed its name to the Eritrean Islamic Salvation Movement (Harakat al-Khalas al-Ertrrya al-Islammiya, or al-Khalas for short) in an effort to defuse the increasingly hostile attention from the international media. Nevertheless, the conference renewed its call for jihad, and EIJ operatives continued to launch attacks into Eritrea, seeking to capitalize on dissatisfaction with the secular regime in Asmara and the perception that the government was controlled by Christian Tigrinya-speakers, who dominated the economy in mostly Muslim western Eritrea. Of particular concern then— and more so as the confrontation with Ethiopia accelerated—were the government's efforts to challenge conservative social mores on gender issues and the conscription of Muslim women into the military.

In the immediate aftermath of the devastating third round of fighting with Ethiopia in May–June 2000, conditions for Muslims living in western Eritrea deteriorated significantly, even as demands on Eritrea's limited capacity for emergency relief multiplied. Dissatisfaction in Muslim communities grew as refugees began returning from camps in the Sudan under a long-delayed UN resettlement program and the military call-ups to guard the still unstable border with Ethiopia continued. The EIJ capitalized on this fact to expand its reach. By 2001, it had begun to operate freely in the Northern Red Sea region, and it became dangerous for government officials or foreigners to travel there without armed escort. This situation worsened when PFDJ cadres, backed by military force, intervened in the Beja Congress to impose a puppet leadership. Afterward, disaffected Bejas began to cooperate with the Sudanese authorities and with the EIJ. Eritrean investigators probing an August 2003 attack on a vehicle in the Sahel region, in which two local employees of the U.S.-based aid group Mercy Corps International were killed, blamed members of the EIJ. Surprisingly, however, the State Department's "Patterns of Global Terrorism 2003" report did not mention the group, though it cited the incident in its chronology of terrorist attacks.[18]

In April 2004, the United Nations reported "a spate of attacks in western Eritrea, believed to have been carried out by the Eritrean Islamic Jihad Movement (EIJM)."[19] Two months later, Eritrean national television broadcast footage of a "confession" by an Eritrean man, identified as Segid Mohamed Kelifa Mentay Ali, who said he had planted a bomb in Barentu on May 25 that wounded ninety people. Ali, who took responsibility for other bombings earlier in the year, said he had carried out the attack on the orders of a group he characterized only as "jihad."[20]

At its August 2004 general conference in Khartoum, the organization altered its name again, to al-Hezb al-Islami al-Eritree LilAdalah Wetenmiya (Eritrean Islamic Party for Justice and Development). It also dropped the image of an automatic rifle on its official emblem. Yet it appeared to have changed little in its strategic orientation.

Secular Opposition Movements

Chronic turmoil within the ELF has produced numerous splinter groups since the 1960s. The EIJ draws heavily on this process. Even the EPLF/PFDJ traces its origins to three groups that broke with ELF in 1969–1970. By 2004, there were more than eighteen organizations committed to the ouster of the Isaias regime, nearly all of them arising from the ELF. Some defined their separate identity by ideological orientation, but most were differentiated by their links to external powers, their regional or ethnic base, or the personalities who led them. Though they quibbled endlessly over seemingly inconsequential points, however, two major issues divided them: whether or not to wage an armed struggle to topple the government, and how closely to work with Ethiopia in pursuing their objectives.

The rise of a vocal but poorly organized opposition within the EPLF/PFDJ in 1998–2000, the government crackdown on dissent that got under way in earnest in 2001, and the creeping split within the PFDJ that followed gave rise to a new trend that drew on the EPLF's legacy even as its adherents denounced the president for hijacking it. In February 2002, the dissenters launched the EPLF-Democratic Party (EPLF-DP) under the leadership of Mesfun Hagos, a founder of the EPLF and a member of G-15, with the goal of establishing "a constitutional system in accordance with the democratic principles laid down in the ratified Constitution of Eritrea."[21] Two years later, its name was changed to the Eritrean Democratic Party (EDP). After defections over the two main issues noted above, it absorbed another small party based on former EPLF/PFDJ supporters, the Movement for Democratic Change, and allied itself with two ELF factions, the ELF and the ELF-Revolutionary Council. This bloc has the greatest potential to undermine the president's support within Eritrean society—and within the Eritrean Defense Forces, where Mesfun retains considerable popularity.

Most of the other secular groups deriving from the old ELF or EPLF are in the thirteen-member Eritrean Democratic Alliance (EDA), which also includes several new secular and religious opposition formations. The EDA is committed to the armed overthrow of the Isaias government and maintains political offices in Ethiopia.[22] Their adherents are drawn mainly from former ELF fighters and from refugees in the Sudan and Ethiopia. They include the ELF-National Congress (the largest of the former ELF factions), the strongly pro-Ethiopia Eritrean Revolutionary Democratic Front (whose name mimics that of the ruling party in Ethiopia), the Eritrean People's Movement (an EDP splinter), and several small regional groups like the Democratic Movement for the Liberation of Eritrean Kunama and the Red Sea Afar Democratic Organization. Three of these opposition formations—the EDP, the ELF-RC, and the EDA—beam weekly short-wave radio programs to Eritrea via satellite.

New parties, civic organizations, and would-be armies drawing their roots from the old ELF emerge and fade frequently. The political culture from which they spring is one of bitter enmity toward the Asmara regime, often mixed with driving personal ambition, and it is bound to keep gestating new groups and alliances. When this volatile political cocktail is stirred by outside interests, the result can be deadly.

While the opposition groups that cooperate with Ethiopia differ over tactics, they share the short-term goal of weakening the Isaias regime in order to displace it. In the absence of significant popular support—badly eroded by their association with Ethiopia—this grouping is most likely to resort to terrorism, the more so if it acts as a proxy for either Ethiopia or the Sudan. Both of these states have interests in destabilizing Eritrea—to promote regime change and to exact retribution for Eritrean support for opposition groups operating in their own territories—and they both see ready opportunities to do so through proxy groups. Thus, the attainment of regional peace and stability are key factors in limiting the potential for terrorism.

The Potential for Terrorism

The likelihood of Eritrea becoming a regional outpost for global terrorist organizations operating on their own is slim. The dangers are that the reciprocal action between domestic repression and external threats will open spaces for acts of terrorism to increase in frequency among indigenous groups, both as political instruments and as gestures of frustration and anger—or simply revenge; and that such groups will seek stronger relationships with and support from global networks to accomplish such attacks. What we have in Eritrea is a set of factors that individually do not equate to a major threat, but, taken together, amount to a dangerous trend. In circumstances where the stability of the regime declines—which many actors seek—this volatile mix could produce America's worst nightmare.

The tenor and direction of the present political situation, coupled with the ripening of related environmental features, create conditions in which terrorist attacks on domestic targets will almost certainly increase in frequency and intensity. At the same time, Eritrea's continuing confrontations with both Ethiopia and the Sudan incubate centers of state-sponsored terrorism that operate in both directions and are aimed at weakening the other's capacity to rule. Should order break down in Eritrea, politically motivated terrorism could spread faster and further. But there is also a danger that the continuing militarization of Eritrean society will lead to an atmosphere of increased criminality within which terrorists of all sorts could thrive.

Eritrea has frequently been implicated in the promotion of unrest in both Ethiopia and the Sudan through its support of rebel groups ranging from Oromo militants in southern Ethiopia to the Sudan People's Liberation Movement (SPLM) in southern Sudan, the NDA coalition in the Sudan's east and northeast, and the newly formed Sudan Liberation Army in Darfur. Both Ethiopia and the Sudan have responded by aiding armed opposition movements that target Eritrea. Recent acts of terror in Eritrea have consisted mainly of land mine detonations and small-scale ambushes near the country's highly militarized borders with Ethiopia and the Sudan or in the coastal lowlands. Most are blamed on the EIJ or on ELF-derived guerrilla groups, but a series of bomb explosions in Asmara in 2002 were ascribed to supporters of the jailed G-15 dissidents. Should Eritrea's security situation deteriorate further, these incidents will grow in scope and potency. So far, none of these acts has targeted U.S. interests, but that also could change.

The United States now finds itself in a peculiar position. On the one hand, it is blamed by the Eritrean government for abetting "treason" during the Border War with Ethiopia, and since then, of supporting "enemies of the state" (political dissidents, jailed journalists, and members of minority religious denominations). On the other hand, it is castigated by the government's opponents for counting the Isaias regime among its allies in the Iraq coalition and continuing to provide it with aid while doing nothing to enforce criticisms of the suppression of democracy. Islamist critics also chastise the United States for promoting closer ties between Eritrea and Israel and use this linkage to buttress their charge that the Asmara government is Christian dominated.

The most important factor shaping Eritrean attitudes toward the United States—and allowing the government to deflect attention from its own failings—is America's toothless protests over Ethiopia's noncompliance with the 2002 findings of the international boundary commission. Many Eritreans see that as the latest slight in a historical pattern going back to Washington's failure to protest Emperor Haile Selassie's abrogation of the UN treaty that federated Eritrea to Ethiopia in the first place. This neglect fuels popular anger at the United States and harrows the ground for future anti-American actions. The unfolding political situation within Eritrea needs to be read and interpreted in this context.

Although the present climate of fear may forestall direct challenges to the regime over the coming one or two years, Eritrea's medium-term prospects for stability and democracy are poor. National elections, when held, will not be free and fair. With no public space for political discussion, let alone protest, and severe constraints on the organizational expression of the most benign social or economic interests—that is, the blanket suppression of civil society—the possibility to contest the PFDJ's grip on power is simply nonexistent. Elections under such conditions can only rubber-stamp the sitting government. With all peaceful avenues for altering the political situation thus closed, those who reject this dispensation are increasingly driven toward extralegal forms of resistance.

Few in the opposition who advocate armed force to topple the regime expect to win a military victory. Their hope is to so weaken the ruling party that the state will collapse from within, perhaps through a popular uprising, perhaps by an assassination, perhaps in the course of a coup d'état, or, more likely, through some combination. The danger comes largely from the possibility of a collapse at the center before the opposition is prepared to fill the vacuum. Under such circumstances, the country could slide into civil war or anarchy, as significant fault lines—regional, religious, and ethnic, as well as political and personal—lie under the social surface.

Meanwhile, a generation of young people has lost the opportunity for education or skill development, apart from in the arts of war, for more than six years. Whatever happens to alter the political situation, this cohort could be a major source of political (or criminal) violence in Eritrea and the wider region for many years to come. The longer this crisis situation obtains, the more serious will be the problem—fostering the development of a warrior class with few personal or political scruples. This is an army united by nationalist values (and coerced into serving for this extended period) but lacking in the culture of social and political responsibility that underlay the liberation movement. Absent nationalism as a unifying dynamic, they could put their martial identities and skills at the service of new and far more dangerous demagogues than populate the scene today. Effective demobilization programs could help to avert this danger, but only if these hardened, disgruntled soldiers are disarmed and in transition soon.

Disenchantment is most advanced among the Muslim population, where grievances against the Isaias regime have grown steadily over the past decade, especially since the outbreak of war with Ethiopia. These sentiments find expression through the EIJ. Issues that feed the EIJ's growth include a litany of perceived cultural slights: the government's refusal to accept Arabic as an official language; the imposition of leaders on Islamic religious institutions, including the grand mufti in Asmara; the virtual colonization of the lowlands by Tigrinya-speaking Christians; the denigration of pastoralism as a way of life; perceptions of unequal representation in state and party leadership; a conviction that the official (but haphazardly implemented) land reform program will impinge on traditional grazing rights; and, most important, outrage over the conscription of women into an army where they reportedly suffer extensive abuse.

Prior to the Border War, the government managed to minimize complaints over such issues by extending new services to areas that had rarely received them in the past, from primary education and rudimentary health care to rural roads and electrification. But its capacity to maintain these services was sharply curtailed by the onset of war, and existing structures were badly damaged in the fighting and the looting that followed. Meanwhile, the program to resettle refugees returning from the Sudan, accelerated after 2001, brought many Eritreans influenced by Islamic values and organizations back to these war-devastated areas—lands where, in some cases, the government was already attempting to resettle highlanders. At the same time, Eritrean Muslims returned from conservative Middle Eastern states where they had been exposed to even more radical interpretations of Islam and Islamist politics. These factors contributed to an atmosphere of increased toleration for—and in some cases direct assistance to—EIJ's organizing efforts among the mostly Muslim western lowlanders.

Should the EIJ escalate its tactics and employ the suicide bombing tactic so rife in the Islamist movements with which it maintains loose connections, the situation in Eritrea could take a drastic turn for the worse. However, military aid to Eritrea to counter terrorist threats in this political environment runs the risk of identifying the United States with the worst excesses of a regime whose days may be numbered—and of inviting those opposed to this regime to regard the United States as a target as well.

Toward a New U.S. Policy

U.S. policy in Eritrea has been adrift since the outbreak of war with Ethiopia. In Eritrea, the political environment has deteriorated substantially, as the society has become polarized over the repression of dissent and as expressions of protest have been rendered infeasible—apart from clandestine acts of violence—both by state repression and by a popular hesitation to confront the state during a time of war. The result is an appearance of order that masks deepening alienation and progressive instability in which the United States is implicated by its inaction. This inaction needs to be reversed.

The United States must articulate a set of objectives for the region as a whole and pursue policies toward Eritrea that arise from and are consistent with them, rather than reacting piecemeal to problems and opportunities that wax and wane within each individual country. An effective strategy to prevent any country in this region from becoming a haven for terrorists demands closer coordination among all of them. These states are too deeply intertwined to do otherwise with any expectation of preventing the spread of terrorism.

The strategy for achieving these objectives must be built around settling disputes, promoting democracy, and destroying emerging terrorist threats, without which such interstate cooperation is impossible. Publicly articulating such an approach would help to isolate those who stand in the way and facilitate linked incentives and penalties to advance policy objectives. But these must be more than rhetorical flourishes.

For Eritrea, sequencing is important; but from the standpoint of U.S. interests, linkage between movement on the border dispute and on democratization—and on leveraging one to achieve the other—is critical. The United States should move aggressively to end the confrontation between Eritrea and Ethiopia. No former colonial power, nor any other state or multilateral institution, is positioned to play this role, from the standpoint either of historical engagement or of current influence. And no other objectives can be effectively dealt with until this issue is taken off the table. But the United States should not act on this in isolation from other objectives.

Both the prospect of more war and the continuing suppression of democracy in Eritrea contribute to a chronically unstable environment in which terrorism will develop. Preventing terrorism must start with a resolution of the border dispute, as intractable as it now seems. However, making clear that the United States is committed to democracy and respect for basic civil and human rights in Eritrea is also essential—and could be a key to moving dispute resolution forward, even as it addresses the gathering alienation within the Eritrean population and the slide toward despotism.

The acceptance "in principle" by Prime Minister Meles Zenawi of Ethiopia in November 2004 of the 2002 border commission ruling raised hopes of movement in the stalled peace process, but the announcement hedged on details, and, despite gestures of support from across the global political spectrum, the Isaias government dismissed the initiative as offering nothing new. The failure of the international community to use this initiative, however flawed, to pry open the stalled peace process represented another in a series of missed opportunities. This failure may come back to haunt all parties involved if, as is likely, it rekindles tensions along the disputed frontier.

If left to fester, this crisis could lead to renewed conflict that would not only devastate the two foes but could also unravel peace efforts in the Sudan and Somalia, while opening the region further to terrorist penetration. That would be a disaster for the peoples of the affected countries and for U.S. policy. Even if full-scale conflict does not ensue, the no-war/no-peace stalemate holds great risk: it tests Eritrea and Ethiopia, both of which are threatened by drought-induced famine; puts the entire region at risk (especially the Sudan); strengthens antidemocratic trends in both states; and undermines confidence in all such international peace agreements, from the Sudan to Israel-Palestine and beyond.

It is in the interest of the United States to move the peace process forward on the basis of the acceptance of the boundary commission's findings, coupled with sufficient incentives to make a settlement palatable. In part this approach involves pressuring Ethiopia to implement the findings as they are; in part it involves offering incentives to both sides to make progress toward peace more acceptable to their constituencies. A new initiative should be coordinated with both the European Union (EU) and the African Union (AU) to strengthen its impact and to signal U.S. intent to work within multilateral frameworks. Doing so would underline the risk of isolation for both states if they drag their feet. But that message must be backed by a credible threat of sanctions that have more than symbolic value. Demands without punch carry no weight with either antagonist.

The United States should also take an aggressive approach to reversing the suppression of liberties and rights in Eritrea. Making this policy a centerpiece of American action while pushing Ethiopia to accept the boundary commission's findings without hedging on details (including Badme) would blunt charges that the United States is somehow tilting toward Eritrea, while implicitly addressing one of Ethiopia's larger concerns—the risk of placating an unpredictable state on its northern border that shuns diplomacy and is prone to violent confrontations. Meanwhile, the United States should refrain from actions (public statements, high level delegations, aid other than that for humanitarian purposes, and so on) that appear to condone or accept the deterioration of the political situation within Eritrea.

The Eritrean government is convinced—and often makes this point in public statements—that the Bush administration is divided over Eritrea, with the Pentagon favoring closer relations out of respect for Eritrea's military prowess and its commitment to the war on terrorism and the State Department advocating the opposite due to concerns over human rights and democracy. As a result, most Eritrean initiatives toward strengthening relations with the United States are targeted at the Defense Department, rather than using conventional diplomatic channels.[23] This contradictory posture must change, so that the United States speaks to Eritrea with one voice on foreign policy—that of the State Department. The United States should not abort the reform process in Eritrea by propping up Isaias's repressive regime with military assistance as a cold-war-style payoff for joining the war on terrorism. To do so makes a mockery of claims that this "war" has anything to do with promoting democracy.

Specific Recommendations

The most urgent priority for the United States is to defuse the border dispute between Eritrea and Ethiopia. All else turns on this reality, and it must be addressed first. To promote a fair and lasting resolution of that conflict, the United States should:

1. Pressure Ethiopia to implement the boundary commission's 2002 decision promptly and fully, without additional conditions or qualifications.

2. Pressure Eritrea to enter into side talks on issues of importance to Ethiopia, without linking them to Ethiopia's acceptance of the commission's findings.

3. Provide the boundary commission and the United Nations Mission in Ethiopia and Eritrea (UNMEE) the necessary support and security guarantees for the border demarcation.

4. Negotiate parallel initiatives with the help of the UN, the African Union, and the European Union to reduce the impact on civilians in the affected areas and to prevent conflict that might result from the demarcation process.

5. Offer material incentives for rapid progress on the resolution of this confrontation and work to build an elite consensus for it within both societies.

6. Spell out a sequence of gradually escalating political and financial penalties for any party that blocks such a resolution of the conflict.

7. Publicize these opportunities and penalties as widely as possible to the populations of both states, through both diplomatic channels and global media, in order to generate pressure from below to accept a settlement.

To promote a stable, democratic, political arena that will be less conducive to terrorist threats, the United States should pressure Eritrea to:

1. Immediately implement the constitution that was ratified in 1997, bringing all of Eritrea's laws into line with it.

2. Release or bring to public trial all political prisoners, including but not limited to the former liberation front leaders and government officials identified with the Group of 15.

3. Grant amnesty to members of opposition political movements based outside the country, allowing those organizations to renounce violence and enter the political process as legal entities competing on a level playing field with the ruling PFDJ.

4. Untangle the complex (and secret) interlocking economic relations between the government and the ruling party and make them transparent—or forgo international development assistance.

5. Permit the reestablishment of a free, independent media, including broadcast as well as print outlets.

6. Provide legal protections for all religious groups, and take prompt legal action against those who attack members of minority faiths.

7. Approve the Party Law tabled in the National Assembly in March 2001, which legalizes multiple parties and lays the groundwork for national elections.

8. Establish an independent commission to organize Eritrea's first national elections, with adequate safeguards for competing parties and open campaigns and with extensive international monitoring throughout the process.

The Eritrean people should not be punished for the sins of the regime. The United States should provide generous humanitarian aid to victims of drought and war, while withholding other assistance until the Eritrean government takes decisive steps to return the country to the path of democratic development.

In the event of significant progress on dispute resolution and democratization, the United States should be prepared to:

1. Commit funds and technical support for the rapid demobilization and reintegration of combat troops.

2. Assist with the resettlement of war-displaced civilians, those who have been expelled from Ethiopia and those returning from the Sudan.

3. Provide support for poverty-alleviation and development programs within the scope of Eritrea's national priorities.

4. Increase support for HIV/AIDS prevention and treatment, particularly among demobilized soldiers.

5. Resurrect the Greater Horn of Africa Initiative, dormant since the outbreak of the Border War, and promote the development of regional infrastructure and the expansion of regional trade.

6. Offer Eritrea enhanced terms of bilateral trade and expedite its inclusion in the Millennium Challenge Account program.

7. Assist Eritrea in modernizing and reequipping a slimmed-down military to identify and destroy terrorist threats more effectively.

Notes

1. The National Security Agency operated the Kagnew Station complex until the mid-1970s, intercepting radio, telephone, and telegraph messages from Soviet missile crews in Egypt, French diplomats in Senegal, African revolutionaries in Mozambique, and Arabs plotting against the British in Aden. It was also a relay station for communications with U.S. ships and submarines in the Indian Ocean, for links to forces in Southeast Asia, and for coded diplomatic traffic. See Connell, *Against All Odds: A Chronicle of the Eritrean Revolution* (Trenton, 1997).

2. Victoria Garcia, "Terrorism: Eritrea" (May 19, 2004), www.cdi.org/program/document.cfm?documentid=2223&programID=73&from_page=../.

3. For a discussion of the underlying complexities of this conflict, see Leenco Lata, "The Ethiopia-Eritrea War," *Review of African Political Economy*, XXX (2003), 369–388.

4. Bureau of African Affairs, U.S. Department of State, "Background Note: Eritrea" (March 2004), www.state.gov/r/pa/ei/bgn/2854.htm.

5. See Connell, "Inside the EPLF: The Origins of the 'People's Party' and Its Role in the Liberation of Eritrea," *Review of African Political Economy*, XXVIII (2001), 345–364.

6. See Connell, "Enough! A Critique of Eritrea's Post-Liberation Politics" (November 6, 2003) http://allafrica.com/stories/200311060876.html.

7. For a narrative account of these measures, see Debessay Hedru, "Eritrea: Transition to Dictatorship, 1991–2003," *Review of African Political Economy*, XXX (2003), 435–444.

8. I was in Eritrea in 2001 as criticism of the president became public and I interviewed several top-ranking dissidents shortly before they were imprisoned indefinitely. These interviews appear in Connell, *Conversations with Eritrean Political Prisoners* (Trenton, 2004).

9. U.S. Department of State, "International Religious Freedom Report 2004" (Washington, D.C., September 15, 2004), www.state.gov/g/drl/rls/irf/2004/35354.htm.

10. "Eritrea 2004," *Amnesty International Report 2004* (January 2004), http://web.amnesty.org/report2004/eri-summary-eng.

11. "VOA correspondent freed in Eritrea, 16 journalists remain in secret jails," Committee to Protect Journalists (March 3, 2005), http://allafrica.com/stories/200503030914.html.

12. "Eritrea Dismantles 'Terrorist Network' Backed by the Sudan: Official," Agence France-Presse (October 20, 2004), www.keepmedia.com/ShowItemDetails.do?itemID=614937&extID=10030.

13. See the EIJM website, www.alkhalas.org/Significant.htm. See also Ruth Iyob, "Shifting Terrain: Dissidence versus Terrorism in Eritrea," in *Terrorism in the Horn of Africa* (Washington, D.C., 2004), www.usip.org/pubs/specialreports/sr113.html.

14. See the Gedab Investigative Report, "The 'Executed': No Smoking Gun, but Plenty of Circumstantial Evidence," www.awate.com/cgi-bin/artman/exec/view.cgi/11/1090.

15. Interview with a defecting Sudanese noncommissioned officer in Tessenei, Eritrea, March 10, 1997, as cited in Human Rights Watch, *Global Trade, Local Impact: Arms Transfers to All Sides in the Civil War in Sudan* (New York, 1998).

16. I observed and photographed these arms at an NDA base in the northeastern Sudan after this attack.

17. "The Governing Regime Is a Terrorist Regime Which Acts with Enmity against the Eritrean People," *Nida'ul Islam* (February–March 1998), www.islam.org.au/articles/22/index.htm.

18. Department of State, "Patterns of Global Terrorism 2003" (April 2004), www.state.gov/s/ct/rls/pgtrpt/2003.

19. Integrated Regional Information Network, "Sudan: Peace and the Region" (April 2, 2004), www.plusnews.org/S_report.asp?ReportID=40388&SelectRegion=East_Africa.

20. "Eritrea Bomb Suspect Admits 'Jihad' Attack Planned from Sudan," Agence France-Presse (June 23, 2004).

21. See the EPLF-DP's founding program (February 2002) at www.eritreaone.com/Docu/publication.htm.

22. On May 2, 2003, Hiruy Tedla Bairu, general secretary of the Eritrean Democratic Alliance, told the BBC that its military wing would attack strategic targets such as television and radio stations. See the EDA website, www.erit-alliance.org.

23. On September 15, 2004, for example, the Ministry of Foreign Affairs issued a statement rejecting recent U.S. criticism of its policies on religious freedom. It cited past Central Intelligence Agency "intervention" in Eritrean affairs and termed it "astonishing to see the United States, which lacks moral and legal high grounds on human rights and respect for religions, make an attempt to become the self-appointed adjudicator."

5

ETHIOPIA
Governance and Terrorism

DAVID H. SHINN

E thiopia has experienced a substantial number of terrorist attacks, the vast majority initiated by indigenous groups or Al Itihad Al Islamiya (AIAI, located in neighboring Somalia). Yet, it generally has been free of international terrorism. Either international terrorists have not yet focused on Ethiopia or the internal situation renders the country a more difficult target than others in the region. The African Human Security Initiative at the Institute for Security Studies in Pretoria, South Africa, recently extensively reviewed the terrorist threat in eight African countries, including Ethiopia. It assigned a high threat assessment to Algeria, Kenya, and Uganda; an intermediate assessment to Nigeria, Ethiopia, and South Africa, and a low assessment to Ghana and Senegal.[1]

Background

Although it may not be in the highest threat category in Africa, Ethiopia has too many inherent weaknesses to be considered a bulwark against terrorism. It shares a boundary with five countries: Djibouti, Eritrea, Kenya, Somalia/Somaliland, and the

Sudan. The borders with Somalia/Somaliland and the Sudan are each about 1,000 miles long, while those with Eritrea (567 miles), Kenya (512 miles), and Djibouti (209 miles) are shorter. Ethiopia's land borders are unusually porous, even by African standards. The Horn of Africa serves as the back door to the troubled Persian Gulf, the source of much of today's international terrorism. The Horn over the past fifty years has been the origin of several conflicts and has been negatively impacted by numerous others. These conflicts have resulted in the direct use of terrorist tactics by indigenous organizations hostile to the government of Ethiopia and have created a receptive environment that international terrorists can use for their own nefarious purposes.[2]

Ethiopia and other countries in the region can minimize the likelihood that terrorism will eventually overwhelm the country. Over the short and medium terms, improvements in security, intelligence, border control, and the technical ability to monitor the movement of people and money will pay significant dividends. But it is addressing the long-term problems of how to improve governance, reduce poverty and social inequality, and treat traditionally disadvantaged ethnic and religious groups equally that will do the most to create an environment that will discourage both indigenous and international terrorists. Doing so will require Ethiopia, supported by the international community, to build democratic structures, reduce ethnic tensions, further improve relations between Christians and Muslims, roll back the HIV/AIDS pandemic, institute effective family planning programs, and launch a comprehensive attack against poverty. It also means that all countries in the region must end their support for opposition groups that are trying to overthrow regimes in neighboring states.[3]

Good governance and open political competition, characteristics that only now are beginning to develop in Ethiopia, have a direct bearing on the ability of terrorism, especially the domestic variety, to take root. Violent opposition groups will find fewer Ethiopians willing to cooperate in such an environment. Even international terrorists will have one less opportunity to exploit and will find a society more unified on basic principles.

Generic Sources of Instability

Ethiopia is one of the poorest countries in the world. Per capita annual income has fallen to about $100. (One must, however, be skeptical about per capita income figures for agriculturally based barter societies.) Only half of the population has access to minimal levels of health care and only a quarter has access to safe drinking water. In 2002, the infant mortality rate per 1,000 live births was 114, higher than the average for sub-Saharan Africa but a notice-able improvement over the figure twenty-five years earlier. In 2002, life expectancy at birth was forty-two years, four years below the average for Africa and unchanged from twenty-five years earlier. Secondary school enrollment was about 17 percent of those eligible. Ethiopia remains highly vulnerable to external shocks, especially drought and low prices for coffee, its major export. Its poverty indicators remain among the most dismal in the world.[4]

Ethiopia has experienced periodic food shortages and famine since the beginning of recorded history. Exacerbated by dramatic increases in popula-tion, the frequency and severity of shortages have steadily increased. Ethiopia has not produced enough food to feed its population since the late 1960s. It now has a structural food deficit during normal crop years that affects about 5 million people. A special advisor to the UN secretary-general commented that Ethiopia's population of 72 million will double every twenty-three years.[5] The United Nations Population Fund projects that Ethiopia's population will reach 170 million in thirty years. The government's goal is to achieve self-sufficiency in food in three years. In view of the modest achievement so far and a major, possibly flawed, land resettlement scheme, it is difficult to envisage success. The combination of poverty, structural food deficits, and a high pop-ulation growth rate will put increasing pressure on Ethiopia's ability to remain politically stable.

Ethiopia has the fourth highest number of persons affected by HIV/AIDS in the world, after South Africa, India, and Nigeria. The prevalence rate is about 5 percent for those between the ages of fifteen and forty-nine—more than 2 million adults. In addition, an estimated 200,000 children were HIV positive in 2001, and 1.2 million children had been orphaned. Ethiopia's preva-lence rate is relatively low compared with countries in southern Africa, but the total number of affected individuals is exceptionally high, because of the large overall population.

HIV/AIDS is an overwhelming problem for a poor country with a primi-tive health care system. Although the government has belatedly taken some impressive steps to stem the pandemic, the prevalence rate continues to rise. The armed forces began a major anti-AIDS program in the mid-1990s. As a result, the prevalence rate in the army is slightly below that for the general adult population. Nevertheless, as in other African countries, HIV/AIDS poses a serious threat to the health care system and the national economy.[6]

Corruption is a problem throughout the region, although somewhat less of an issue for Ethiopia than for most of its immediate neighbors. In a world-wide assessment of 145 countries in 2004, Transparency International ranked

Ethiopia 114 (down from 92 the previous year), along with eight other countries. By comparison, the Sudan ranked 122, Kenya 129, and Eritrea 102. (The
higher the number, the more serious is the problem of corruption. Somalia
and Djibouti were not included in the survey.)[7] Most allegations of corruption have been aimed at political figures, bureaucrats, bankers, and
businessmen. The government has launched a spirited anticorruption campaign, but it tends to focus excessively on the private sector. The fact remains
that corruption threatens the integrity of the government. The bribing of
public officials is a common practice with a long tradition. It also opens possibilities for persons with nefarious plans, including international terrorists,
to obtain local assistance from poorly paid Ethiopian security and immigration personnel.

The Impact of Religion

Ethiopia is located on a religious fault line. This diversity can be a source of stability or instability. Over the past 100 years Ethiopia's complex mélange of
religious communities has generally lived side by side in harmony. Increasing
proselytism by fundamentalist sects, primarily Islamic Wahhabis but also a few
Christian groups, has begun to disturb this relative tranquility. The last
Ethiopian census, in 1994, indicated that 51 percent of the population was
Ethiopian Orthodox, 10 percent Protestant, 33 percent Muslim, and most of
the remainder followers of indigenous beliefs. Many observers believe that
the census overstated the percentage of Ethiopian Orthodox and understated
the number of Muslims. In addition, there is some evidence of a more rapid
expansion of the Islamic population since 1994. The U.S. State Department's
International Religious Freedom Report for 2004 states that between 40 and 45
percent of the population is Ethiopian Orthodox and 10 percent is Protestant,
while about 45 percent is Muslim.[8] No one knows with certainty the percentage of Christians and Muslims living in Ethiopia. It is likely, however, that
they are nearing parity. This result has important implications for political
power and stability. Ethiopia (tied with Morocco) now has the eleventh highest number of Muslims in the world; it has more Muslims than Saudi Arabia,
the Sudan, Iraq, or Afghanistan.[9] Ethiopia is no longer a "Christian nation."

Ethiopian Muslims reside throughout the country but tend to concen-
trate along the southern, eastern, and western peripheries. The Oromo
constitute about 40 percent of Ethiopia's population. Oromo leaders differ on
the Muslim-Christian distribution, but most estimate that it ranges from a
50-50 split to 60 percent Muslim and 40 percent Christian. Ethnic groups that

are almost entirely Islamic include the Somali (6 percent of the population), the Afar (4 percent), the Harari, and a number of smaller groups along the Sudanese border and scattered elsewhere in the country. Because of their heavier concentration on the peripheries, their tendency to function as separate communities, and the long tradition of Christian control, Ethiopian Muslims have not yet exercised political influence commensurate with their numbers.

Although the leadership continues to be largely Christian, Ethiopia now officially recognizes both Christian and Muslim holy days. The government accorded legal status to the Supreme Council of Islamic Affairs in 1992 and tries to guarantee the rights of Muslims. In 1992, it lifted restrictions on travel to Mecca and repealed its ban on the importation of non-Christian religious literature. The number of private Islamic publishing houses is increasing in Addis Ababa. In general they publish Amharic translations of Islamic material in Arabic and English; one is translating the Qur'an into Amharic. On the other hand, a clash between police and Muslims at the al-Anwar mosque in Addis Ababa in 1995 interrupted otherwise cordial relations. Some Muslims complain that the government has interfered in the internal affairs of the Supreme Council and that some Pentecostal preachers disparage Islam in their services. The Supreme Council also claims that it has more difficulty than the Orthodox Church in obtaining land from the government.[10]

Sufism is the predominant form of Islam in Ethiopia. Over the centuries distinct orders have developed, with their own sheikhs, tolerant of one another. Significant sheikhs became regarded as saints, credited with powers of healing and other miracles. Upon death they were deified and their tombs became centers of worship. However, a growing number of Ethiopian Islamic scholars, fluent in both Amharic and Arabic, have been studying in Saudi Arabia and are now returning to spread Wahhabism. They strongly oppose the Sufi-inspired traditional practices that have permeated Ethiopian Islam. The Wahhabists have encouraged the desecration of Sufi tombs; there have also been reports of the destruction of mosques frequented by followers of Sufi Islam. Young scholars returning from Islamic universities abroad increasingly are replacing the older, traditional, uneducated sheikhs. The young sheikhs also bring substantial funding and build impressive mosques and Islamic schools. These actions put additional pressure on the traditionalists to forsake their worship at the shrines and tombs of their ancestors. In many parts of Ethiopia such Wahhabi ideas are meeting strong resistance.[11] This conflict manifests itself within the Supreme Council, which voted in 2004 to replace all executive members of the Council with strong anti-Wahhabists.[12] The battle between traditional followers of Sufism and the advocates of Wahhabism has been joined; it is not clear where it will end.

There is considerable disagreement among Ethiopian scholars concerning the impact of Wahhabism in the country. Some consider it a serious threat to traditional Islam and long-standing cordial relations between Muslims and Christians. They point to the growing influence of radical elements within Islamic communities, aided by funding from Saudi Arabia and the Gulf States. They cite the significant growth of mosques and Islamic schools constructed with funding from Wahhabi charities. They claim that Wahhabis are changing the outlook of many Ethiopian Muslims, especially the young and the poor. Medhane Tadesse, author of a book on Al Itihad, argues that Ethiopia's "religious equilibrium is collapsing very quickly" and "incubating violent confrontation."[13] He adds that "the contemporary religious militancy should be seen as a wholly new phenomenon and a threat to the peace, stability and independence of the country."[14]

Others emphasize that Ethiopian Muslims have long had a reputation for being tolerant and that their traditional Islamic beliefs will make it difficult for Wahhabism to be accepted. Mesfin Woldemariam, a human rights activist, similarly argues that as the major religions, including Islam, entered Ethiopia, they all attempted to replace its "Ethiopianness"—but they all failed, and instead "each became Ethiopian."[15] In a study of religion and the Oromo, Abbas Haji Gnamo acknowledges that in recent decades increasing numbers of Oromo have made the pilgrimage to Mecca and completed advanced studies at Islamic universities, often in the Wahhabi tradition. He notes that the Wahhabis returned and tried to oppose the Sufi cult of saints, but argues that they have been largely unsuccessful in this effort. His primary thesis suggests that Oromo nationalism has nothing to do with an Islamic resurgence in the Arab world. The Oromo, he insists, are liberal and tolerant and will not easily fall into zealous religious fanaticism and militancy.[16] He does warn, however, that one cannot exclude "the possibility that unsatisfied aspirations and frustration, inequality, deprivation, etc., may manifest themselves" in religious fundamentalism as the only available alternative.[17]

The money provided by the Wahhabis is significant for a country as poor as Ethiopia. Some Ethiopian Muslims explain that there has long been a shortage of mosques and that the Wahhabis are filling the void. They look favorably on the Islamic schools and services provided by organizations such as the Saudi-financed International Islamic Relief Organization (IIRO), which donated food and medicine to the Tigray and Somali states during the drought in 2003.[18] Ethiopia's minister of justice commented a year earlier that "many people in Ethiopia had benefited from the services of the IIRO," which had provided help to the poor, refugees, displaced people, orphans, widows, and the physically handicapped.[19] Another Saudi charity, the al-Haramain Islamic Foundation, had completed construction of sixteen mosques in Ethiopia as of 2000 and had plans to fund 259 more over the next four years.[20] During a meeting in 2003 with the Saudi-based Muslim World League, the president of Ethiopia's Supreme Council of Islamic Affairs praised the Saudi charities for their assistance, particularly those relating to the teaching of Islamic values and culture to the new generation of Ethiopians.[21]

Internal Ethnic Threats to Stability

With more than eighty-five ethnic groups, some of them subjugated and added to the empire just over 100 years ago, and a population of 72 million, it is not surprising that Ethiopia has experienced its share of ethnic tension. Most of these conflicts pose no serious threat to the integrity of the state. These include, for example, long-standing disputes involving a number of small ethnic groups in southwestern Ethiopia, such as the Surma and the Dizi, and the Sheka and the Bench-Maji.[22] There are also periodic conflicts between the Somali, on the one hand, and the Afar and Oromo, on the other. Although there are many reasons for these disputes, they often reflect competition for scarce resources such as land, water, and pasturage. Late in 2003, in Gambela state, a significant conflict broke out among Nuer, Anuak, and highlanders that resulted in the death of at least sixty-five persons and forced more than 9,000 to flee, some taking refuge in neighboring Sudan. Although the incident was more serious than acknowledged by the government, it never threatened the regime.[23]

One ethnic issue that does threaten Ethiopia's territorial integrity is Somali irredentism. From its independence in 1960 until it became a collapsed state in 1991, the Somali Republic claimed all of southeastern Ethiopia inhabited by Somali. Much of this region is known as the Ogaden. With the Derg regime preoccupied in a war with Eritrean nationalists, neighboring Somalia briefly conquered most of this territory in the late 1970s. There continues to be considerable sympathy for autonomy among Somalis living in Ethiopia's Somali state. When Somalia rejoins the community of nations, Somali living in Ethiopia may even demonstrate a desire to join that country. In the meantime, two organizations have engaged in antigovernmental activity in Ethiopia's Somali state: Al Itihad Al Islamiya operates out of Somalia; the other is an indigenous group known as the Ogaden National Liberation Front (ONLF), which periodically attacks civilian and military government personnel. The Ethiopian People's Revolutionary Democratic Front (EPRDF), since it came to power in 1991, has not been able to restore control throughout the Ogaden.[24]

Another, and in some ways more serious, challenge to the government concerns the future of Oromia. Because of their large numbers, the Oromo potentially are in a position to exercise significant influence over any future Ethiopian government. Unlike the Somali state, Oromia cuts through the heart of Ethiopia. An independent Oromia, a goal of some Oromo, would effectively result in the total disintegration of Ethiopia. Although Oromo nationalism is strong, there is no consensus on their future. In a truly democratic Ethiopia, most Oromo would probably be satisfied with seeking their goals through the electoral process. In the meantime, some have aligned with the EPRDF by joining the Oromo People's Democratic Organization (OPDO). Supporters of the Oromo National Congress function as an internal opposition party within the political system. There also is a new Oromo Federalist Democratic Movement.

The most important Oromo group, the Oromo Liberation Front (OLF), continues to operate in exile with headquarters in Eritrea. It seeks to overthrow the EPRDF. The OLF occasionally attacks government forces inside Ethiopia and then issues exaggerated press releases. Conversely, the government often blames the OLF for terrorist attacks against hotels, restaurants, and public transportation. The OLF, however, says that it does not engage in terrorism and denies complicity with these acts. Complete agreement is lacking within the OLF on the direction that it should take to achieve power. Some OLF leaders want to continue the armed struggle, while others have concluded that doing so will lead nowhere. They believe that the time has come to rejoin the political process if the EPRDF can offer sufficient guarantees for free and open participation in elections. There are also several small illegal Oromo groups, such as the Islamic Front for the Liberation of Oromia and Oromo Abboo, that on rare occasion conduct attacks inside Ethiopia.[25]

External Threats to Ethiopian Stability

Ethiopia enjoyed cordial relations with Eritrea between 1991 and 1998, when a seemingly small border incident developed into all-out war. With the benefit of hindsight, there were many antecedents to this conflict.[26] Fighting came to an end in 2000, after Ethiopian forces penetrated deep inside Eritrea. Following binding arbitration that demarcated the border between the two countries, Eritrea accepted the outcome while Ethiopia interposed objections.

In 2005, some 3,500 United Nations monitors (the number is scheduled to decline) continue to occupy a fifteen-mile-wide buffer zone along the Eritrean side of the border while a tenuous peace remains in effect. Ethiopia physically occupies the territory that it claims along the border; consequently, it has no incentive to resume fighting. Eritrea grows increasingly frustrated that Ethiopia has not accepted the binding arbitration but is forestalled by UN troops in the buffer zone, the knowledge that it lost the last war with Ethiopia, and growing internal challenges to the government of President Isaias Afwerki. In the meantime, Ethiopia is supporting several small Eritrean opposition groups, known as the Eritrean National Alliance, while Eritrea backs anti-Ethiopian Somali and Oromo armed groups, including the ONLF and the OLF.[27] The situation is ripe for further conflict.

Islamic fundamentalism outside Ethiopia remains near the top of its list of perceived external threats. When Hassan al-Turabi held positions of power in neighboring Sudan, during most of the 1990s, the EPRDF believed rightly that his National Islamic Front was trying to export Islamic fundamentalism to Ethiopia. Sudanese support for anti-Ethiopian groups like the OLF and Beni-shangul Liberation Front (while Ethiopia supported the Sudan People's Liberation Army), combined with the long and porous border, underscored the threat. The Sudan also assisted an Egyptian terrorist group in the failed assassination attempt against Egyptian President Hosni Mubarak when he visited Addis Ababa in 1995. This event deeply embarrassed Ethiopia and resulted in a sharp downturn in relations with the Sudan. The ties returned to normal only after Sudanese President Omar al-Bashir detained Hassan al-Turabi and conflict broke out between Ethiopia and Eritrea.[28] Ethiopia concluded that it needed the Sudan's support, or at least its neutrality, while it dealt with Eritrea. Relations between Ethiopia and the Sudan continue to be good, although the crisis in Darfur in western Sudan and the implementation of the comprehensive peace agreement between Khartoum and the Sudan People's Liberation Movement could raise new challenges. As alliances and regimes change in the Horn of Africa, Ethiopia will keep a watchful eye on the possibility of renewed efforts by the Sudan to export Islamic fundamentalism.[29]

The other major external threat to Ethiopia's territorial integrity comes from neighboring Somalia. This issue is more complex, because it has an important domestic component. The external part of the threat emanates from a future Somali government that might conceivably decide to revive the issue of Somali irredentism. More significant are the potential activities of the Somalia-based Al Itihad Al Islamiya, whose goal is to create an Islamic Somali state that would incorporate Ethiopia's Somali population. The group carried out a series of attacks inside Ethiopia in the mid-1990s. Ethiopia responded forcefully by crossing into Somalia in 1996 and attacking Al Itihad's bases. Ethiopia has subsequently crossed into Somalia whenever it believes hostile groups are organizing.[30] There are reports that Ethiopia continues to provide arms to friendly political factions inside Somalia, although both the government of Ethiopia and the Somali faction leaders deny such allegations.[31]

Governance Structures in Ethiopia

Ethiopia's 1994 constitution is a sharp departure from its previous constitutions. It creates a federal multiparty system that accords unusual importance to the ethno-linguistic groupings in the country. It states that "all sovereign power resides in the Nations, Nationalities and Peoples of Ethiopia."[32] Article 39 allows every nation, nationality, and people, after complying with certain conditions, "an unconditional right to self-determination, including the right to secession."[33] Reflecting this emphasis on ethnicity, the government divided the country for administrative purposes into nine ethnically based states and two self-governing city states. Although some of the states—such as Somali, Afar, and Tigray—are overwhelmingly inhabited by one ethnic group, others—such as Southern, Gambela, and Benishangul-Gumuz—remain ethnically highly mixed.

Since 1991, the EPRDF has been the principal governing structure in Ethiopia. Although headed from the beginning by current Prime Minister Meles, there is considerable debate on key issues within the party's central committee. The Tigrayans, reflecting their major role in removing the Marxist Derg regime, exercise disproportionate power in the upper ranks of the EPRDF. Representatives from other ethnic groups, however, are increasingly affecting the decision-making process. The EPRDF maintains close control over the military, the police, and the intelligence service. Although Ethiopia's system of government emphasizes ethnic federalism and delegation of authority to the state governments, the EPRDF continues both subtly and sometimes not so subtly to retain complete control over the security forces. But on a continent that has eschewed federalism, Ethiopia grants a surprising amount of latitude to its state governments.

Elections to the national bicameral parliament, which consists of the House of Peoples' Representatives (lower chamber) and House of Federation (upper chamber), occur every five years. The last national elections took place in 2005. The people directly elect the 547 members of the lower house, the more important of the two, from single-member districts. Each member represents a constituency of about 100,000 persons. State assemblies choose the representatives for the 108 member House of Federation. Parliament, although slowly improving, continues to be largely ineffective; its authority remains weak and its leadership is discouraged.

The president of Ethiopia is elected for a six-year term by a two-thirds vote of the two houses in joint session. As chief of state, his role is largely ceremonial. The House of Peoples' Representatives elects one of its own members as prime minister for a five-year term. The prime minister is head of government and, together with the council of ministers or cabinet, holds the highest executive powers. Meles Zenawi has been prime minister since 1995.

The 2005 Elections

In 2004 political parties affiliated with the EPRDF held 481 seats in the lower house, or 88 percent of the total.[34] The most significant party in the EPRDF was the Tigray People's Liberation Front (TPLF). Also important are the Amhara National Democratic Movement (ANDM), the Southern Ethiopian People's Democratic Movement (SEPDM), and OPDO. Although representing a significant number of constituents, SEPDM and OPDO are particularly weak and subservient members of the EPRDF.

Opposition parties have existed in Ethiopia since the fall of the Derg regime in 1991. One important group is the Oromo Liberation Front, which aligned itself with the EPRDF initially but left the government after a year. Its leadership is now in exile, primarily in neighboring Eritrea, and the OLF is trying to overthrow the EPRDF government with force. Other opposition parties continued to operate inside the country, but they were not strong, well organized, or even unified until 2005.[35] Fifteen opposition parties joined together under the banner of the Union of Ethiopian Democratic Forces (UEDF) in the summer of 2003. These groups agreed to replace the EPRDF by peaceful and legal means. The UEDF claimed to seek genuine multiparty democracy, the right of self-rule for all ethnic groups, freedom of the press, and a market economy. It also insisted on negotiating security guarantees with the EPRDF, so that its members could compete fairly and transparently in the election.[36]

Only five of the fifteen parties that originally constituted the UEDF had meaningful support inside Ethiopia during the 2005 national parliamentary election. Most of the others remained outside the country and had little chance of electing candidates to parliament. The most important members of the UEDF coalition are the Oromo National Congress (ONC), Ethiopian Social Democratic Federal Party (ESDFP), Southern Ethiopia People's Democratic

Coalition (SEPDC), All Amhara People's Organization (AAPO), and Ethiopian Democratic Unity Party (EDUP). An even more important coalition developed early in 2005. Known as the Coalition for Unity and Democracy (CUD), it includes the following parties: Ethiopian Democratic League (EDL), All Ethiopian Unity Party (AEUP), United Ethiopian Democratic Party and Medhin Party (UEDP-MEDHIN), and Rainbow Ethiopia: Movement for Democracy and Social Justice (REMDSJ).[37]

Prior to the 2005 election, the EPRDF held a low opinion of opposition parties, and perhaps even of the concept of opposition politics. The governing party did not see them as offering original ideas for solving Ethiopia's problems and tended to dismiss them as exile organizations. It is not surprising, therefore, that legitimate opposition parties found it difficult to operate in Ethiopia. Until 2005, they had no access during campaigns to government-controlled radio and television and they still do not have the advantage of using the government bureaucracy that extends throughout the country. There have been a number of documented cases of harassment, intimidation, and manipulation during recent elections.[38]

The government decided to permit a more level playing field for opposition parties in the period preceding the 2005 election. For the first time, it sat down with opposition party leaders to discuss possible changes in electoral law, the composition of the national electoral commission, and guarantees to allow opposition parties to engage in normal political activity. It allowed opposition parties to hold large rallies, convey their views on government radio and television, and debate the issues with the EPRDF and invited significant numbers of election observers from the African Union, the European Union, and the United States. Approximately 23 million Ethiopians, or more than 90 percent of eligible voters, participated in the election for 524 out of 547 seats in the House of Peoples' Representatives. Elections for the remaining 23 seats in Somali state took place in August 2005. In addition to the EPRDF, CUD, and UEDF, a number of smaller parties, some aligned with the EPRDF and others in opposition, contested some of the seats. Outside observers generally described the May 2005 voting as free and fair, but were quick to condemn vote-counting procedures and harsh actions against demonstrators.[39]

Almost immediately after the balloting closed, both the EPRDF and the opposition claimed victory. The government began dribbling out election results that showed the EPRDF winning a majority, while acknowledging that the opposition had increased significantly the number of seats it won as compared to the 2000 elections. Tension began to rise, and the government imposed a ban on demonstrations in Addis Ababa. In effect, the ban applied to the entire country. The opposition took heart from a leaked copy of an internal European Union report dated May 24 and covering 552 polling stations, which suggested that the opposition won 57 percent of the vote. Although the polling stations did not constitute a random sample and the results exceeded the expectations of virtually all neutral observers, the EU report did raise serious questions about the honesty of the ballot counting process. Of particular concern was the finding that about one-third of the ballots were invalid.[40] Illegal demonstrations, possibly encouraged by the opposition, broke out during the second week of June. Overreacting, government security forces killed at least thirty-six unarmed persons, injured many more, and arrested several thousand demonstrators. Before complete chaos ensued, on June 10 the EPRDF, CUD, and UEDF signed a declaration in which they agreed to end the violence and establish a procedure for adjudicating contested election results in the presence of international observers.[41]

The government subsequently released most, but not all, of the detainees and began the adjudication process in the face of continuing complaints from the opposition. Investigation teams consisting of representatives from the National Election Board (NEB), opposition parties registering a complaint, and an international observer began to review those cases judged by the NEB to have merit. One of the problems was that not enough international observers remained in the country. By the beginning of July, there were only about a half dozen from the EU and ten from the Carter Center. The government extended the ban on demonstrations. Several foreign governments floated the idea of a government of national unity that included significant opposition representation. The EPRDF expressed no interest in that suggestion. Official NEB results as of early September accounted for 545 out of the 547 constituencies; two were still in doubt. The EPRDF and affiliated parties won 371 seats (68 percent), the opposition parties won 173 seats (32 percent), and an independent captured one seat.[42] The opposition parties continued to contest the outcome, and as of this writing it was not clear that they would take up their seats in parliament. Failure to do so could create a political environment that will lead to major political conflict. Nevertheless, it is clear that this election marked a turning point in Ethiopia's march toward democracy. It is now up to the EPRDF and the opposition to gain the trust of the Ethiopian people.

Ethnic consciousness in Ethiopian politics has increased since 1991 and the EPRDF has been reluctant to compromise or bargain with opposition and autonomous political groups. Clapham argues that the EPRDF must create political mechanisms that allow the government to cope with ethnicity and ethnic voting. Doing so should include efforts to establish national loyalties that could reduce the role of ethnic groups as the only channels for political representation. It should also permit increased real autonomy at the local level by allowing opposition parties to contest free and fair elections and local officials to wield administrative control without harassment from the central government.[43]

The opposition parties did better in the election than just about anyone predicted. Nevertheless, they are not united on all issues and may well find themselves in disagreement on some key questions, such as the future of ethnic federalism and policy toward Eritrea. The losses for the ruling EPRDF may reflect more a vote against its continuous rule since 1991 than a vote of confidence in the various opposition parties and their policies. The CUD, the opposition party that won the most seats, did best in Addis Ababa and was strong in Amhara state. But it also won seats in other regions such as Oromia and ethnically mixed Southern. The UEDF showed strength in Southern and Oromia, while the OFDM won all of its seats in Oromia. Ethnic politics played a role in the election, but it would be a mistake to attribute opposition success solely or even primarily to ethnicity.

How the Government Maintains Control

Ethiopians, at least those from the central highlands, take great pride in the length and richness of their history. Ethiopia is one of the oldest countries in the world. Although conquered briefly by the Italians, it was never colonized by a foreign country. The rugged highlands helped to guarantee Ethiopia's long history of independence until the arrival of airplanes and all-terrain vehicles. An element of xenophobia is still present in Ethiopian highland society. The people are tough, secretive, and accustomed to deprivation. They tolerate considerable hardship, but respond with extraordinary force when threatened.

Looking back over more than 2,000 years, whether the government was feudal, communist, or based on ethnic federalism, there has always been an effort to exercise strong control from the center, especially concerning security and political power. The present government operates in this manner, too. The vast majority of Ethiopians, 85 percent of whom are peasant farmers, seem to accept such a tradition. Hierarchy and obedience are important parts of Ethiopian culture. Woldemariam put it starkly: "We have failed to develop any other alternative to the use of force for administration. We differentiated ourselves between those who are superior and inferior, between those who have obligations as masters and servants in an uncomfortable relationship."[44] He also argues that Ethiopia has not been able to institutionalize political power; Ethiopian governments link power to guns, and if democracy is to prevail it is necessary to change this dynamic.[45] The EPRDF says that it wants to create democracy in Ethiopia. Assuming that this is a sincere goal, it must overcome more than two millennia of experience to the contrary.

The TPLF, a peasant-based revolutionary party in Tigray state, continues to play a preponderant role in the EPRDF. The TPLF established the EPRDF in order to build a national party and legitimize its authority throughout the country. It never fully succeeded. Most of the EPRDF's member organizations are weak. The exiled OLF continues to challenge the government at the political level but does not pose a serious security threat. Certainly not all Oromo support the OLF, but because they constitute about 40 percent of Ethiopia's population, the EPRDF dismisses the OLF at its peril. In addition, the political and administrative weakness of many ethnically based local governments and EPRDF-affiliated political parties has forced the TPLF to become more involved at the regional level than it intended to or is desirable. This situation has increased the perception that Tigrayans are trying to dominate local government and raises questions about their commitment to ethnic federalism. Close ethnic ties between Tigrayans and Eritreans add to the perceptual problem and encourage some to conclude that Meles yielded unnecessarily on Eritrean independence, leaving Ethiopia as the world's most populous landlocked country.[46]

A twenty-member politburo of five representatives from each of the major constituent parties coordinates EPRDF policy. Each party is organized in typical Marxist-Leninist hierarchical style. Within the TPLF, the most important component, serious policy differences arose in 2001. These were primarily due to concerns that the TPLF was drifting away from its base and disagreements related to the handling of the 1998–2000 war with Eritrea. The debate resulted in a split in the TPLF. Meles survived the challenge by reaching out to other nationalities, especially the Amhara, to shore up his support within the broader EPRDF. There was a major purge of EPRDF and especially TPLF cadres who did not support Meles. Although his position within the party was not in question before the surprising outcome of the 2005 election, this episode illustrates the potential fragility of leadership in the ruling party.[47]

The military, especially the army, has long been a bulwark of the regime. Ethiopia has a history of producing tough and effective soldiers, in the battles centuries ago against Islamic invaders, against the Italians in 1896, in Korea in the early 1950s, and against the Eritreans during the 1998–2000 war. But there is no guarantee that the military will always support the state. The emperor's imperial guard almost succeeded in overthrowing Haile Selassie in 1960. Later, he was deposed by revolutionary elements of the armed forces in 1974. Morale and discipline largely broke down toward the end of the Derg regime, making it easier for the EPRDF and the Eritrean People's Liberation Front to topple its leader, Mengistu Haile Mariam. Since 1991, the EPRDF has paid enormous attention to the military and has purposely limited its size to meet realistic security threats. It has worked hard to build a national army that tends to reflect Ethiopia's ethnic groups, at least below the level of most senior officers. Civilian authorities control the armed forces, which generally have the respect of the people.[48] For the moment, the military does not appear to pose a threat to the EPRDF government.

The Role of Foreign Assistance

As a poor and populous country, Ethiopia receives a substantial amount of for-eign assistance. Recent statistics on the total amount vary widely, probably because some figures reflect only development aid while others include food aid and money to combat HIV/AIDS. Ethiopia currently receives $900 million in aid per year, according to a UN advisor to Secretary General Kofi Annan. He emphasized, however, that Ethiopia needs $5 billion annually if it is to have any chance of meeting its antipoverty goals.[49] Another recent account suggested that Ethiopia receives about $1.3 billion annually, although 60 percent of that figure constituted food aid and emergency assistance.[50] The UN Development Program concluded that aid to Ethiopia increased from $605 million in 1997 to $1.937 billion in 2003.[51] Even if the higher figure does reflect the current sit-uation, on a per capita basis foreign aid to Ethiopia remains low.

During times of severe drought, Ethiopia is dependent on the donor com-munity to stave off famine and keep people alive. Likewise, Ethiopia cannot deal with the HIV/AIDS pandemic unless it receives substantial outside sup-port. It is somewhat better positioned to implement its development program with more modest foreign assistance. Ethiopia has traditionally followed a conservative fiscal policy and works hard to keep debt to a minimum. An exception occurred during the Derg period, when internal rebellions and Eritrean opposition resulted in the creation of a large military establishment and consequently high debt. Most of this debt has been cancelled. Although Ethiopia spent heavily during the 1998–2000 war, it purchased many of its hardware needs with cash and quickly cut back military expenditures at the end of the war. Spending on the armed forces reached 11 percent of GDP in 1999, but had fallen back to 6 percent by 2001.[52]

The Terrorism Threat

Ethiopia has experienced a significant number of terrorist acts. Those that have occurred since the current government took power in 1991 have usually been bombings of hotels, restaurants, government buildings, and public transportation and assassination attempts. The most embarrassing incident occurred in 1995, when Egyptian terrorists associated with al-Gamaa al-Islamiyya (Islamic Group) attacked President Hosni Mubarak while he was en route from the Addis Ababa airport to a summit meeting of the Organization of African Unity.[53] A former Al Qaeda member testified that the Qatar Charitable Society bankrolled the plot with $20,000.[54] The government attributes most terrorist attacks, however, to one of three organizations operating in Ethiopia or from neighboring countries: Al Itihad Al Islamiya, the OLF, and the ONLF. With the notable exception of the unsuccessful attempt on the life of Mubarak, terrorist groups from outside the Horn of Africa seem to have been minimally active in Ethiopia.

Al Itihad, which originated in neighboring Somalia, acknowledged responsibility for several terrorist attacks in the mid-1990s. Ethiopia also implicated Al Itihad in the attempted assassination of Abdulmejid Hussein, its minister of telecommunications, in 1996. Ethiopia asserts that Al Itihad has links to Al Qaeda. The United States includes the organization on its list of terrorist groups, and there is substantial independent confirmation of links between Al Itihad and Al Qaeda.[55] In recent years, however, Al Itihad seems to have significantly curtailed its acts of terrorism against Ethiopia. This result may reflect the fact that Ethiopian security forces were quick to attack Al Itihad's bases inside Somalia and to increase efforts to patrol the long border. The threat has not, however, disappeared. In 2004 the U.S. embassy in Addis Ababa issued a warning that Al Itihad militants were planning to attack American citizens and Ethiopian security officials in Jijiga, capital of Somali state, and to plant land mines along roads in the area.[56] As the United States focused attention on Somalia after 9/11, Al Itihad may have concluded that it was time to go underground. One expert believes that it no longer functions in Somalia, although it is still active in Ethiopia's Somali state.[57]

The militant wing of the ONLF and the quiescent Islamic Front for the Liberation of Oromia (IFLO) have resorted to terrorist tactics in pursuit of their political goals. But these acts seem to be confined to the areas in which they have indigenous support: Somali state in the case of the ONLF, and the area around Bale for the IFLO. The situation involving the OLF is much more complex. The Ethiopian government regularly assigns responsibility for some terrorist attacks to the OLF. It claimed, for example, that the OLF was responsible for attacks on the Dire Dawa railway station in June 2002 and the Tigray Hotel in Addis Ababa in September of the same year, various attacks in recent years against the Ethio-Djibouti railway, and several blasts in Addis Ababa in 2004.[58] The OLF generally denies responsibility for these incidents and claims that it is not a terrorist organization and does not target innocent people. It did take responsibility for an attack in 2002 against a warehouse along the Ethio-Djibouti railway, claiming that it was a legitimate military target.[59] The OLF does not deny that civilians may be in the wrong place at the wrong time when it attacks a facility that in its opinion constitutes a military target. But this caveat still does not resolve the discrepancy between the government's allegations and OLF's denials of attacks against clearly civilian targets.

Ethiopia has a tough, effective security apparatus that dates from the TPLF's long conflict with the Derg regime. Many personnel in the Ethiopian Security, Immigration, and Refugees Affairs Authority (SIRA) are veterans of the military campaign. Their tactics are firm, some would say harsh, and they have developed an impressive intelligence capacity. Corruption appears to be minimal in SIRA. As a result, Ethiopia does not offer so soft a target as such nearby countries as Kenya, Tanzania, and Uganda. But SIRA is far from infallible, particularly in countering attacks and plots from indigenous organizations.[60] As long as there continue to be alienated groups in Ethiopia who believe, rightly or wrongly, that they cannot achieve their goals through the political process, such attacks will continue and may worsen. Taken in isolation, however, they do not threaten the ability of the EPRDF to govern the country.

Attacks perpetrated by organizations based outside the Horn of Africa are much less likely but pose a serious threat if an Al Qaeda affiliate decides to target Ethiopia. Wahhabi influence could provide a beachhead, and perhaps has already done so. In 2004, Saudi Arabia and the United States named the Ethiopian branch of the Saudi-based charity al-Haramain as a channel of terrorist financing, and Riyadh subsequently ordered the dissolution of that organization worldwide.[61] Ethiopia currently is not a center of international terrorism. But a combination of poor Ethiopian decisions on political and economic policy, further alienation of Oromo and Somali, and disenchantment or demoralization within the security service and the army could make it so.

U.S.-Ethiopian Cooperation on Counterterrorism

The United States sees Ethiopia as one of its most important African partners in the battle against terrorism. President George W. Bush invited Prime Minister Meles and former Kenyan President Daniel arap Moi to Washington in late 2002 to discuss the subject. President Bush lauded Ethiopia's assistance in the global war on terrorism and assured Meles that the United States would work closely with him to disrupt any terrorist plans aimed at Ethiopia. Meles in turn expressed appreciation for American leadership in countering terrorism and stated that Ethiopia would cooperate with the United States.[62] A week later Secretary of Defense Donald Rumsfeld visited Ethiopia and other countries in the Horn of Africa to thank them for their assistance in the war on terrorism. Speaking in Addis Ababa, Rumsfeld warned that the Horn of Africa had provided a home for Al Qaeda. Meles promised to do whatever was necessary to fight terrorism in the region.[63] During a visit to Ethiopia in early 2003, Major-General John F. Sattler, commander of the Combined Joint Task Force-Horn of Africa (CJTF-HOA), commented that the United States considered "Ethiopia a valued partner in our mission to detect, disrupt and defeat terrorists, who pose an imminent threat to coalition partners in the Horn of Africa region."[64] General John Abizaid, commander of the U.S. Central Command, visited Addis Ababa in July 2003 and February 2004. During the first visit he announced the establishment of an eleven-nation African regional task force to combat disasters and ward off terrorism. On the second visit, he said that a clear terrorist threat still existed in the region.[65]

The principal American structure for dealing with terrorism in the region, including Ethiopia, is the Djibouti-based CJTF-HOA. Staffed at any given time with between 1,400 and 1,600 military and civilian personnel, it works with countries in the Horn of Africa and Yemen to improve their ability to prevent terrorist attacks. In the case of Ethiopia, CJTF-HOA has provided infantry skills training and small unit tactics against terrorism to the Ethiopian National Defense Forces at the Hurso training camp, northwest of Dire Dawa. The ultimate goal is to establish three new Ethiopian antiterrorism companies. The United States established a temporary training facility called Camp Unity at Hurso to carry out the program. In addition, American civil affairs personnel conduct medical and veterinary civic action programs and refurbish schools in the area.[66]

Ethiopia benefits from the $100 million U.S.-financed East Africa Counterterrorism Initiative (EACTI). Begun in 2003, it provides military training for border and coastal security, programs to strengthen capacity-building, and assistance for regional efforts to combat terrorist financing and train police. It also includes an education program to counter extremist influence. The U.S. Terrorist Interdiction Program (TIP) operates at airports in Ethiopia. The TIP hardware/software package is designed to hinder the movement of terrorists between countries with a computerized name-check network that enables immigration and border control officials to identify suspect persons. In 2002, the State Department also began funding a police development program, although this is not specifically focused on counterterrorism.[67]

Recommendations for a U.S. Counterterrorism Policy for Ethiopia

To be successful, any counterterrorism program must be developed as a regional effort. The countries of the region are too interlinked and their borders too porous to design a policy in isolation. The long history of tit-for-tat support of opposition groups by one country against its neighbors complicates an effective counterterrorism strategy and underscores the need to end this practice. For purposes of developing a plan to counter terrorism in Ethiopia, the region should include the Sudan, Eritrea, Djibouti, Somalia/Somaliland, Yemen, Kenya, Uganda, Tanzania, and the Comoro Islands.

U.S. counterterrorism policy in Ethiopia must take careful account of the fact that the country has as many Muslims as Christians and that the government, like most foreign governments, will use the American preoccupation with terrorism for its own purposes. The United States should also give far more attention to the long-term elements of its counterterrorism policy. It is necessary, of course, to share intelligence, interrupt terrorist plans when they become known, and provide training and technical assistance to Ethiopia for countering terrorism. These steps are not nearly sufficient, however, to improve an environment that allows indigenous or international terrorists to operate in the country and manipulate a small number of Ethiopian nationals for their own causes. The bulk of the long-term effort depends on good economic and political policies and a firm commitment by the Ethiopian government to combat terrorism. For its part, the international community must provide substantial resources if it is really serious about helping a country as poor as Ethiopia to battle terrorism effectively.

Ethiopia was one of five African countries (the others were Angola, Eritrea, Rwanda, and Uganda) to join the "coalition of the willing" against Saddam Hussein's Iraq. Although the Ethiopian government offered no tangible support, Muslim leaders in the country reportedly regretted that the government had publicly taken the side of the United States in the war. They said that it would have been better if Ethiopia had adopted a neutral position, so as not to create additional tension within the Muslim community.[68] This raises a legitimate question: is U.S. policy better served by having the moral support of Ethiopia in the war against Iraq while creating another problem within

Ethiopia's Muslim community, or is it wiser to forgo moral support and avoid the internal problem?

Ethiopia has shared useful counterterrorism intelligence with the United States. One must wonder, however, if such cooperation is occasionally driven by ulterior motives. Ethiopia is anxious to prove that terrorist organizations such as Al Itihad operate out of Somalia against Ethiopia. As a result, it seeks U.S. understanding in dealing with such groups inside Somalia. The United States needs to avoid being drawn into counterterrorist activity in Somalia that is driven more by Ethiopian political objectives than by a serious terrorist threat.[69] Ethiopia also asserts that the OLF engages in terrorism and wants the Oromo organization placed on the U.S. list of groups that engage in terrorism. The United States should only respond to information for which it has independent corroboration.

Ethiopian authorities must bear the primary responsibility for curbing terrorism in their own country. They know the local cultures and languages. How many American soldiers and civilian counterterrorism experts working on Ethiopia speak fluent Amharic or the languages of the Oromo, Somali, and Afar peoples? It is unrealistic for Americans (or others who do not come from the region) to deal successfully at the grassroots level with terrorism. The United States should long ago have expanded significantly its area expertise and understanding of key regional languages so as to undertake independent "ground truthing" and conduct more effective liaison with local authorities. The United States also needs personnel in Ethiopia and elsewhere in the region that possess a good understanding of Islam.[70]

The United States should encourage the Ethiopian government to improve relations with its Muslim community and urge that state resources be shared equitably among its different religious groups. More directly, the United States needs to identify innovative ways of its own to increase outreach to and interaction with Ethiopia's Islamic population. Such an effort began several years ago when the United States provided assistance for countering HIV/AIDS to the Supreme Council of Islamic Affairs.[71] In 2004, the U.S. Secretary of State's Africa Policy Advisory Panel recommended an allocation of $200 million to reach out to Muslim communities in Africa.[72] This kind of program could pay huge dividends in a country like Ethiopia.

Finally, and controversially, there are the links in a country such as Ethiopia among terrorism, poverty, and social and economic inequality. Some terrorism experts argue that these connections are too weak to merit serious attention. Although they constitute a costly and very long-term challenge, it is short-sighted to dismiss the interrelation of such factors. This is not to say that poverty and inequality are root causes of terrorism, but they do create an environment within which committed external terrorists can thrive. The problem becomes even greater in weak and failed states.[73] Even President Bush's National Security Strategy acknowledged that "poverty, weak institutions, and corruption can make weak states vulnerable to terrorist networks and drug cartels within their borders."[74] British Prime Minister Tony Blair, during a recent visit to Ethiopia, stated that "we know that poverty and instability leads to weak states, which can become havens for terrorists and other criminals."[75] Most Ethiopians agree with that analysis.

U.S. counterterrorism policy can only achieve long-term success in Ethiopia by working to ameliorate the myriad economic, political, and social issues throughout the region in addition to strengthening and working with local security forces. Doing so will require a major attack on poverty and inequality by the international community. There must also be a total commitment by regional governments to improving internal policies so that external resources will be more effective at resolving the economic, political, and social problems of which terrorists take advantage. Ethiopia, supported by the United States and others, must therefore combat corruption, expand democracy, improve living conditions for ethnic and religious minorities, and share state resources more equitably. These are huge tasks for the government of Ethiopia and expensive ones for the international partner community. Anything less, however, will leave Ethiopia and the region susceptible to terrorism and U.S. counterterrorism policy hopelessly chasing advancing domestic and international terrorists.

Notes

1. Anneli Botha, "Terrorism, African Commitments to Combating Organized Crime and Terrorism: A Review of Eight NEPAD Countries," II, The Africa Human Security Initiative, Institute for Security Studies (Pretoria, 2004), www.iss.co.za/pubs/Other/ahsi/Goredema_Botha/Contents.html.

2. Shinn, "Terrorism in East Africa and the Horn: An Overview," Journal of Conflict Studies, XXIII (2003), 80–81.

3. Shinn, "Promoting Stability in the Horn of Africa," Economic Focus, VI (2004), 1–8.

4. Global Coalition for Africa, African Social and Economic Trends, 2003/2004 Annual Report (Washington, D.C., 2004); International Monetary Fund press release no. 04/194 (September 12, 2004).

5. Jeffrey Sachs, "Ethiopia: Country Living on the Edge, Says UN Adviser," IRIN news release (July 5, 2004).

6. Shinn, "HIV/AIDS in Ethiopia: Past, Present and Future," Horn of Africa Journal of AIDS, I (2004), 65–72.

7. Transparency International, *Corruption Perceptions Index 2004*, www.transparency.org/cpi/2004/cpi2004.en.html#cpi2004.

8. U.S. Department of State, *International Religious Freedom Report 2004* (Ethiopia), www.state.gov/g/drl/rls/irf/2004/35355.htm.

9. Shinn, "Ethiopia: Coping with Islamic Fundamentalism before and after September 11," *CSIS Africa Notes*, VII (2002), 2.

10. U.S. Department of State, *Religious Freedom Report*; Paul Balisky, "Religious Practices in Ethiopia," unpub. manuscript, November 2003.

11. Balisky, "Religious Practices."

12. U.S. Department of State, *Religious Freedom Report*.

13. Medhane Tadesse, IRIN news release (May 8, 2003). Johannes Sebhatu provides an even more alarming account of the alleged threat from Islam, "The Emergence of Radical Islam in Ethiopia (1991–2004)" (July 3, 2004), www.ethiomedia.com/commentary/radical_islam_in_ethiopia.html.

14. Tadesse, IRIN news release.

15. Mesfin Woldemariam, "Vision 2020: Whither Ethiopia?" *Economic Focus*, VI (2003), 10.

16. Abbas Haji Gnamo, "Islam, the Orthodox Church and Oromo Nationalism (Ethiopia)," *Cahier d'Études Africaines*, XLII (2002), 109–114.

17. Ibid., 114.

18. "International Islamic Relief Organization Donates Relief Food," Global News Wire (July 1, 2003).

19. "Justice Minister Praises International Islamic Relief Organization," Global News Wire (October 7, 2002).

20. "Riyadh Group Launches Mosques Project Abroad," Middle East News File (August 17, 2000).

21. "Muslim World League Chief Meets with Ethiopian Muslim Leader," Global News Wire (March 12, 2003).

22. U.S. Department of State, *Ethiopia 2003 Country Report on Human Rights Practices*, www.state.gov/g/drl/rls/hrrpt/2003/27727pf.htm.

23. Government of Ethiopia, "A Statement on the Situation in Gambella," March 2004; "Independent Inquiry Commission Issues Its Findings on Killings in West," Global News Wire (July 10, 2004).

24. Shinn, "An Overview," 84–85; Sarah Vaughan and Kjetil Tronvoll, *The Culture of Power in Contemporary Ethiopian Political Life* (Stockholm, 2003), 131.

25. Shinn, "An Overview," 84–85; Siegfried Pausewang, "Democracy and Human Rights in Ethiopia—Not for the Oromo?" unpub. paper prepared for an Oromo conference in Bergen, Norway, September 28–October 1, 2004.

26. There have been numerous analyses of this subject. See, for example, Tekeste Negash and Kjetil Tronvoll, *Brothers at War: Making Sense of the Eritrea-Ethiopian War* (Oxford, 2000); Leenco Lata, "The Ethiopia-Eritrea War," *Review of African Political Economy*, XXX (September 2003), 369–388; Christopher Clapham, "War and State Formation in Ethiopia and Eritrea," unpub. paper delivered at the Failed States Conference in Florence, Italy, April 10–14, 2001; Ruth Iyob, "The Ethiopian-Eritrean Conflict: Diasporic vs. Hegemonic States in the Horn of Africa, 1991–2000," *Journal of Modern African Studies*, XXXVIII (2000), 659–682.

27. Jon Abbink, "Ethiopia-Eritrea: Proxy Wars and Prospects of Peace in the Horn of Africa," *Journal of Contemporary African Studies*, XXI (2003), 413–415. See also Dan Connell,

"Eritrea: On a Short Fuse," chapter 4 in this volume; and Timothy Carney, "The Sudan: Political Islam and Terrorism," chapter 6 in this volume.

28. See also Carney, "The Sudan."

29. Shinn, "Islamic Fundamentalism," 2–3.

30. Ibid., 4–6.

31. United Nations, *Report of the Monitoring Group on Somalia Pursuant to Security Council Resolution 1519*, Report 04.43773 (2004).

32. Fasil Nahum, *Constitution for a Nation of Nations* (Lawrenceville, NJ, 1997), 214.

33. Ibid., 229.

34. Government of Ethiopia, the Parliament of the Federal Democratic Republic of Ethiopia, *Political Parties and Their Seats*, www.ethiopar.net/English/hopre/politi.htm.

35. Shinn, "Ethiopia: The 'Exit Generation' and Future Leaders," *International Journal of Ethiopian Studies*, I (2003), 28.

36. UEDF Press Release (September 3, 2003).

37. National Election Board of Ethiopia website, www.electionsethiopia.org/Political%20Coalitions.html.

38. Kjetil Tronvoll, "Voting, Violence and Violations: Peasant Voices on the Flawed Elections in Hadiya, Southern Ethiopia," *Journal of Modern African Studies*, XXXIX (2001), 697–716; Siegfried Pausewang and Lovise Aalen, "Shattered Promises and Hopes: The 2001 Local Elections in Southern Region," in Siegfried Pausewang, Kjetil Tronvoll, and Lovise Aalen (eds.), *Ethiopia since the Derg* (London, 2002), 201–229, U.S. Department of State, *Human Rights Practices*.

39. National Election Board of Ethiopia website: www.electionsethiopia.org/Index.html; Abraham McLaughlin, "Democracy Gains in Ethiopia," *Christian Science Monitor* (May 31, 2005).

40. European Union, *Election Observation Mission Situation Report* (Addis Ababa, May 24, 2005), 1–24.

41. *Joint Declaration by UEDF, CUD and EPRDF on the NEBE Complaints Review and Investigation Process* (June 10, 2005).

42. National Election Board of Ethiopia website, www.electionsethiopia.org/Index.html.

43. Christopher Clapham, "Ethiopia and the Challenge of Diversity," *African Insight*, XXXIV (March 2004), 50–55; September 14, 2004, conversation with the leader of one of the opposition parties; "Meles Zenawi Switches on the Charm," *Indian Ocean Newsletter*, MC (September 4, 2004), 1.

44. Woldemariam, "Vision 2020," 18.

45. Mesfin Woldemariam, comments made at the University of the District of Columbia, September 14, 2004.

46. Medhane Tadesse and John Young, "TPLF: Reform or Decline?" *Review of African Political Economy*, XXX (2003), 398.

47. Ibid., 389–391; Vaughan and Tronvoll, *The Culture of Power in Contemporary Ethiopian Political Life*, 16, 113–116, 121–122.

48. Tsadkan Gebretensae, "A Vision of a New Army for Ethiopia," paper presented by the Chief of Staff of the Armed Forces at a Symposium on the Making of the New Ethiopian Constitution, Addis Ababa, May 17–21, 1993.

49. Sachs, "Country Living on the Edge."

50. "President Calls for Increased Economic Development," IRIN news release (September 13, 2004).

51. "IMF Urges More Effective Use of Aid," IRIN news release (September 16, 2004).

52. Global Coalition for Africa, *African Social and Economic Trends 2003/2004*, 87.

53. "Three Suspects Arrested in Failed Attempt to Assassinate Mubarak," Associated Press (August 2, 1995).

54. "Government's Evidentiary Proffer Supporting the Admissibility of Co-Conspirator Statements," United States of America vs. Enaam M. Amaout. U.S. District Court Northern District of Illinois, Eastern Division. Case # CR 892, January 31, 2003, 103.

55. Meles Zenawi, informal English translation of interview contained in Eritrean Tigrinya-language magazine *Hwyet* (May 1997); Rohan Gunaratna, *Inside Al Qaeda: Global Network of Terror* (New York, 2002), 154–155; International Crisis Group, "Somalia: Countering Terrorism in a Failed State," *Africa Report*, XLV (May 23, 2002), 15–19; Matt Bryden, "No Quick Fixes: Coming to Terms with Terrorism, Islam and Statelessness in Somalia," *Journal of Conflict Studies*, XXIII (2003), 30. Although it does not draw a direct link between Al Qaeda and Al Itihad, the *9/11Commission Report* states that scores of Al Qaeda trainers entered Somalia following the arrival of American troops in 1992. *The 9/11Commission Report* (New York, 2004), 60.

56. U.S. Embassy Addis Ababa, warden message, dated September 13, 2004.

57. Matt Bryden, Horn of Africa Project Director, International Crisis Group, comment made June 30, 2005, at the Woodrow Wilson Center, Washington, D.C.

58. U.S. Department of State, *Patterns of Global Terrorism 2002*, Washington, D.C. (April 2003), 4–5, www.state.gov/s/ct/rls/pgtrpt/2002/; "Terrorist Attacks Can Only Come from Oromo Liberation Front, al-Ittihad," *Addis Tribune* (June 13, 2003); "OLF Denies Having a Hand in Bomb Explosion in Train," *Addis Tribune* (October 3, 2003); "Ethiopian Police Blame 'Terrorist Elements' for Train Attack," Ethiopian News Agency website (January 19, 2004); "Two Blasts Rock the Ethiopian Capital, No Casualties: Police," Agence France-Presse (August 1, 2004).

59. "International Campaign against Terrorism Must Apply on OLF as Well," Ethiopian News Agency (July 9, 2002); "Ethiopia: Oromo Rebel Group Condemns Addis Ababa Hotel Bombing," BBC monitoring of Voice of Oromo Liberation audio web site on September 17, 2002; "Ethiopian Rebel OLF Official Comments on Recent Meeting with US Officials," BBC monitoring of Voice of Oromo Liberation audio web site on December 11, 2002; "OLF Denies Having a Hand in Bomb Explosion in Train," *Addis Tribune* (October 3, 2003).

60. United States Institute of Peace, "Terrorism in the Horn of Africa," Special Report 113 (Washington, D.C., January 2004), 5-6.

61. "Remarks of Treasury DAS Juan Zarate on Joint U.S. and Saudi Action," Global News Wire, June 2, 2004; *al-Riyadh* (October 6, 2004).

62. Scott Lindlaw, "Bush Meets with Leaders of Kenya, Ethiopia," Associated Press (December 5, 2002); Leon Harris and Suzanne Malveaux, "Bush Meets with African Leaders," CNN Transcript 120501CN.V54 (December 5, 2002).

63. "Rumsfeld Tours Horn of Africa with Terrorism in Focus," Deutsche Presse-Agentur (December 11, 2002). See also Lange Schermerhorn, "Djibouti: A Special Role in the War on Terrorism," chapter 3 in this volume.

64. "Ethio-US Collaboration against Terrorism," *Daily Monitor* (Addis Ababa) (February 23, 2003).

65. "Ethiopia: Anti-Terror Regional Task Force Set Up," IRIN news release (July 30, 2003); "Abizaid: Clear Terrorist Threat in East Africa," Associated Press (February 16, 2004).

66. www.globalsecurity.org/military/facility/camp-united.htm (a website on global security issues published from Alexandria, Virginia); Chris Tomlinson, "U.S. Forces Training in

Ethiopia, Developing New Allies," Associated Press (December 20, 2003), www.addistri-bune.com/Archives/2003/07/11-07-03/US.htm.

67. Testimony of Karl Wycoff, Associate Coordinator, State Department Office of the Coordinator for Counterterrorism, before the House Subcommittee on Africa, April 1, 2004; remarks by William Pope, State Department Deputy Coordinator for Counterterrorism, at the East Africa Counterterrorism Initiative Conference in Kampala, Uganda, April 21, 2004.

68. "Support for the USA Causes Problems," *Indian Ocean Newsletter* (April 5, 2003).

69. Shinn, "An Overview," 84-85; United States Institute of Peace, "Terrorism," 6.

70. Shinn, "Fighting Terrorism in East Africa and the Horn," *Foreign Service Journal*, LXXXI (September 2004), 42.

71. United States Institute of Peace, "Terrorism," 6.

72. Africa Policy Advisory Panel for U.S. Department of State, *Rising U.S. Stakes in Africa: Seven Proposals to Strengthen U.S.-Africa Policy* (Washington, May 2004), 115.

73. Jakkie Cilliers, "Terrorism and Africa," *African Security Review*, XII (2003), 102. For an excellent discussion of the link between development and security, including the question of terrorism, in weak states, see "On the Brink: Weak States and US National Security," A Report of the Commission on Weak States and US National Security sponsored by the Center for Global Development (Washington, D.C., 2004).

74. George Bush, September 17, 2002, cover letter for *The National Security Strategy of the United States of America* (Washington, September 2002).

75. Andrew Cawthorne, "Blair Says Africa's Woes Make It Terrorist Haven," Reuters (October 7, 2004).

6

THE SUDAN
Political Islam and Terrorism

TIMOTHY CARNEY

A s the only nation in the Horn of Africa on the U.S. list of
six state sponsors of terrorism, the Sudan holds a key to
any successful effort to combat terrorism in both Africa and the
Middle East. To this end, Washington, despite serious concerns
about humanitarian and human rights issues within the Sudan,
has successfully engaged the Khartoum authorities since 2000 to
gain vital information about Islamic groups that have had a presence in the Sudan. This collaboration has increased U.S.
understanding of various Middle Eastern networks and, especially, individuals. While the Sudanese have answered most of
the United States' concerns about terrorism, humanitarian and
human rights issues have continued to make the bilateral relationship difficult. The United States, long interested in seeing an
end to the grinding conflict between the North and the South,
applauded the agreement forged by the government of Sudan
and the Southern People's Liberation Movement early in 2005 to
end the North-South civil war. Resolution of the insurgency and
brutality in Darfur is needed to end serious American objection
to normalizing relations with Khartoum.

Introduction

Over the last three decades, the Sudan has experienced several terrorist attacks; that is, attacks on resident foreigners as well as against Sudanese. Numerous groups, including Osama bin Laden's Al Qaeda, have used the Sudan as a base for training. Some of his Sudanese recruits figure spectacularly in the news, but no evidence suggests that Al Qaeda recruited large numbers of Sudanese.[1] Moreover, some organizations, most notably the Egyptian Gamaa Islamiya (Islamic Group), have mounted international operations from Sudanese soil.

The present authorities in Khartoum inherited a complicated relationship with major Middle Eastern terrorist groups on assuming power after their 1989 coup. The Sudan's relationship with those terrorist organizations dates to 1969, just after Jaafar Nimeiri and a group of army officers seized power. Nimeiri rechristened the country the "Democratic Republic of the Sudan." His only civilian member of cabinet described it as "leftist, socialist, but not extremist or fanatic."[2] That regime initially adopted the policies of the Sudanese Communist Party toward socialist and Arab states, including a total commitment to the Arab cause against Israel. This commitment, argued a recent interlocutor in Khartoum, is what lay behind the permission granted later in 1969 to the Palestinian opposition group Fatah to establish an office in Khartoum.[3] By 1971, the Nimeiri government was hanging communists, and relations with the Soviet bloc had significantly deteriorated. However, despite some problems with Libya and Egypt, the Sudan generally enjoyed good relations with the Arab world. Today, Khartoum has friendly relationships with members of the Arab League, although some in Khartoum doubt the status of relations with Qatar, whose emir is close to deposed Sudanese Islamist Hassan al-Turabi (who is said to have publicly supported the emir's coup against his father in 1995).

Throughout the 1970s, Khartoum continued to welcome Middle Eastern radical groups as a matter of policy, although relations with the Palestine Liberation Organization (PLO) suffered temporarily after the "Black September" murder of two Americans and a Belgian diplomat in 1973. That welcome expanded after the 1989 coup that brought the Sudan's Islamists to power. Significant numbers of "Afghan-Arabs" who had fought the U.S.S.R. in Afghanistan began to arrive in the Sudan as Osama bin Laden and his followers accepted the invitation of Sudanese Islamist Hassan Turabi to live in Khartoum. Turabi, the theorist of the Sudan's Islamist movement, aimed not only to create a modern Islamic state in the Sudan, but to advance political Islam worldwide. He sought international Muslim recognition by expanding contacts with Islamic organizations and welcoming militants, notably Osama bin Laden.

That approach began to change in the mid-1990s after Sudanese officials were implicated as accomplices before and after the fact in the 1995 attempt to assassinate Egyptian President Hosni Mubarak in Ethiopia. In large part as a response to pressure from the international community, more sober individuals in Khartoum began to assess the costs of alienating key members of the UN and, especially, powerful neighbors such as Ethiopia and Egypt as well as the more distant United States. Unsuccessful initiatives to ease relations with the latter included asking bin Laden to leave the Sudan in 1996, as well as repeatedly trying to engage the United States in discussions on terrorism.

The United States finally answered these calls in early 2000 and sent a counterterrorism team to Khartoum. By the end of 2000, the Sudan had signed all twelve international conventions against terrorism, and then in 2002 it took the initiative within the Intergovernmental Authority on Development (IGAD) to discuss combating terrorism.

The future of political Islam is very much in question in the Sudan today. While the country is no longer the Islamist firebrand it was a decade ago, the political transition that began with the split in the Islamist movement in 1999 remains fragile. Turabi and his followers have been removed from positions of authority. They remain, however, a very powerful and potentially destabilizing political force. Deep bitterness within the Islamist ranks has left the government weaker, and Turabi, among others, has been quick to exploit its vulnerabilities. For example, Darfuri members of the former National Islamic Front (NIF), which was led by Turabi, have emerged as the leaders of the Justice and Equality Movement (JEM), one of Darfur's key rebel groups.

By the late 1990s, the government of the Sudan was also beginning to contemplate political reforms. A 1998 constitution established the Sudan as a federal entity. In 2002, under international pressure, its leadership began to focus seriously on negotiating an end to the war with the South. The 2005 peace agreement heralds fundamental political change in the Sudan. It creates a six-year transitional period under a new national government and army composed of both northerners and southerners. The agreement mandates a more genuine federal structure. Recently, senior Sudanese officials have argued that the accords reached with the South can be applied throughout the Sudan to answer local grievances.[4]

A Terror Balance Sheet

In the Sudan, both internal and international terrorism, loosely defined as violence against noncombatants for political ends, have existed. Radical Islamic infighting has resulted in shooting deaths. Attacks on mosques of the

very fundamentalist Ansar al-Sunna sect in 1994, 1997, and 2000 at Omdurman and Wad Medani resulted in deaths and injuries. In the incident in 2000,
police killed an assailant whom they identified as a member of the extremist
group Takfir wal-Hijra, also fundamentalist, but espousing violence. Takfir is
believed to have been responsible for the earlier attacks. The group accused the
National Islamic Front of being an infidel government, and in 1995 Khartoum executed its founder, who held dual Tunisian and Libyan nationality.

Some reports claim that a Takfir agent tried to assassinate bin Laden as
part of the 1994 operation against the Ansar al-Sunna mosque. Bin Laden's
house and office were also targets of a drive-by shooting in 1995. Four armed
foreigners opened fire, prompting a shootout with bin Laden's guards. The
government arrested and later hanged the two surviving assailants.[5]

Acts of international terrorism within the Sudan began, for the purposes of
this chapter, with the 1973 seizure of guests at the Saudi Arabian ambassador's
farewell reception for the American deputy chief of mission in Khartoum.
With PLO leadership knowledge and concurrence, the Black September team
beat and killed the departing deputy, whom they believed had been involved
in Jordan's military attack against the PLO in 1970. They also killed the newly
arrived U.S. ambassador and the Belgian chargé d'affaires.[6]

Two more well-publicized acts of international terrorism took place in the
Sudan in the 1980s. In 1988, the Abu Nidal Organization (Fatah—Revolutionary Council) of the late Sabri al-Banna, alias Abu Nidal, who had been named
head of the Fatah office in Khartoum in 1969 before he broke with the late
Yasser Arafat, bombed the Acropole Hotel and the Sudan Club in downtown
Khartoum. Two years previously, on the day U.S. jets attacked Tripoli, gunmen
from the Libyan embassy in Khartoum had shot and wounded a telecommunications technician as he returned home after working late at the U.S. embassy.

Only after Turabi and the Islamists, essentially the core of the Sudan's Muslim Brotherhood, operating as the *shura* (council) of the NIF, came to power
in 1989 did the United States become seriously concerned about the Sudan's
involvement with terrorist groups and the export of terror.[7] Turabi, a man of
revolutionary zeal, had begun his political career decades earlier by taking
over a Sudanese branch of the Muslim Brotherhood. He liked to depict himself as a modernizer who could help spread political Islam worldwide.
Ultimately, his "Islamic Project" for the Sudan failed, "leaving Turabi the leader
of a small minority movement in the urban communities where the Blue and
the White Niles meet."[8]

Turabi probably first focused on bin Laden as a source of the financial capital that he badly needed to fund his ambitions. In 1989, he sent three NIF

intelligence agents to talk to bin Laden in Pakistan.[9] Knowing that bin Laden and his "Afghan-Arabs" were hoping to leave the Afghanistan theater in the wake of the Russian defeat there, Turabi offered them sanctuary in the Sudan. Bin Laden responded by sending his own scouting mission to Khartoum. Although each side had serious suspicions about the credentials and intentions of the other, they reached an agreement by the end of 1990. Bin Laden, his four wives, their children, and dozens of Arab veterans of the Afghan war arrived in Khartoum in 1991.[10]

The Sudan served as a financial base for bin Laden's international efforts. Al Qaeda, according to Jamal Ahmed al-Fadl, a member-turned-FBI-informant, ran a series of international businesses in the Sudan. A shell corporation established in Khartoum as Wadi al-Aqiq held many of these businesses. Al-Shamal Islamic bank in Khartoum opened accounts for two of bin Laden's companies, including a foreign currency account. It was replenished from outside the Sudan and was used to transfer money through al-Shamal's network of correspondent banks.[11]

The Sudanese Islamist government had a long-established policy of waiving visa requirements for all Arab nationals. However, Islamist security personnel went further. They made sure that some of bin Laden's followers received Sudanese passports bearing aliases, and, on occasion, ordered immigration authorities to let them come and go without stamping their passports. In some cases, government officials went so far as to provide them with official diplomatic documents.

The open door policy attracted radical Islamists from all over the Middle East and North Africa. In addition to Al Qaeda, these entities included Abu Nidal, the Islamic Jihad, and Hamas from Palestine; Hezbollah from Lebanon; Iran's Revolutionary Guards; Egypt's Gamaa Islamiya and Islamic Jihad; as well as individual radicals from Algeria, Libya, Eritrea, Ethiopia, and Tunisia. And as a special case, members of the Lord's Resistance Army, the non-Islamic fanatic movement, came from Uganda. The Sudan soon acquired a reputation as a haven for militant groups. Some used the Sudan only as a sanctuary; others set up offices and actively planned operations.

The Sudan's neighbors grew increasingly alarmed as their intelligence networks picked up information about money laundering schemes, arms smuggling, and plots. Egypt, Eritrea, Ethiopia, and Uganda were among the first to complain. Egypt was especially worried because Egyptian radicals, rooted in the Muslim Brotherhood, had a long tradition of opposition to the government and had been part of bin Laden's inner circle from the very beginning.

The Sudan's initial support for the Ethiopian insurgency's 1991 victory over the Derg resulted in promising relations after the two key Tigrayan movements took power in Ethiopia and Eritrea became independent. Khartoum's support for opposition Islamist movements, however, soon alienated the leadership of both countries. The Sudan was particularly supportive of the Eritrean Islamic Jihad that was engaged in operations against the government of Isaias Afwerki in Asmara. That support eventually resulted in Eritrea's breaking relations with the Sudan in December 1994 and becoming the base for northern armed Sudanese opposition, the National Democratic Alliance.

Khartoum also assisted the Islamic Oromo Liberation Front and the Benishangul Liberation Front, a smaller Ethiopian organization.[12] In response to Sudanese support for Islamist insurgents, Ethiopia slowly resumed ties to the southern rebels, the Sudanese People's Liberation Army (SPLA), whom it had expelled following the victory over the Derg.

On a broader front, actions by Sudanese intelligence and security officers, perhaps exceeding their instructions, caused some alarm in New York in the early to mid-1990s and in New Delhi in 2001. The concern flowed from suspicion of a Sudanese role in the 1993 World Trade Center bombing. An Egyptian resident in the Sudan was among those ultimately convicted, causing some analysts to believe that Sudanese authorities had supported the action. In 1996, the U.S. expelled a diplomat from the Sudan's mission to the UN, contending that, by the testimony of a Sudanese man who had pleaded guilty in 1995 to complicity in New York City bomb plots, the diplomat and a colleague had offered access to the UN headquarters in support of the bomb plot.[13] And in what may be the last international terror action with Sudanese involvement, in 2001 the authorities in India arrested a Sudanese-born student in whose car police had found explosives and detonators that he said had been supplied by two diplomats at the Sudanese embassy. An Al Qaeda lieutenant hatched the plot, he said. According to the press report, a Sudanese diplomat became aware of the plot and informed Khartoum, which appears to have informed Washington. The journalist heard that Khartoum had blamed the incident on Turabi.[14]

In the early 1990s, the Sudan's neighbors complained, expressing both publicly and privately their increasing doubts about the Sudan's contacts with and policies toward a broad range of terrorist groups. Algeria, Morocco, and Tunisia added their voices to those of Egypt, Ethiopia, and Eritrea. The U.S. Department of State responded by putting the Sudan on its list of state sponsors of terrorism in 1993.

State Sponsor of Terrorism

The Sudan initially figured on the U.S. list of state sponsors of terrorism not because it created terrorist groups or designated targets for terrorist action, but rather because it afforded sanctuary, gave facilities, and offered a training venue to a broad range of Middle Eastern and neighboring terrorist organizations. One State Department official instrumental in putting it on the list later described the Sudan as a "Holiday Inn for terrorists."[15]

Popular Arab and Islamic Conference (PAIC)

In direct response to the first Gulf War, Turabi, the country's de facto political force for much of the 1990s, launched, and became the first secretary-general of, the PAIC, an organization intended to set the Sudan forth as a model and energizer of modern Islam.[16] He designed the PAIC as a joint forum, using the word "Arab" to bring in Arab nationalists as well as Islamic fronts in an effort to rally Islamist movements from around the world. He argued that it assembled all Muslims for the first time, overcoming Sunni and Shia divisions. The PAIC met three times, in 1991, 1993, and 1995. Hundreds of delegates from Islamist bodies attended the second and third conferences.

Turabi dismissed the Organization of the Islamic Conference (OIC) as unrepresentative and inactive.[17] In fact, however, Turabi assembled a motley crew of the world's most notorious Muslim radical groups, a counterculture version of the OIC. Turabi's explanation of the purpose of the PAIC differed depending on his audience. In 1996, he described the conferences to American Muslim Mansoor Ijaz as "venting sessions."[18] To some he described the PAIC as a front against imperialism and foreign intervention in the Islamic world. One of his goals was surely to put the Sudan on the map as the principal mediator between governments and their Muslim populations.

The Sudan's neighbors and other countries argued that the PAIC's more sinister intentions included sparking an Islamist revolution throughout the Middle East and fomenting the development of a worldwide armed Islamist movement.[19] Indeed, regarding the desire to bring Sunni and Shia together against a common enemy, Central Intelligence Agency (CIA) analysts believed that in late 1991 or 1992 Al Qaeda and Iran held discussions in the Sudan and informally agreed to cooperate in supporting, if only for training, actions against Israel and the United States.[20] U.S. government officials described the PAIC meetings as terrorist planning sessions and demanded that Turabi stop hosting the conferences. The list of attendees, coupled with the rhetoric at the conferences, only exacerbated international concerns about the Sudan's role in the support of terrorist groups.

In 1996, with his election to parliament and selection as speaker of that body looming, Turabi told me (as the U.S. ambassador to the Sudan) that he would end his activities with the PAIC. He formally turned the organization over to Ibrahim Senoussi, his close associate. The organization did not hold any further conferences in Khartoum, but continued to be active. Following Turabi's own eclipse in late 1999 after a political confrontation with President Omar Hassan al-Bashir, in 2000 the Sudanese press reported that the PAIC would seek a headquarters outside the Sudan. Senoussi attributed the termination of the PAIC's presence in the Sudan to unnamed foreign pressure.[21]

At the same time as he was creating the PAIC, Turabi decided to launch an inter-religious dialogue in Khartoum. The inter-religious dialogue met twice, in 1993 and 1994. Turabi explained his belief that Islam was in a period of renaissance, and specifically, that the Sudan's Islamic renaissance had a "worldwide influence" because of its political, social, and economic dimensions. It would spark a "resurgence of Islamic energy worldwide." One purpose of the dialogue was to define a common ground between Islam and Christianity, to mobilize, as Turabi put it, "Christians and Muslims against the irreligious in a common front."[22]

Attempted Assassination of Egypt's President

Increasing regional and international concerns raised by the presence of so many radical Islamist groups and the rhetoric generated by the PAIC proved justified when Egyptian radicals, based at least temporarily in the Sudan, attempted to assassinate President Mubarak shortly after he arrived in Addis Ababa to attend the 1995 summit of the Organization of African Unity (OAU). The Gamaa Islamiya assassination team had been formed under the aegis of Islamist militant Ayman al-Zawahiri, although apparently without his direct participation. From its base in Khartoum, the team sent weapons to Addis Ababa on a Sudan Airways flight, and members established themselves in Addis Ababa, using false identities.[23] They tried to shoot Mubarak as he drove in from the Addis Ababa airport, but were foiled by security officials. Three surviving members of the team fled back into the Sudan and disappeared. Sudanese authorities from the security section of the Islamist shura and, likely, elements of the government's External Security Bureau, were accessories before and after the fact of the failed assassination attempt. The clear case for official complicity resulted in the imposition of limited UN sanctions in 1996, restricting the travel of Sudanese officials, reducing the Sudan's diplomatic staff abroad, and prohibiting the holding of conferences in Khartoum. Shortly thereafter, a second resolution restricted the places where Sudan Airways could land. Those sanctions ended only in 2001.[24]

The attempted assassination of Mubarak triggered the first serious debate over the issue of "foreign guests" within the Islamic movement. It not only proved to be a costly embarrassment to the government, but also revealed the degree to which Turabi had miscalculated the reaction of the international community. Contemporary Islamist sources in Khartoum said that Bashir was surprised and angered by the scope of official collusion with the Egyptian assassins and insisted that Turabi come to him, rather than his going to Turabi, to discuss the matter. Indeed, Bashir fired Nafi ali Nafie, the head of the External Security Bureau, who has nevertheless long since returned to Bashir's good graces. More thoughtful members of the Islamist movement began to reconsider the Sudan's ties to radical Islamists. Many of them now believe that the beginnings of the internal tensions that led to the 1999 split in the Islamist movement can be traced to this ill-considered adventure.

United States Intelligence

Between 1990 and 1995, the U.S. generated a large volume of dubious intelligence about the Sudanese government's intentions to engage in terrorist actions against American targets. Much of this material, dating to the early to mid-1990s, has been discredited.[25] The CIA withdrew a large number of reports early in 1996, after determining that its sources had lied or exaggerated earlier reports. Those withdrawn reports had prompted the evacuation of dependents from the U.S. mission to the Sudan in 1993.

The tenor of much of this intelligence, including separate reports in late 1995 of Sudanese plans to murder Anthony Lake, then U.S. national security advisor, exacerbated the climate of suspicion and anger against the Khartoum authorities. The source of the Lake murder plan was dropped as unreliable within six weeks of his walking in to provide the report, even as CIA Director John Deutch was using that information to push then Secretary of State Warren Christopher to close the U.S. embassy entirely. In early 1996, Christopher ultimately decided to reduce staff and move the diplomats offshore, but leave the embassy open under local Sudanese staff.

The Departure of Osama bin Laden

By 1996, the Sudan's international relations had reached their nadir. By harboring and supporting various radical Islamist groups, it had successfully alienated almost all of its immediate neighbors. Its relationship with the United States plummeted to historic lows, reduced to a once-a-month visit by an ambassador residing in Kenya.

On the eve of the diplomatic staff's departure from Khartoum—ultimately to end up, reduced in number, in Nairobi—David Shinn, head of the State Department's Directorate for East African Affairs, and I met with Ali Osman Taha, then foreign minister of the Sudan. Taha clearly understood that more was at issue than U.S. public protestations about security threats to embassy staff in Khartoum. We spoke candidly to each other in the first real dialogue between the United States and the Sudan about its support of terrorism. Earlier discussions had centered on more formal presentations that included accusations and the occasional threat. The Sudanese had always responded by rejecting the charges and obfuscating the facts.

Shinn and I raised questions about the Middle Eastern, anti-Eritrean, and anti-Ethiopian radical Islamist groups that Khartoum was abetting, as well as the issue of the Sudan harboring terrorist financier Osama bin Laden and his Afghan-Arabs. We urged the Sudan to expel the various groups. Taha listened and then argued that Hamas and others were legal groups, not terrorists. This issue would figure on my first visit back to the Sudan.

Bashir, whom Taha no doubt briefed, quickly recognized that he needed to become more actively engaged with the United States. Bashir's personal style was generally to operate by consensus, moving on issues after the Islamist council had debated and agreed on positions. However, since the exposure of the major Sudanese intelligence role in support of the Egyptian Islamic Jihad's hit team against Mubarak the previous summer, he had begun to use his authority more readily. He asked Major General El-Fatih Erwa, his military intelligence colleague and deputy minister of defense, to represent him to the intelligence community in Washington. Fatih Erwa, an intelligence professional, was well known to the United States, having been instrumental in the successful movement of Falasha Jews from Ethiopia through the Sudan to Israel in 1985.

By early 1996, within a month of the U.S. diplomatic staff's departure from Khartoum, a two-track effort was well under way to deal with terrorism in the Sudan. On the intelligence track, the CIA presented Fatih Erwa with an eight-point agenda jointly composed by the State Department, the National Security Council, and the CIA. His main meetings were with CIA staff. Back in Khartoum, Taha led the Sudanese side of the diplomatic track. He and I met during my seven- to ten-day monthly visits to Khartoum. At the same time, Erwa and I would sometimes talk in Khartoum. In addition, I began a series of meetings with the External Security Bureau chiefs: first, the Bashir loyalist who had replaced Nafi, and then his successor, Qutbi al-Mahdi, former ambassador to Iran.

We made significant progress during March and April on several of the agenda items. The Sudan announced that it had asked some Middle Eastern groups to leave, and offered to let the United States examine sites that we had argued were being used to train terrorists. In July, I accompanied a U.S.-based officer who filmed the empty Sudan Military Academy camp north of Omdurman. This permanent installation received troops for training annually. We then went on to Merkhyiat, a smaller, permanent center somewhat further north into the desert, where we watched young men field-stripping AK automatic rifles. The Sudanese said the men belonged to the Sudan's Islamist militia, the Popular Defense Force, and were training for the civil war in the South.

Deutch, the principal architect of the U.S. withdrawal, had passed through Nairobi in April 1996. We had an extended conversation in which he acknowledged that his people were anxious to get back to Khartoum. We agreed to meet on my next visit to Washington.

The two-track negotiations continued. Much of the U.S. discussion with the Sudanese government was focused on bin Laden and his Afghan-Arabs. The Saudis were especially worried about bin Laden and the fanatics whom he was attracting to his cause. They had stripped him of his Saudi citizenship in 1994 because of his campaign against the Royal House of Saud. He ran a construction company and several other businesses in the Sudan, including the Khartoum Tannery.

Although the United States knew that bin Laden financed terrorist organizations, it did not, at that time, have sufficient proof of his direct involvement with terrorists to issue an indictment. Nevertheless, by early 1996 the United States was determined to have him removed from the Sudan, which was, after all, just a short leap across the Red Sea from Saudi Arabia.

Talks on the U.S. agenda obtained mixed results. The Sudanese initially claimed that they did not know how many bin Laden loyalists were in their country. They pointed out that they had abolished visa requirements for Muslims in 1989 and claimed to have inadequate records. However, they said that they were willing to expel bin Laden and send him home to Saudi Arabia. But the Saudis were not willing to take him back on any terms. The White House at that time did not feel that it could force the issue. The dickering over what to do with bin Laden continued until the Sudanese finally decided that they just wanted to be rid of him.[26]

On May 20, 1996, three and a half months after we started our negotiations on terrorism, Taha sent a fax to my Nairobi office informing me that bin Laden had left the Sudan. I replied with thanks and asked about the disposition of bin Laden's assets.

Bin Laden's expulsion should have opened opportunities for greater cooperation with the Sudanese. By then, Deutch had fully repented of his enthusiasm to close the embassy in Khartoum. His staff was cognizant both of the bad intelligence that had skewed American views of the Sudan and of the urgent need to get good people back into that complicated country. They knew that no developing country can be covered adequately with open sources, much less by reports from allies. The CIA had already become too dependent on third-country intelligence reports, and officers knew the inherent danger of relying on other countries, each with its own political agenda, for information about a place as important and as complex as the Sudan.

I met with Deutch in his offices at CIA headquarters. Deputy Director George Tenet, who replaced him as director in the second Clinton administration, joined us along with Barbara Bodine, who had replaced Shinn at the State Department. Other, less senior officials on both sides also attended the meetings. Deutch agreed that the U.S. staff needed to return to Khartoum. Tenet, who is said to have since privately described the withdrawal of Americans from the Sudan as the worst decision made during his tenure at the CIA, wanted to move back at once.[27] With caution and great regret, I argued that no one in the administration would risk the Sudan becoming a presidential election issue, and the move should be delayed until after November's poll. Deutch agreed.

Immediately after the election, I contacted Deutch to begin the process of returning American officers to the Sudan on a permanent basis. He quickly raised the issue at senior levels of the State Department, but got nowhere. Deutch's influence waned because of his public position on controversial issues; he ultimately did not continue as director in the second Clinton administration. It would take another three and a half years before the United States seriously engaged with the Sudan. In 2000, the Clinton administration changed its policy and accepted the Sudan's long-standing invitation to send a counterterrorism team to Khartoum.[28]

Hamas

Of all the resident Middle Eastern groups, it was the Palestinian Hamas that Sudanese officials, in discussions with the press and with American officials, consistently argued in support of, contending that this group was political and not terrorist. Foreign Minister Taha made that point when Shinn and I met with him in Khartoum on February 6, 1996. Officials had argued that Hamas members had settled into communities in Khartoum and were engaged in business. In 1998, during a visit to the Sudan by the group's founder, the Khartoum state governor gave Hamas office space, land, and farms, calling on other Muslim and Arab nations "to follow the Sudan's example and allocate endowments for backing the Palestinian struggle."[29]

Over the years since, Hamas representatives have maintained a presence in Khartoum. Public reports are not totally clear. Hamas resident representatives were said to have left the Sudan in late 2003, citing U.S. pressure. It has also been said that Hamas did not have any office in Khartoum; instead, there was a "representative" of the movement, and a new representative took up residence on February 24, 2004.[30]

Governance and Terror

International and internal pressures helped the Sudan's government to recognize that it was on the wrong tack and should cooperate with the West on issues involving terrorism, as well as embark on internal political reforms. The regime is no longer at the cutting edge of political Islam and its seeming acceptance that the nation is plural and diverse has implications for governance.

The military authorities who conducted the 1989 coup initially dissembled, causing the Egyptians, among others, to welcome then Brigadier General Bashir's overthrow of elected Prime Minister Sadiq el-Mahdi. At first no one was sure exactly who these people were or what the orientation of the new government would be. Turabi, who had managed to get himself jailed to create an alibi in case the coup failed, was in Kober Prison for the first six months.

By the time that Turabi left his prison cell, the Islamist core of the NIF was in charge. When Turabi and Bashir finally fell out in 1999, both men made statements that demonstrated the calculated game played at the time of the coup. Bashir said publicly: "I carried out the orders and instructions of the movement without hesitation, when it came to taking over power I did so too, without hesitation, then we dissolved the Military Council. I am a member of the movement. I carried out the Engaz [coup] for it."[31]

A few weeks later, Turabi publicly repeated the history lesson, echoing Bashir's explanation. The Islamist figure had, in fact, spoken about the coup privately to young Muslims in London in 1992, but with a broader appreciation for the implications of the sham of the coup period. He argued then, with the sophistry that so maddened his interlocutors in the following years, that public denial was not "lying," but rather "*taqia*," the Shiite principle of dissimulation to avoid confronting a superior or damaging force.[32]

The key issue following the coup was loyalty and chain of command. The solution was in the Qur'anic concept of allegiance—*bay'a*. The goal was allegiance to the victory of religion, and Turabi's authority was its assurance. Thus, all the Islamists in the Revolutionary Command Council (RCC) made allegiance to Turabi, and all, including Bashir, then head of the RCC, were obedient to Turabi, as disciples to a sheikh.[33]

The NIF, a broad organization that served as the vehicle for the Islamic Movement in the Sudan, had at its core the clandestine Muslim Brotherhood, an Egyptian import active in the Sudan since the 1940s. Turabi disbanded the NIF after the coup, arguing that political Islam was now in charge. He also engineered the resignation of the NIF shura, made up entirely of Muslim Brothers, and reconstituted it with a mixture of former members and new officers, on the logic that disarming possible suspicion required membership by the officers' group. Many Islamists remained unhappy with the dissolution of an entity specifically devoted to their cause, even though a shura continued to exist. After a lapse of a few years, a new Islamic Movement was created and joined the National Congress party. Called the Special Entity (*al kayan al khas*), it is made up of Islamists who support the government after the eclipse of Turabi. The body has a shura that is broader than the NIF shura. In 2003, Vice President Taha was picked as secretary-general of the entire Islamic Movement while he was in Naivasha, negotiating with the SPLM. Previous heads of the new movement's shura were the director of the Arab Institute in Khartoum and, before him, the director of the International University of Africa. Among the activities of the new movement are education and training in Islamic studies.[34]

Parallel Organizations

After 1989, the Islamists both ruled through the formal bureaucratic structures of government and at the same time used parallel party structures that wielded great power. The government quickly announced a new Revolutionary Command Council that was only disbanded in 1993, with Bashir's assumption of the title of president. It also created a Transitional National Assembly in 1992 and, ultimately, an elected parliament in 1996. Turabi became its first speaker.

In parallel with those structures were the various, and, as yet, little eluci-
dated, bodies of the Islamist shura. In the mid-1990s, NIF members in
Khartoum claimed to me that the party no longer existed and protested at my
use of the name. Indeed, the movement formally dissolved when Turabi gave
senior members each a copy of the Qur'an. He argued that the Islamist movement had control of the government and an Islamist party was not needed.[35]
Turabi said that the NIF dissolved, "indeed, because our work has outgrown
it," pointing to new areas of responsibility to make the Sudan "a land of Islamic
revival and to face all the challenges that come with it."[36]

In fact, Turabi dissolved the National Islamic Front in 1990 because he
wanted to eliminate the old guard of the Islamic movement. He closed the
existing shura, claiming that it might pose security problems for the new government and that he would create a new shura composed equally of Islamists
from the old ranks and Islamists from the officer corps. The old shura's main
function had been strategic planning, from the Qur'anic term *al temkin* (the
use of which legitimizes the function through association with the scriptures).
The new shura acted similarly, but effectively built consensus around the ideas
of Turabi himself.[37]

The Islamist movement reemerged as the core of the National Congress—
a "national structure" as Turabi called it, envisaged as the only legal political
organization, providing a forum both for political action and from which the
government drew its leadership.[38] In the mid- and late 1990s, the leading body
remained the modified NIF shura, a consensus policy-making entity of forty
or more, elected from among the leading Islamists, almost all of whom were
closely associated with Turabi. Agencies or bureaus of the shura included one
for intelligence/security, as well as a military office and an external relations
office, the last under Ibrahim Senoussi. There was also a separate military
bureau. Indeed, Islamist rule included an attempt to create a parallel army in
the form of the Popular Defense Force, a militia created outside the military
structure. That body, regarded as the armed wing of the Islamic movement,
recruited young men and women. Interlocutors in Khartoum in October 2004
stated that former military bureau of the shura membership was involved in
the abortive coup effort in September 2004 on behalf of Turabi and his
eclipsed section of the Islamist movement.

With some irony, it was the shura of the modern National Congress Party,
some 582 strong, that Bashir used in 2000 to end Turabi's role completely. A
strong majority effectively endorsed Bashir's decision to dismiss Turabi as
secretary-general by picking for the post another Islamist, known to be
opposed to Turabi.[39]

International Dimensions

Since the expulsion of bin Laden, the Sudan has worked assiduously and with success to rebuild its relations with its neighbors and the West. The Sudan's efforts to clamp down on Islamist groups within its borders, and the split within the Sudan's Islamist movement, have enabled Khartoum to mend relations with its neighbors. The Egyptians, who are totally preoccupied with the life-giving Nile waters, also finally recognized that they must be a player in any scenario to resolve the civil war with the South. These considerations brought Cairo around to a more constructive role in the Sudan. Bilateral relations are now normal. By late 2004, Egyptian doctors were traveling throughout government zones in the Sudan to work at clinics and hospitals, and Cairo was supporting Khartoum's position on the insurgency in Darfur.

After the 1995 attempt to assassinate Mubarak, the Ethiopians downgraded their representation in Khartoum. The Sudanese, however, kept a very capable ambassador in Addis Ababa. The 1998 war between Eritrea and Ethiopia, and the eclipse of Turabi in 1999, have resulted in improved relations between Khartoum and Addis Ababa.

To the frustration of the United States, Europeans have generally stayed close to Khartoum. Terrorist Ilich Ramirez Sanchez, alias Carlos the Jackal, was arrested by the Sudanese government and extradited to France, leading France to enter into a complicated relationship with the Islamist government. Turabi, a graduate of a French university, saw a role for himself in the francophone world, notably brokering a truce between the Algerian authorities and the opposition Front Islamique du Salut. France also has been engaged in a forty-year archaeological effort in the Sudan. Finally, French companies entered into mining agreements with Khartoum in 1991, and export five tons of gold annually.

The United Nations has been the scene of both Sudanese Islamist diplomatic triumph and comeuppance. Until the final stage of talks to end the civil war in the South, Khartoum tried to keep UN political and security elements out of the Sudan, while at the same time becoming more active within the UN family. Operation Lifeline Sudan (OLS), created in 1989 by a unique agreement between the UN and the Sudan, allowed the UN to establish conditions for the safe delivery of food and medical supplies in the South.

International conventions against terrorism can be a benchmark to test behavior on the issue of terrorism. Conversations in Khartoum began in early 1996 when research in Washington indicated that the Sudan had signed and ratified only four of the dozen conventions related to terrorism. The Sudan is now a party to all twelve conventions, and, as described, closed down the PAIC offices. The Sudan is also a party to the various African Union and Arab League conventions on terrorism.[40]

The dispatch of CIA, FBI, and Department of State diplomatic security officers to Khartoum in 2000 began a productive dialogue about U.S. terrorism concerns.[41] The team, according to Sudanese External Security Bureau officials, brought with it a six-point list that the Sudanese believed they had satisfied by early 2001.[42] The new Bush administration agreed, deciding in 2001 to name a presidential envoy to try to energize the North-South peace process. The president introduced special envoy Senator John Danforth a week before the 9/11 attacks. Counterterrorism cooperation became significantly greater after 9/11, and in late 2001 Secretary of State Colin Powell acknowledged the Sudan's assistance. Khartoum delivered hundreds of intelligence files to the U.S. team after 9/11, clear evidence that despite the waiver of visas for Muslims, the Sudan's security services had kept watch on a range of Middle Eastern groups in Khartoum.[43]

Weapons of Mass Destruction

Closely allied to the issue of terrorism, largely due to dubious U.S. allegations, is the matter of the Sudan's acquisition of weapons of mass destruction. The Sudan had contracted with various countries for military purposes. Bulgaria, for example, established a factory to make military pistols. The Iraqi military arrived for work in the Sudan in the early to mid-1990s on still unknown projects. Over this period, press reports from the SPLA cited the use of chemical weapons in the South. I spoke regularly with former Vice-President Abel Alier, a respected Dinka statesman, in Khartoum about these reports. Neither of us had specifics or anything credible to go on. Nor did "samples" that others collected ever test positive. In August 1996, seven Iraqis returning home hijacked a Sudan Airways craft destined for Jordan and forced it to fly to Stansted, near London. My understanding is that British officials questioned the Iraqis about weapons of mass destruction but received no information that such projects were under way in the Sudan.

The case in support of the U.S. cruise missile attack on the Al-Shifa pharmaceutical plant in 1998 centers on allegations of storage, transport, or creation of a chemical weapon precursor to the nerve gas VX. No other element of the supporting charges has survived with any credibility: Washington did not know who owned the plant, falsely stated that it was part of the Sudanese "military-industrial" complex and heavily guarded, and then froze the assets of Salah Idris, its Saudi-resident Sudanese owner, who was in regular conversation with U.S. embassy officers. Idris successfully sued, forcing the U.S. Treasury to unblock his assets, and has separately sued for damages to his plant. A number of American visitors to the plant cast doubt on the allegations, noting that no significant guard force was present.[44]

Conclusion and Outlook

The Islamist vision of the Sudan as a modern Islamic outpost has blurred following Turabi's eclipse. No one can argue successfully that the broad Islamist role that he and his collaborators set for the Sudan in the late 1980s and 1990s was one of mere communication with other—including violent—Islamic movements rather than active cooperation with these groups.[45] At the very least, their welcome provided bin Laden and his people a breathing space to regroup and maintain coherence for future actions.[46] Some Sudanese joined Al Qaeda, but recruitment does not appear to have taken place on a large scale. Enough evidence exists to accuse Khartoum itself of venturing into operations; for example, the Addis Ababa assassination attempt and the work of intelligence officers overseas, some of whom seem to have exceeded their brief as collectors and ventured into action. This trend clearly met with considerable debate in Khartoum itself. By 1996, the debate had ended in a decision to address U.S. concerns. Tardy U.S. acceptance of the Sudan's invitation resulted in a delayed peace process, and more serious delays in building relationships with Sudanese intelligence and security officials.

The Sudan is now in transition. Expectations and anxieties over the country's political and economic future have put governance into question in both the North and the South. The split in the Islamist movement continues to echo with allegations that Turabi loyalists tried to effect a coup at the end of September 2004. The government has engaged in peace talks in three venues: in the first, Naivasha, the text of peace with the South was signed on January 9, 2005, and a coalition government established in Khartoum on July 9, 2005; in the second, Cairo, the talks successfully brought the armed opposition NDA back into a peaceful political process; and in the third, Abuja, the objective—not yet achieved—was to end the insurgency that began in Darfur in February 2003. In July, 2005, the government and the two Darfuri insurgent groups did sign a Declaration of Principles that could form the bases of peace, but failed to reach a comprehensive agreement to stop the violence. Meanwhile, the UN has concluded that genocide did not take place in Darfur, but major human rights violations did. Should the Sudan fail to satisfy the conditions of a UN Security Council Resolution on resolving the crisis in Darfur, sanctions may follow that strike at the Sudan's oil industry, its major foreign exchange earner.[47]

Notes

1. Jamal Ahmed al-Fadl, a Sudanese who joined Al Qaeda in Afghanistan, turned FBI informant and testified in 1993. Guantanamo detainee Ibrahim al-Qosi was recruited in the Sudan and acted as a bodyguard, accountant, and treasurer, according to U.S. government allegations charging him with war crimes. See Peter Bergen, "The Bin Laden Trials: What Did We Learn?" *Studies in Conflict & Terrorism*, XXIV (2001), 429–434, www.polisci.taylorandfrancis.com/pdfs.ter_article.pdf; "Prisoners: Ibrahim al Qosi," www.cageprisoners.com/prisoners.php?pri_id=243.

2. Quotes from Peter M. Holt and Martin W. Daly, *A History of the Sudan* (Harlow, England, 2000, 5th ed.), 167.

3. Interview in Khartoum, September 2004. Also in Holt and Daly, *A History*, 169.

4. Conversation with the governor of South Darfur, September 2004.

5. Jonathan Randal, *Osama: The Making of a Terrorist* (New York, 2004), 148–149, citing the *Washington Post* (August 27, 1998) and remarks of then Saudi intelligence chief Prince Turki al-Faisal.

6. A compelling description of the event and its aftermath can be found in David A. Korn, *Assassination in Khartoum* (Bloomington, 1973).

7. Hassan Mekki kindly provided a history and outline of the Islamist movement and its institutions when we met in Khartoum in January 2005.

8. J. Millard Burr and Robert O. Collins, *Revolutionary Sudan: Hasan al-Turabi and the Islamist State 1989–2000* (Leiden, 2003), 279. This study provides great detail on the National Islamic Front and its relationship to governance in the Sudan in the period named.

9. Randal, *Osama*, 117. He cites testimony in the New York trial of East African terrorists (308, fn. 2).

10. Personal communication from Robert O. Collins.

11. See John Willman, "Attack on terrorism—Inside al-Qaeda: Trail of terrorist dollars that spans the world," *Financial Times*, November 29, 2001, http://specials.ft.com/attackonterrorism/FT3RNR3XMUC.html; Victor Comras, "Al Qaeda Finances and Funding to Affiliated Groups," *Strategic Insights*, IV (2005), www.ccc.nps.navy.mil/si/2005/Jan/comras-Jan05.asp.

12. See David Shinn, "Ethiopia: Governance and Terrorism," chapter 5 in this volume.

13. U.S. Department of State, *1996 Global Terrorism: Overview of State-Sponsored Terrorism*, www.fas.org/irp/threat/terror_96/overview.html. The other diplomat had rotated home as the U.S. contemplated taking action.

14. Karl Vick, "The Sudan, Newly Helpful, Remains Wary of U.S.: Officials Share Files but Deny Ties to Foiled Attack," *Washington Post* (December 10, 2001).

15. Barbara Bodine had been the State Department's acting director for counterterrorism and was, at the time of the quote, country director for Horn of Africa Affairs.

16. In a personal communication, Collins argued that Turabi likely had long harbored the idea of such a body, and that the arrival of numbers of Afghan-Arabs triggered his efforts to realize it.

17. Muriel Mirak-Weissback, "Sudanese Leaders Deal with the Issues," *Executive Intelligence Review*, XXI (1994), www.aboutthe Sudan.com/interviews/hassan_al_turabi.htm.

18. Author's discussions with Mansoor Ijaz, 2002.

19. See the discussion about the PAIC in Claes-Johan Sorensen, "The Islamic Movement

in the Sudan: External Relations and Internal Power Struggle after 1989," unpub. master's thesis, American University of Beirut (2002), 52–54, http://sudansupport.no. Yossef Bodansky, "Peres and the New Middle East," *The Maccabean Online* (December, 1995), www.freeman.org/m_online/dec95d.htm, argues that the 1995 PAIC meeting decided on an Islamist offensive.

20. National Commission on Terrorist Attacks against the United States, *The 9/11 Commission Report* (New York, 2004), 61 and fn. 468.

21. Muhammad Ali Saeed, "Khartoum closes Turabi's international organization," Agence France-Presse, 2004, www.metimes.com/2k/issue2000-7/reg/khartoum_closes_turabis.htm.

22. Mirak-Weissback, "Sudanese Leaders Deal with the Issues."

23. Lawrence Wright, "The Man behind Bin Laden," *The New Yorker* (September 16, 2004). He writes that Ayman al-Zawahiri and his Egyptian Islamic Jihad formed the backbone of Islamic terrorism, and that, specifically, Zawahiri presided at an April 1995 meeting in Khartoum at which both the Islamic Jihad and the Islamic Group decided to kill Mubarak.

24. UN Security Council Resolution (UNSCR) 1054 (1996) and UNSCR 1070 (1996) required all states to reduce the staff of their Sudanese diplomatic and consular posts and to limit the movement of remaining staff, to limit transit through their territory of Sudanese civilian and military officials, to refrain from convening any conferences in the Sudan, and in resolution 1070, to deny airspace or landing rights to aircraft registered, owned, leased, or operated by the Sudan.

25. Timothy Carney and Mansoor Ijaz, "Intelligence Failure? Let's Go Back to the Sudan," *Washington Post* (June 30, 2002), B5. See also Randal, *Osama*, 122–139; Steve Coll, *Ghost Wars* (New York, 2004), 320–326.

26. I had broached the idea of sending bin Laden to Saudi Arabia during an informal dinner with Taha on January 20, 1996. In the same period, the Saudi ambassador had told me that bin Laden needed to apologize and then would be accepted back home.

27. Tenet's private view came from a senior CIA official at a seminar for American ambassadors-designate whom we both briefed in 2001.

28. Omar al-Bashir, "Bashir's Letter to Congressman Hamilton, April 5, 1997," *Newsday*, 2004, www.newsday.com/news/nationwide/world/ny-the Sudanletter,0,3511829.story?col=-ny-top-headlines.

29. "HAMAS Given Office, Land in the Sudan," Agence France-Presse, www.vitrade.com/the Sudan_risk/terrorism/980602_hamas.htm.

30. "Khartoum: Hamas New Representative Assumes Work" (February 25, 2004), www.arabicnews.com/ansub/Daily/Day/040225/2004022516.html; "Hamas Representative Left the Sudan under American Pressure" (November 15, 2003), www.arabicnews.com/ansub/Daily/Day/031115/2003111506.html.

31. Khalid Al Mubarak, *Turabi's Islamist Venture: Failure and Implications* (Cairo, 2001), 62, citing a press conference reported by daily *Al Ray al Aam* (Khartoum) (December 16, 1999).

32. Khalid, *Turabi's Islamist*, 63, citing *Al Ray Al Amm* (January 7, 2000). In fact, a perfectly good term exists for politically inspired lying in Sunni jurisprudence. It is *al hid'a al sharia* and translates as "legal cheating." As Hassan Mekki explained to me in January 2005, Turabi, as a politician, would not choose a term that included the word "cheating" lest he alienate his audience, and so used the Shia term instead.

33. From my conversation with Mekki, who himself was an Islamist and official of the new authority, January 2005.

34. Interview with a senior Sudanese official, November, 2004; and discussion with Hassan Mekki, January, 2005.

35. Discussion with a senior Sudanese official, November, 2004.

36. Mohamed ElHachmi Hamdi, *The Making of an Islamic Political Leader: Conversations with Hasan al-Turabi* (Boulder, 1998), 63.

37. Conversation with Mekki, January 2005.

38. Sorensen, "The Islamic Movement in the Sudan." Sorensen cites Abdelwahab el-Affendi, "Sudan: Turabi and His Detractors," *Middle East International*, DCXII (1999), http://meionline.com.

39. Ibrahim Omar, who became acting secretary-general, had been at odds with Turabi for years. See "The Sudan's Regime Poised to Self-destruct," *Jane's* (July 6, 2000), www.janes.com/security/international_security/news/jiaa/jiaa000706_1_n.shtml.

40. The twelve conventions against terrorism are: Convention and Certain Other Offences Committed on Board Aircraft (Tokyo 14/06/63); Convention for the Unlawful Seizure of Aircraft (The Hague 16/12/70); Convention for the Suppression of Unlawful Acts against the Safety of Aircraft (Montreal 23/09/71); Convention on the Prevention and Punishment of Crimes against Internationally Protected Persons, Including Diplomatic Personnel (New York 14/12/73); Convention against the Taking of Hostages (New York 17/12/79); Convention on the Physical Protection of Nuclear Materials (Vienna 03/03/80); Protocol for the Suppression of Unlawful Acts of Violence at Airports Serving International Aviation, complementary to the Convention for the Suppression of Unlawful Acts against the Safety of Aircraft (Montreal 24/02/88); Convention for the Suppression of Unlawful Acts against the Safety of Maritime Navigation (Rome 10/03/88); Protocol for the Suppression of Unlawful Acts against the Safety of Fixed Platforms on the Continental Shelf (Rome 10/03/88); Convention on the Marking of Plastic Explosives for the Purpose of Detection (Montreal 01/03/91); UN Convention for the Suppression of Terrorist Bombings (New York 15/12/97); UN Convention for the Suppression of Financing of Terrorism (New York 09/12/99).

41. This change in U.S. policy remains unexplained. I believe it reflects a recognition of the failure of the continuing Clinton administration effort to require more concessions from Khartoum before engaging with the Sudanese authorities. Of particular relevance is the dissolution of the regional states' collaboration to support the SPLA with troops, command and control staff, and hardware following the Eritrea-Ethiopian war of 1998.

42. Conversation at External Security Bureau headquarters in Khartoum, mid-January 2001. In this general context, I recall a trial in 1998 related to intelligence adventurers in Khartoum who provided false information to foreign embassies. Also relevant are various trials and expulsions of foreigners; thirteen Saudis, for example, accused of plotting against their homeland from residences in the Sudan. For a report citing a government statement, see "Syrian Convicted in the Sudan Terrorism Trial" (August 28, 2003), www/phillyburbs.com/pb-dyn/news/91-08282003-149666.html.

43. Interview in Khartoum, January 2001; Vick, "Sudan, Newly Helpful," 3.

44. A good summary of the matter is in Henry L. Stimson Center, "U.S. Case for Al Shifa Attack Disintegrates," *CBW Chronicle*, III (2000), accessed October 26, 2004, www.stimson.org/cbw/?sn=cb2001121262.

45. Sorensen ("The Islamic Movement," 87–88) says that the Sudanese Islamists' relations with foreign groups were almost entirely based on communication, rather than cooperation.

46. This point is abundantly made in Ann M. Lesch, "Osama bin Laden's 'Business' in the Sudan," *Current History,* CI (2002), 203–207.

47. For more detail on the negotiations and Darfur, see Robert I. Rotberg, "Sudan and the War in Darfur," *Great Decisions 2005* (New York, 2005), 57–67.

7

YEMEN

Political Economy and the Effort against Terrorism

ROBERT D. BURROWES

Yemen, in the middle of the first decade of the twenty-first century, is not yet a "bastion of terror." On the contrary, and especially by mid-2005, it has become an increasingly stalwart ally of the United States in the effort against transnational revolutionary political Islam and terrorism.[1] Nevertheless, within the next several years Yemen could easily become a major arena in which transnational revolutionary political Islam openly contends for rule. It could also become a major incubator and exporter of this variant of Islam, much as Afghanistan was in the 1980s and again after 1994 with the rise of the Taliban. If something along those lines occurred, Yemen could no longer be counted on by the United States to be an ally in the effort against transnational revolutionary Islam; it would be less a part of the solution than a part of the problem.

The possibility of Yemen's becoming a bastion of terror, and its relationship to both the United States and the American effort

The author wishes to thank his colleagues at the University of Washington for their encouragement and support. Special thanks are due his dear friend Jere Bacharach and the current director of the Henry M. Jackson School of International Studies, Anand Yang.

against transnational revolutionary Islam, turn largely on its domestic politics. It depends on whether Yemen's political regime has the will and capacity to adopt and implement quickly the major political and socioeconomic reforms needed to restore the country's viability and to make it again a land of promise for most of its people.[2] It also hinges to some degree on whether the United States can both redefine the effort against transnational revolutionary Islam and terrorism in other than military terms and adopt policies for the greater Middle East region and the Horn of Africa that will help eliminate their root causes. Such a redefinition and change in policy would make it politically easier for Yemen to partner with the United States in this critical effort.

The economy of Yemen has been weak for much of the decade since 1994. Yemen in 2005 is in great need of major socioeconomic reforms. The failure to effect such reforms is likely quickly to undermine the ruling regime and its political system. Failure will drain away support and legitimacy, thereby increasing Yemen's chances of becoming a failed state.[3] Under these circumstances, Yemen will be vulnerable to revolutionary political Islam, and unreliable as an ally.

The reform—or rather, the reconstitution—of the coalition that makes up the current political regime would also seem to be required in order to increase its will and its capacity to effect required reforms.[4] The goal must be a ruling coalition more able, if only for the sake of survival, to act in terms of its enlightened self-interest. The ability of Yemen rapidly to effect these political changes, as well as to bring about required socioeconomic reforms, is overwhelmingly a domestic issue. There is only so much that the United States can to do to further this process.

Yemen: Land and People

Yemen occupies the southern corner of the Arabian Peninsula, bordering on Saudi Arabia and Oman and facing, across the Red Sea and the Gulf of Aden, the countries of the Horn of Africa—Djibouti, Eritrea, Somalia, Ethiopia, and the Sudan. Yemen contains most of the mountains and highlands of the Arabian Peninsula.[5] For this reason, it receives most of the monsoon rains that fall on that overwhelmingly arid rectangle of land, and this rainfall has for millennia supported intensive agriculture and a relatively dense pattern of settlement at higher elevations. Dwarfed in area by neighboring Saudi Arabia, Yemen's population of about 20 million is roughly equal to the combined populations of Saudi Arabia, Oman, and the four mini-states of the peninsula.[6]

Apart from the western mountains and the southern uplands, however, much of Yemen is arid and thinly populated, in some places only by nomads. This paucity of people is especially true of the eastern reaches that gradually slope down to the Empty Quarter of Saudi Arabia. Indeed, life in most of Yemen is constrained severely by a shortage of water, and the water table in many areas is now falling at an alarming rate.

Yemen has long ranked as one of the poorest countries of the world, its poverty contrasting sharply to the great oil-based wealth of Saudi Arabia and most of the Arab Gulf States. Throughout most of the twentieth century, and to some extent in earlier centuries, its chief export and a principal source of wealth was the men who worked and did business abroad and remitted relatively large sums of hard currency; those who remained at home engaged mostly in subsistence agriculture. Beginning in the 1960s, Yemen became the recipient of a considerable amount of development aid. Since the late 1980s, moreover, the country has received significant revenue from the exploitation of its very modest reserves of oil.[7] Unfortunately, rapid population growth and corruption have consumed much of aid and oil revenues.

The Republic of Yemen (ROY) was the quick and surprising result in 1990 of the union of the Yemen Arab Republic (YAR), or North Yemen, and the People's Democratic Republic of Yemen (PDRY), or South Yemen.[8] From the 1840s, rule by different colonial powers—the Ottoman Empire in the north and the British in the south—had pulled Yemen in two directions, the north toward inland Sanaa and the south toward the port city of Aden. This process of differentiation continued under the revived Hamid al-Din imamate in the north in the first half of the twentieth century, and then with the revolution and the independence struggle that led, respectively, to the YAR and the PDRY in the 1960s.[9] Growing inter-Yemeni conflict between two very different regimes, the military-dominated conservative republican YAR and the Marxist one-party PDRY, was a product of the 1970s and 1980s. The two Yemens fought brief border wars in 1972 and 1979, and those wars led oddly in each case to agreements for unification that were soon largely ignored.

North Yemen prior to its 1962 revolution was a very conservative Islamic country, as South Yemen, with the exception of Aden Colony, had been before independence from Britain in 1967. The great Hamid al-Din imams, Yahya (1904–1948) and Ahmad (1948–1962), had isolated and insulated the north's Muslim population from the modern twentieth-century world, as had British colonial administrators through their policy of indirect rule in the "independent" protectorates west, north, and east of Aden. As a result, Yemen to this day remains one of the most uniformly conservative and traditional Islamic countries in the world, despite considerable modernization in the north and an effort at socialist transformation in the south. Not surprisingly, Yemeni politics have largely been consumed by the politics of development and nation-state building over the past forty years.[10] Yemen was and is strikingly similar to Afghanistan.

Despite the fact that Yemen and the Yemenis have rarely been united under a single government, a consciousness of being Yemeni and a strong sense of Yemen as a place—of historic or geographic Yemen—go back hundreds of years if not millennia. This has facilitated the growth of a modern Yemeni nationalism over the past half a century or so. Indeed, nationhood stole the march on the state in recent decades, calling for an emphasis on state building.

State, Regime, and Governance

Serious and sustained efforts toward Yemeni unification really began only in the late 1980s, largely at the initiative of a newly confident YAR and partly because of the new economic and political weakness of the PDRY after the end of the cold war. With unification in 1990, Ali Abdullah Salih became president of the Republic of Yemen; a career soldier with strong tribal ties, he had been president of the YAR since 1978. During the next few years of transition, the newly created republic was ruled jointly by the leaders and the political-military forces of the YAR and the PDRY. Escalating political conflict and second thoughts about unification, mostly by southerners, led to a brief war of secession in 1994; Yemen remained intact, as predominantly northern forces prevailed over those of the south. Since then, the far more populous north has dominated unified Yemen and power has been concentrated in the hands of a loose coalition of mostly northern elements led by President Salih.[11]

Salih frequently offers up Yemen as a model emerging democracy for the Middle Eastern region, perhaps most recently and prominently in 2004 at the G-8 meetings at Sea Island, Georgia.[12] Many say Yemen is the most democratic country on the Arabian Peninsula and one of the most democratic in the larger region, and rightly so; this assertion, however, does not say much. In fact, Yemen is not now a very democratic country, and much of its democracy is more apparent than real, mostly a formal façade with shallow foundations. Nevertheless, the beginnings of democracy are in place in Yemen; it could evolve into a much more democratic country in the near future, but only under the right conditions and in the right environment.[13]

The Republic of Yemen's three parliamentary elections—in 1993, 1997, and 2003—were free and fair to a considerable degree.[14] They were, however, elections for a legislature that has and asserts almost no power. Because that body has been rendered so irrelevant, the public has dismissed and paid little attention to it, thereby diminishing its role in public discourse and in shaping public opinion.[15]

Salih, who celebrated twenty-seven years in office in mid-2005, was virtually unopposed in the country's first direct presidential election in 1999.[16] Nearly everyone assumes that he will run again in 2006 and win easily; many also assume that his son, Ahmad Ali, is being groomed to succeed him. The local council elections in 2001, themselves marred by irregularities, were overshadowed by a referendum at the same time that, with strong regime support, increased the term of the legislature from four to six years and, more important, extended the presidential term from five to seven years. If things go as predicted, this change means that Salih will be in office until 2013—for a total of thirty-five years.[17]

Several opposition parties have been officially recognized since 1990 and are active and vocal. With the exception of the Reform Grouping (Islah), a party that combines Islamic elements and the tribes and has considerable organization and grassroots support, none of the other opposition parties even begins to pose a challenge to the ruling party, the General People's Congress (GPC). The Yemeni Socialist Party (YSP), the vanguard party that had ruled the PDRY, once had ideology, organization, and a broad base of support in the south and in pockets of the north; in disarray since 1994, it could rise from the ashes and be a political force in the future. The various Baath and Nasirite parties have little popular support, live in the pan-Arab past, debate irrelevant issues with one another, and are of no real consequence today. Other tiny parties, such as al-Haq and the United Front of Popular Forces (conservative Islamic parties), are just that—tiny.

The opposition press and individual notables of the opposition are outspoken and can be very critical of the regime and its perceived shortcomings; organized interest groups—now commonly referred to as NGOs or civil society organizations—are growing in number, activity, and expertise.[18] However, they do not produce much in the way of a public opinion or public action that can significantly constrain or affect the government. Large protests and demonstrations are still rare in Yemen, partly because there is little tradition of public protest and, until recently, the organizational and material infrastructure for protest has been lacking.

Compared to the two Yemens in the 1970s and 1980s, and to many other countries, there is little physical repression—arbitrary jailing, torture, execution, and disappearance—in today's Yemen. This may, in part, be so because the regime is now able to resort to more subtle means of eliciting or discouraging certain actions. Moreover, most Yemenis have remained passive and accepting in the face of the obvious shortcomings of their government and its failure to meet expectations, which in any case have tended to be low.

The trappings and beginnings of democracy notwithstanding, the Republic of Yemen is best described as an oligarchy, an example of rule by the few. Most of the relatively small number of persons and families who get the most of what there is to get—be it political power, economic well-being, good health, or high social status—come from the northern highlands of old North Yemen. They have strong tribal or military (or security) connections, or both. To the military-tribal complex of the late 1960s and 1970s was added a northern commercial-business element after 1980.[19] Political power was increasingly concentrated in the hands of these sheikhs, officers, and northern businessmen in the 1980s, a trend that accelerated after the war of secession in 1994 eliminated or weakened politicians from the old South Yemen and their party, the YSP.[20] Their tribal and military or security positions and connections are more important than the offices or titles they have in government or the GPC.

Late in the 1980s—the decade in which the current regime crystallized and took form—Yemen for the first time became the recipient of oil revenues as well as increased economic assistance from abroad. The state quickly became the principal source of wealth and private gain for a well-placed and fortunate few. The transformation of the republican state into such a source—a role the relatively poor imamate had not played—began when significant amounts of aid began to flow into the YAR in the mid-1970s.[21] Oil revenues arrived in the late 1980s.

As a result, the Yemeni system has evolved largely into a special variant of oligarchy: a kleptocracy—that is, a government of, by, and for the thieves.[22] The occupants of the key government posts and offices through which flow revenues and development aid have been able to enrich themselves, usually at the expense of policy goals. The oligarchs have used their positions in the state—their "profit centers"—to extract a price for the rendering of services or granting of permissions, thereby increasing the cost of government and development.[23] The associates, friends, and relatives of occupants of key posts and offices are also enriched in this manner, the reaping of riches being a matter of connection as well as location.

Graft, bribery, and other forms of thievery pervade the system at all levels of a steep-sided pyramid of patronage.[24] At the broad base of this pyramid are the hundreds of thousands of employees of the government and the military who are paid extremely low salaries and have to take petty bribes—"eat money"—in order barely to make ends meet. Perhaps the most visible measures of corruption toward the top of the pyramid are the growing number of high-end SUVs and new villas—some virtual castles—on the outskirts of Sanaa, most of which are owned by high government officials receiving modest salaries.

The social structure and political culture of the kleptocratic state is new to Yemen. In centuries past, the tribes and their sheikhs enjoyed freedom on the periphery at the expense of relative wealth at the center, in the towns and cities—that is, they paid a hefty price in terms of comfort for their freedom. Now, the sheikhs have both affluence and a new kind of freedom—as well as continuing autonomy on the periphery—by virtue of the power and access afforded by their positions and connections at the center. In a way unimaginable in 1948, when they literally looted the city of Sanaa, the sheikhs have been participating in the virtual serial sacking of Sanaa since the late 1970s.

A new aristocracy of sheikhs, officers, and businessmen has been born with its own set of motives and values. Its newness is masked by a pervasive, unquestioning sense of entitlement. The second generation of this aristocracy is now slipping silently into key positions and is even more sure and less questioning of its entitlement.[25] This small part of the total population is on the take, and without apology; an even smaller part senses that this state of affairs cannot last much longer, and that it must get as much as it can while the getting is still good. These are the kleptocrats of contemporary Yemen. They regard oil revenues and aid from donors in terms of, first, enrichment of self and associates, and only second, if at all, in terms of public policy and the public good.[26]

Yemen also suffers from what might be described as "arrested statehood," a legacy of the recent political history of North Yemen. The Hamid al-Din imamate, in place from the early twentieth century until the 1962 revolution, did not approximate Weber's classic definition of a state.[27] It did not have a monopoly on the legitimate use of violence in its territory, whether for the purpose of maintaining internal order and providing defense or for the purpose of realizing other goals; nor did the imamate have instruments of coercion—army and police—that were subservient and readily available for use in its pursuit of order, defense, and other goals. In this regard, the old description of the Hashid and Bakil tribal confederations as "the wings of the imamate" is suggestive. The major tribes and their leaders conceived of themselves, and were conceived by others, as outside—not in or under the imamate, not subject to or "subjects" of it. They often acted accordingly, and were able to use their armed tribesmen sometimes to support and protect the imamate and sometimes to contain or oppose it in defense of perceived tribal interests.

North Yemen's first generation of modernists and republicans was prevented by events after the 1962 revolution from creating the modern state to which they aspired.[28] The several-year civil war between the republicans and the royalists diverted the modernists from the task of state building; the Egyptians, who intervened on the side of the republic, ended up doing much of whatever state building occurred, as well as most of the fighting. In 1968, the breaking of the royalist siege of Sanaa determined that the republic, not the imamate, would prevail. However, the Sanaa mutiny that followed quickly on the siege determined that the republic would be a conservative one. It would preserve much of the traditional order, political as well as socio-cultural; in particular, it would ensure a prominent role for tribal leaders and the tribal system. The failure of Ibrahim al-Hamdi's brief attempt at modern state building and development from 1974 to his assassination in 1977 paved the way for the formation in 1978 of the regime headed by Salih.[29] During the 1980s, that regime coalesced into its current form.

As a result, the Republic of Yemen today is in vital ways more like the old imamate than like a modern state. Even in 2005, the state was severely limited in terms of what it had the power and authority to do and where it could do it. An incident in late 2003 illustrates the generally accepted limits of state power and authority as they apply to the tribes in their territories. On this occasion, state security forces intervened for the first time in Marib province in a dispute between two tribes. They became involved after a member of one tribe was killed by a member of the other. When the security forces chased and killed one of the escaping tribesmen, his fellow tribesmen killed three of the security officers. Leaders from *both* tribes expressed outrage at this interference by the state in "tribal affairs." "The government should not have interfered," said a prominent sheikh. "We have ways to settle our disputes and this loss of life is merely a result of the government's interference. . . . We have our own rules . . . and our own ways to deal with things and we want the government to stay out of trouble."[30] This episode, one of dozens if not hundreds, tells much about the state and its lack of a monopoly of the legitimate use of violence in its territory.

The arrested statehood of the YAR and now the Republic of Yemen is both cause and effect of the predominantly tribal-military regime that remains firmly in place today. It has made possible both the maintenance of this group in power for a quarter-century and the beginning of a succession to its second generation. In turn, this group has used its power to oppose and minimize further efforts at state building, especially those that require the reining in of rampant corruption and incompetence.

In combination, the kleptocratic and arrested natures of the Yemeni state raise big questions. Can a regime driven by such motives and values, and a state limited as to how far and deep it can reach, do what has to be done to assure a country's survival in an increasingly globalized world? Can it, at the same time, meet the domestic demands and expectations for a better life for this and future generations? In short, does it have the will and capacity to adopt and implement quickly major political and socioeconomic reforms? If not, can such a regime, of its own volition or under pressure from others, acquire appropriate motives and values, even if only for the sake of survival, and appropriately increase and redirect the capacities of the state?

Yemeni Society and Economy: Crisis, Reform, and Crisis

Many North Yemenis regard the period from the mid-1970s through the 1980s as their halcyon years, the best of times in living memory. Remittance money was flooding into the country from the more than 800,000 Yemenis working abroad, mostly in Saudi Arabia. Because of the labor shortage at home resulting from this emigration, nearly anyone who wanted to work could find a job, and wages in the cities and the countryside were pushed up to new levels. Remittances were distributed widely—as if sprinkled from above—with some going directly or indirectly to nearly all families in all parts of the country; only a little passed through the hands of gatekeepers in the state or the banks. People possessed money for consumer products new to Yemen. Returning workers or recipients of remittances had the capital to add a second story to their stone houses, buy a four-wheel-drive Toyota to use as a taxi, or open a new store or shop. Local development associations mixed remittances with other funds to build thousands of feeder roads, schools, clinics, and cisterns.

At end of this period, in the late 1980s, oil in North Yemen began to gush, with the promise of much more to come; and the country continued to be the beneficiary of much economic aid from a wide range of sources. Yemenis were upbeat and hopeful.[31] To top things off, Yemeni unification and the creation of the Republic of Yemen in 1990 held out the prospect of a stronger and more prosperous Yemen.

These expectations came tumbling down in a matter of months with Iraq's occupation of Kuwait in August 1990 and the onset of the first Gulf crisis and war. The failure of the just-created Republic of Yemen to join the U.S.- and Saudi-led coalition against Iraq prompted the United States, Saudi Arabia, and most of the Arab Gulf States to drastically reduce relations with Yemen and sever virtually all economic assistance.[32] In just a few months, Yemen went from being hailed as the new embodiment of the old dream of Arab unity to being an outcast in the eyes of much of the Arab world. In the most punishing act, Saudi Arabia savaged Yemen's economy by expelling several hundred thousand workers, thereby both denying Yemen the remittances upon which it had become dependent and creating for the first time a massive unemployment problem. The virtual end of the remittance system and the high costs of unification and the war of secession in 1994 were the one-two punches that devastated the Yemeni economy. By late 1994, the economy was in free fall and well on its way to becoming fragile, as then structured, despite modest oil revenues.

It would be hard to exaggerate the grimness of Yemen's situation and prospects in the mid-1990s. The gross domestic product (GDP) for 1995 was less that half its size in 1990; the value of the Yemeni riyal continued a precipitous decline, raising the cost of goods, especially needed imports. Because of massive unemployment and loss of remittances, gross inequality and abject poverty increased at alarming rates throughout Yemen. In the shrunken economy, urban workers, especially the new middle class, were quickly pauperized; the modern institutions in which they worked, and in which they had come to place their hopes for a better future, were hollowed out.[33] Only the privileged few had access by family or position to a constant or growing share of the smaller economic pie and the hidden economy. As much of modern Yemen withered, new villas continued to grow like weeds in Sanaa's new suburbs.

Yemen in 1995 provided a textbook case of a country in economic crisis, requiring immediate triage and then a regimen of long-term reform. In mid-year, the Salih regime agreed with the International Monetary Fund (IMF) and the World Bank that Yemen required economic stabilization followed by a multifaceted program of structural reforms. Belt tightening and other sacrifices required of the Yemeni people would, moreover, soon produce an economic environment that would attract from abroad the investment needed to create jobs, enterprise, and wealth.

It was also understood at the time that it would be necessary for Yemen to reorder its regional affairs so as to create an external environment safe for foreign investment, a tall order given the lasting effects of the first Gulf crisis and war. As it turned out, in the second half of the 1990s Yemen did deal in a statesmanlike way with two regional crises that, if left unresolved, could have scared investors away. Although it took the Yemenis by surprise, armed conflict in 1995 with newly independent Eritrea over claims to a group of Red Sea islands was resolved rather quickly and amicably, by submitting the dispute to the World Court. Far more significant was the old dispute with Saudi Arabia over their long unmarked border, very recently the object of strong words and even armed exchanges. After protracted negotiations, this thorn in the side of Saudi-Yemeni relations finally was removed in 2000 with an agreement demarcating the entire border. More generally, Yemen worked hard over the second half of the 1990s to undo the negative effects of the first Gulf crisis and the internal war of secession on relations with Saudi Arabia and the Arab Gulf mini-states. Unfortunately, a few months after the border agreement with the Saudis was signed, suicide bombers slammed their boat into the destroyer USS *Cole* in the port of Aden, thereby dramatically challenging the investor-friendly regional image of Yemen.

The sequence of events after mid-1995 regarding Yemen's collaboration with the IMF/World Bank on domestic reform followed very closely the script of the best-case scenario. Indeed, major events through the first half of 1997 seemed orchestrated by the Salih regime, the IMF/World Bank, the European Union (EU), and Japan to portray Yemen in the best possible light.[34] From the outset, the relationship between the Salih regime and the two international bodies was collaborative, not adversarial. The regime for the most part stuck to its agreements, and the IMF and the World Bank provided promised aid and were understanding of Yemen's political problems and the need for "social safety net" projects for those least able to bear the burden and pain of the reforms.[35]

In late 1995 and 1996, the Salih regime put in place stabilization measures and an initial set of structural reforms designed to, among other things, bring inflation under control.[36] The several exchange rates for the Yemeni riyal were unified and allowed to float.[37] The budget deficit was narrowed through a combination of spending restraints and increased oil revenues; imports were suppressed, with the result that the current accounts situation improved and foreign exchange reserves rose considerably. In late 1996, the regime took a cautious first step toward lifting state subsidies of essential goods. It took further steps to cut these subsidies in 1997 and 1998.[38] In return, the IMF and the World Bank lent Yemen roughly U.S. $1 billion to support reform projects; in addition, they were among the sponsors and organizers of two donors conferences that yielded pledges of another $2 billion in aid. An IMF pledge of financial support paved the way for a big reduction in Yemen's foreign debt by the Paris Club of creditor nations.

Although other efforts to revive and develop the Yemeni economy gained momentum into 1998, the IMF/World Bank structural reform program faltered in late 1997.[39] Political problems and a sharp decline in oil revenues were major culprits. The government became hopelessly deadlocked in late

1997 and resigned in early 1998; from the outset, in mid-1998, its successor ran into serious resistance in its effort at reform.[40] Oil prices, which had held fairly steady at about $20 per barrel for some years, plunged in 1998 to $10 per barrel. That decline in revenues greatly limited the ability of the government to soften the painful effects of the reforms through development and social spending, and caused widespread unrest.[41]

A new IMF/World Bank agreement negotiated in 2000 was demanding, and called for the broadening and deepening of reforms in exchange for new credits worth hundreds of millions of dollars. All subsidies for essential goods were to be lifted, despite the evidence that the hardships endured by most of the population over much of the 1990s were not triggering much new investment and job-creation.[42] Moreover, the required downsizing of the civil service and the privatization of bloated public corporations meant the loss of jobs for many Yemenis.

Perhaps more important, the new reforms reached beyond the poor and the working class and directly touched some of the prerogatives and benefits of the privileged and highly placed. Among them were measures designed to fight corruption, increase transparency in government, make the courts fairer and more efficient, and reform the banking and financial sectors. For many of the well off, the reforms were getting too close for comfort; many lost whatever appetite they had for reform as the process began to threaten their interests.

After the good start in 1995–1997, the program of structural reforms had by 2001 virtually been abandoned. Most of the measures in the agreement of 2000 were not implemented or were done so partially and half-heartedly. Reforms of the judiciary and the civil service lagged, and rampant corruption in the public and private sectors was barely addressed, except verbally. Although the bombing of the USS *Cole* in 2000 and the attacks of September 11, 2001, caused the reforms to be upstaged by the issue of transnational revolutionary Islam and terror, the reform program had in fact already collapsed.

The Salih regime seemed by 2001 to have suffered a failure of will and a decline in its capacity to effect structural reform. Since then it has resisted IMF/World Bank pressure to revive the process. In 2004, these bodies publicly expressed their growing impatience and displeasure with Yemen, particularly regarding its failure to completely lift subsidies for petroleum products and to implement civil service reforms designed to address corruption and inefficiency. These criticisms were accompanied by not-so-veiled warnings that continued aid remained contingent on Yemen keeping its part of the old bargain on reform. A few months later, the Salih regime, caving in to domestic political pressure and fear of popular unrest, postponed the elimination of diesel fuel subsidies and the imposition of a sales tax. In announcing the delay on subsidies until "our situation improves," President Salih put himself between the people and the IMF and the World Bank and said that it was "a sovereign issue."[43]

In mid-2004, the outgoing head of the United Nations Development Program noted that Yemen's dependence on oil revenues inflated by high oil prices was made more dangerous by "signs of increasing budget deficits and, indeed, initial signs of fiscal difficulties." He emphasized that the government in Yemen suffered from an absence of transparency and from pervasive corruption. "A pessimistic scenario will include a situation whereby corruption not only continues but also expands, further taking resources away from development."[44]

Major development projects also failed to move forward rapidly or to live up to expectations after 2001. Yemen was told in the mid-1990s that the window for the development of its significant natural gas reserves was small; other producers—for example, Qatar and Oman—were pushing ahead to develop their reserves and to secure the long-term marketing agreements required to secure financing. Fighting between two groups of Yemeni politicians, each with its preferred multinational gas developer as client, caused one delay after another, with the result that the window closed and the development of Yemen's gas was shelved sometime around 2001. This fact is important, because timely exploitation of Yemen's gas would more than make up for the decline in oil output—and revenues—expected in the near future.

An Aden free zone and container port was touted in the early 1990s as Yemen's most important development project. It promised to create thousands of jobs and much wealth.[45] Up and running in 2000 after numerous delays, the project soon fell far short of expectations. True, much of the problem resulted from soaring insurance costs and the drop in business in the port of Aden following the bombings of the USS *Cole* in 2000 and the French tanker *Limburg* in 2002. Another big part of the problem apparently was bad planning, mismanagement, and corruption. Similarly, Yemen lost considerable time and money regarding the increase of refinery capacity that had promised both to lower the import of petroleum products and to capture some of the added value coming from downstream petroleum activities. Endless debate focused on whether the emphasis should be on upgrading and expanding the old Aden refinery or on the construction of new facilities, and on whether the Aden refinery should be privatized. Little progress has since been made on resolving these matters.

The failure to attract investment from abroad during these years is not explained primarily in terms of investors being alarmed by security issues after the USS *Cole* incident and 9/11, especially in the case of potential Yemeni investors, at home as well as abroad. Wealthy Yemenis who had jumped in early, especially those with origins in Wadi Hadhramawt, quickly retreated because of bad personal experiences and other tales of woe. Many potential foreign investors decided that the risks were too great relative to potential gains, based partly on a number of well-publicized cases of corruption, nepotism, and political favoritism. It was widely understood that Procter & Gamble, a highly visible foreign manufacturer, had decided to end production in Yemen after concluding that the high costs of corruption were greater than the generous tax relief and abatements provided by the government. Also widely known is the story of how the son of a leading sheikh virtually stole a wealthy Egyptian investor's large share in one of Yemen's two cell phone companies; it was said that the Egyptian could not get a fair hearing in Yemen's courts. There was also the tale of the Saudi investor who, after twice buying and losing title to the same agricultural land in Yemen, was unable to recover his money despite a personal request by Crown Prince Abdullah of Saudi Arabia that President Salih intervene. Embarrassed by the president's failure, the crown prince reimbursed his subject but presumably then had little good to say about investing in Yemen.

As a result of what happened—or, as often, what did not happen—over the decade 1995–2004, Yemen's economy and society was largely dysfunctional by 2005. The problems and their causes are endemic and structural, not cyclical, and they have their origins in events at the beginning of the 1990s. Yemen's economy and society were rendered nonviable in 1994, were subjected to the first stages of a program of reform in the second half of the 1990s, and have again gradually become more problematical as the later stages of that program were delayed, diluted, or discarded. The economy has been bouncing along on the bottom of a low range of output and performance.

As of the end of 2004, the Yemeni economy was barely creating enough jobs and economic enterprise to keep up with a very high population growth rate of 3.8 percent. The unemployment rate has held persistently at about 40 percent, as have the percentages of those malnourished and those below the poverty line.[46] The middle class has probably shrunk further and its pauperization continues relentlessly; at the same time, the gap between the rich few and the many poor has grown much wider, and more visibly so. On the personal level, most people are desperately just trying to make ends meet; they are being ground down and worn out by the effort, and many openly lack any hope for the future. Institutionally, education and health systems are increasingly weakened, and most other social services have almost ceased to exist. The quality of education has declined up to and through the university level, and illiteracy remains very high, especially in rural areas and among women; medical services are in short supply and of poor quality. In short, most institutions have decayed—having been hollowed out and starved of cash. For most Yemenis, the past decade has been one of much pain and no gain.

In addition, the poorly performing Yemeni economy is vulnerable. It is dangerously dependent on oil revenues and on the economic aid and other forms of assistance it receives from the IMF and World Bank, as well as from the many donors who take their lead from those two bodies. The flow of external aid from most donors would largely dry up if, in exasperation, the IMF and the World Bank were to judge Yemen unworthy of further support, a prospect that was hinted at twice in early 2004. More worrisome, since the mid-1990s the condition of the Yemeni economy has been determined almost solely by wide fluctuations in oil revenues. These revenues are increasingly less a function of Yemen's oil production, which has leveled off and is beginning to decline, than of the price per barrel, which is determined by forces over which Yemen has no control. The flipside of life on $50 a barrel oil is life on $20 or even $10 a barrel oil, and the recent past suggests that such quick swings are the rule rather than the exception.[47] The impact of a collapse in oil prices on discretionary social spending, budget deficits, the balance of payments, and economic activity in general, not to mention the quality of life and general welfare, would be wrenching.

The persistently poor performance of the Yemeni economy urgently demands action by the Salih regime.[48] Can Yemen's kleptocrats and its arrested statehood provide the will and capacity needed quickly to effect much-needed, long-deferred socioeconomic reforms? If they have not done so over the past several years, after a good start in the mid-1990s, what reason is there to believe that they can or will do so now? Unfortunately, failure to implement the reforms within a few or several years will undermine the regime and the political system. It will drain away support, legitimacy, and stability, risking Yemen's becoming a failed state. This result would increase the chance of Yemen sliding into anarchy (like Somalia), civil war (like Lebanon), or a revolutionary situation (like Afghanistan). As of 2005, the Republic of Yemen is a fragile state that is failing, and it could easily become a failed state in the very near future.[49]

The unraveling of the Yemeni state and political system could be sudden, given the still-rising levels of anger and despair born of a decade of unfulfilled expectations, as well as the conditional nature of the regime's support and legitimacy.[50] Indeed, the Republic of Yemen is like a rubber band or balloon that has been stretched over time to a surprising degree, only suddenly to reach a breaking point.[51] Yemen's political system at mid-decade is probably only several years from such a point. Widespread popular protests and demonstrations are more likely today than even a decade ago, both because of recent experience with these political forms and because of the further development of the organizational and material infrastructure of popular protest. At the same time, popular protest could easily get out of control and escalate in magnitude and violence, because neither Yemeni protesters nor the security forces have had enough experience to know how to direct or contain this type of civil action. Popular opposition to the lifting of subsidies in 1998 led to demonstrations and riots that, in turn, triggered "police riots"—and many injuries and deaths.

The Salih regime is not likely to be overturned or voted out of office during the next several years. Accordingly, to avoid the slide into anarchy, civil war, or revolution, it must reform—or rather, reconstitute—itself so as to acquire the will and capacity to adopt the social and economic reforms required to make Yemen viable. In an act of enlightened self-interest, the top leadership must take the risks involved in both stripping itself of those elements unwilling or unable to accept major reform and adding to the ruling coalition those elements of the modernist middle-class opposition who are committed to the reforms upon which the future of Yemen depends. For their part, major elements of the currently weak and divided modernist middle-class opposition must unite organizationally and programmatically to create a credible political force. The watchword for both the enlightened members of the Salih regime and the modernist middle class must be *urgency*.

The likelihood that a sense of urgency will prevail and that major action will be taken soon is uncertain. The likely alternative is Yemen's slide into anarchy, civil war, or revolution. Yemen would thus become vulnerable to transnational revolutionary Islam and, at the very least, become an unreliable ally in the effort against terrorism.[52]

Yemen and Transnational Revolutionary Islam

The fact that Yemen remained one of the most uniformly conservative and traditional Islamic countries in the world into the last third of the twentieth century probably inhibited the growth of revolutionary political Islam—and partly immunized Yemen against it. In any case, at least well into the 1970s, Islam in Yemen was assumed to be a given. It did not imply an aggressively defensive posture.[53] This attitude seemed to foster a moderate, nonideological brand of Islam even among those who took the faith very seriously and put it at the center of their lives.

Modern political Islam came to North Yemen in 1947, when an agent of the Muslim Brotherhood (the Ikhwan), the religio-political organization founded in Egypt a decade earlier, visited Yemen. The Ikhwan took root in Yemen and survived into the more modern republican era that began in 1962. Due to its organization and grassroots support, the Ikhwan was regarded as the key political competitor by both the al-Hamdi and the Salih regimes from the mid-1970s onward. In 1990, with unification and the perceived threat of the south's Marxist YSP, the Reform Grouping (Islah) was created. A party of seemingly strange bedfellows, the northern tribes and a spectrum of Islamic elements, Islah was headed by Abdullah ibn Husayn al-Ahmar, Yemen's most powerful sheikh of sheikhs, and Abd al-Majid al-Zandani, well known as the head of the Ikhwan in the 1970s. As with the Ikhwan during the previous two decades, Islah has come to be regarded as the most formidable challenge to the Salih regime since the mid-1990s, again, largely because of its organization, its grassroots support, and the social and education services that it provides.

Unlike in Saudi Arabia, support for and promotion of Islamic fundamentalism were never pillars of the foreign and domestic policies of the YAR or, most certainly, the PDRY, in the last third of the twentieth century. Nonetheless, North Yemen was caught in the wake of its conservative neighbor's use of Islam for political purposes since the 1960s. First, the Saudis fostered and funded Islam as a way of influencing, if not controlling, the YAR in the 1970s and 1980s; they built and staffed hundreds of mosques and schools that espoused the export version of Wahhabism, their fundamentalist brand of Islam. Second, and more important, the Saudis in the 1980s recruited many Yemenis to be leaders and followers in the Islamic struggle in Afghanistan against the armed forces of the Soviet Union. A disproportionately large number of Yemenis participated in this Saudi- and U.S.-supported armed struggle, which unintentionally served as the incubator for the transnational revolutionary political Islam so prevalent by 1990.[54]

When Soviet forces withdrew and fighting subsided at the end of the 1980s, many of the militant chickens came home to roost. Many radicalized and battle-hardened Yemeni "Afghani Arabs" streamed back into Yemen; many of their colleagues from Egypt, Algeria, Jordan, and elsewhere, often unable to return their own countries for political reasons, found sanctuary in Yemen due to its porous borders and large areas beyond the control of the government. In the early 1990s, many of these veterans of the struggle in Afghanistan, even some of the non-Yemenis, got caught up in the politics of both the first Gulf

War and Yemeni unification, the former convincing them that the United States and Saudi Arabia, not the defunct Soviet Union, were the major enemies of Islam. As relations between the two main parties to Yemeni unification became increasingly conflictual after 1991, the political and military leaders around President Salih folded many of the returnees from Afghanistan into units of "their" army and turned a blind eye to their killing of southern politicians and officials. Many of the returnees participated in the war of secession in 1994 on the side of unity and the Republic of Yemen. Doing so placed the Salih regime in their debt. In the mid-1990s, when the regime balked at some of the militants' demands, there were battles between them and the security forces. Many of the militants had also found their way into a new organization, the Yemeni Islamic Jihad.

Through the mid-1990s, the Salih regime, when it could not ignore militant political Islam, treated it largely as a troublesome domestic matter. At the time, it had a lot of seemingly more important and immediate matters on its political plate. In particular, it remained preoccupied with unification and its problems, as it had been when Iraq entered Kuwait several years earlier.

The Goldmur Hotel bombing in Aden captures much of the tone of the period. In the last days of 1992, this small hotel was bombed, causing two deaths. A similar attempt to bomb the larger Aden Hotel was foiled in the course of its execution. These incidents, as well as what quickly followed, indicated—at least in hindsight—that the United States had become a target of terrorism by transnational revolutionary Islam, that Yemen had become a venue for the activities of this growing movement, and that the movement and efforts to deal with it were deeply intertwined with the domestic politics of the new Republic of Yemen. The acts against the hotels by militant Islamists targeted a handful of American military personnel and were meant to hamper U.S. relief efforts in nearby Somalia, as well as to protest against the Republic of Yemen's logistical support of those efforts. In early 1993, Yemeni security forces responded with the siege of a mountain redoubt and the arrest of Tarik al-Fadhli, an Afghani Arab who was also heir to one of the sultanates abolished nearly three decades earlier by newly independent South Yemen. Al-Fadhli's subsequent "escape" was followed by his and his followers' co-optation by the Salih regime. Al-Fadhli had been a leader of the Yemeni Islamic Jihad, and some of those who refused to go over to the regime with him soon became the backbone of another organization, the Aden-Abyan Islamic Army. The Salih regime and some of al-Fadhli's former colleagues quietly waged a low-intensity fight against each other during the mid-1990s, especially in Abyan province. Still, the threads connecting militant Islamists in Yemen, the Salih regime, and the United States to the Goldmur incident were not so evident at the time; they were to become stronger, tighter, and more apparent in just a few years.

U.S.-Yemeni Relations from 1970 to the Present

During the 1970s and 1980s, U.S. policy toward the YAR was little more than an addendum to its policy toward Saudi Arabia; its policy toward the PDRY, regarded as a satellite of the Soviet Union, like Cuba, was very hostile and unforgiving. Simply put, because of its overriding concern for Saudi Arabia and its oil, the United States urged the YAR to do what the Saudis wanted.[55] Nevertheless, the YAR did gain some leverage over the United States when the cold war revived at the end of the 1970s and made North Yemen a bulwark against the PDRY, the Soviet Union's surrogate on the Arabian Peninsula.[56] At the same time, by playing the two superpowers off against each other, the YAR was able to secure considerable economic and military aid from both sides. Still, it was almost always Saudi Arabia that was on the United States' mind, not the YAR or the PDRY.

In the second half of the 1980s, the United States began to look upon the YAR more favorably, for two reasons. First, the discovery by a Texas-based company of then-unknown quantities of oil gave the United States a material stake, possibly a big one, in North Yemen. Second, the start of the Yemeni unification process promised to make the PDRY disappear and to dilute the influence of its Marxist leaders, as well as to provide greater political stability on the corner of the Arabian Peninsula sandwiched between Saudi Arabia and the countries of the Horn of Africa.[57]

In late 1990, however, U.S. policy toward the just-created Republic of Yemen suddenly turned nearly 180 degrees with the failure of Yemen to join the U.S.- and Saudi-led coalition against Iraq's occupation of Kuwait. In November, after joining Cuba in voting against the UN Security Council's "all necessary means" resolution against Iraq, Yemen's UN ambassador was told by a U.S. assistant secretary of state that it had been the most expensive vote he would ever cast. Shortly thereafter, the United States drastically reduced relations with Yemen and suspended virtually all assistance.

U.S. relations with Yemen began to thaw during the short war of secession in mid-1994. Going against Saudi wishes, the United States, after some wavering and ambiguity, quietly came down on the side of a unified Yemen. Slow to renew bilateral ties, it did put its support behind the IMF/World Bank package of reforms adopted by Yemen in 1995. At about the same time, and as something of a first, the United States publicly chided Saudi Arabia for its heavy-handed attempt to pressure foreign oil companies to refrain from activity in the area adjacent to the long-disputed border between Yemen and Saudi Arabia. The revival of strategic political-military ties began modestly in 1997 with a training program in mine removal, limited joint military exercises, and the refueling of U.S. warships in Aden. In early 2000, the United States said publicly that it would be happy to use its good offices to help Yemen and Saudi Arabia to settle their border dispute. Still, the rebuilding of relations between the United States and the Republic of Yemen meandered, and direct material aid remained modest. Yemen was simply not high on the U.S. list of priorities in the post–cold war world of the mid-1990s.

Before the late 1990s, Yemen did not have to follow the U.S. lead on the issue of transnational revolutionary Islam and terrorism because the United States was not as yet doing much leading on this subject, especially as it applied to Yemen.[58] Two events caused the United States to take the lead on this issue and also alerted the Salih regime that the issue was a threat to both its domestic politics and its external relations, especially with the United States: the bizarre sequence resulting in the death of four tourists taken hostage by the Aden-Abyan Islamic Army in late 1998; and, more salient, the bombing of the USS *Cole* in 2000, which cost seventeen American lives and left a gaping hole in the destroyer's side.[59]

It was the destruction of the twin towers of the World Trade Center on September 11, 2001, that made the effort against transnational revolutionary Islam and terrorism *the* issue for U.S. external relations and made Osama bin Laden and Al Qaeda the embodiments of those evils. Three events in 2002 further underlined the linkage between these evils on the one hand, and Yemen on the other: (1) the October suicide bombing of the French oil tanker *Limburg* off the southern coast of Yemen; (2) the assassination about three months later of Jarullah Omar, Yemen's leading secular socialist thinker-activist, by an Islamic militant; and (3) the murder two days later of three American medical missionaries by another militant, a colleague of the first, at their hospital in rural Yemen.[60]

By this time, the United States and the Republic of Yemen were acting together on this linkage and U.S. aid, economic and especially military, revived significantly. About a month after the bombing of the *Limburg*, a Yemeni leader of Al Qaeda named Qaid Salim Talib Sinan al-Harithi was killed near Marib by a Hellfire missile. The missile was fired by U.S. forces from an unmanned U.S. Predator aircraft in Yemeni airspace but controlled from Djibouti, apparently with the consent of the Yemeni government.

With the USS *Cole* bombing and then 9/11, the dynamic of U.S.-Yemeni relations became, on the one hand, U.S. insistence on Yemeni help in the effort against transnational revolutionary Islam, as defined by the United States; and on the other, Yemen's attempt to do as much as politically possible to meet U.S. requests for help.[61] A major motive of Yemen at this time was the desire to avoid a repeat of the punishment meted out by the United States for its stand during the first Gulf crisis, a decade earlier.[62] When Salih visited Washington, D.C., shortly after 9/11, he is said to have assured President Bush of his commitment to fight terrorism. He acted on this assurance in a major way in late 2001, and with disastrous results. When he sent troops to Marib to capture al-Harithi, the Islamist later killed by the United States with a Hellfire missile, a large number of his troops were killed and wounded by tribesmen. Nevertheless, the Salih regime has continued to step up its effort against militant Islamists in Yemen, most notably by arresting many alleged militants and placing some of them on trial.[63]

The new relationship between the United States and Yemen has its rough spots. The two have differed over how much Yemen can do and how it should do it. They have also differed over what the United States has said and done regarding both the effort against transnational revolutionary Islam and other issues sensitive to or of special concern to either or both parties.

The USS *Cole* investigation by the United States and Yemen provided the paradigm. The Yemeni government, which agreed that Al Qaeda was behind the bombing, wanted to execute the jailed alleged participants, and to stop at that; the United States, and, especially FBI investigators, wanted to continue the investigation until all the dots were connected back to bin Laden and Al Qaeda in Afghanistan. The problem was that people in high places in Yemen suspected or knew that the dots would come close to other persons in high places in Yemen. The Yemenis won, in part because U.S. diplomats in Sanaa intervened on their side against the FBI.[64] Nevertheless, the two countries sparred for two more years over the questions of when the accused would be tried and whether they would be tried separately or with the group accused of the *Limburg* tanker bombing. After bad feelings and acrimony, these issues were more or less resolved. The two groups were tried separately in 2004, and six of the convicted *Cole* defendants were sentenced—two of them, one Saudi and one Yemeni, to death.

Since 9/11, the Salih regime has had difficulty explaining or justifying to the United States its relationship—and those of its individual leaders and friends—to militant Islamists in the 1980s or even in the early 1990s. This difficulty arises partly because the Islamic revivalism of 1980 and earlier was not the political Islam of 1990 and later. As a result of the events of the 1980s, especially in Afghanistan, much of the earlier local or "national" Islamic revivalism, both nonpolitical and political, morphed after 1990 into, among other things, transnational revolutionary Islam; just as political Islam changed over time, so too did the Islamic political orientations of prominent Yemenis. Abd al-Majid al-Zandani, co-leader of Islah, has covered the spectrum of political Islam and is hard to label today; whatever he is now, many inside and outside the regime find him too close to the regime for comfort—and too influential.

Ali Muhsin, the president's half brother and arguably both his chief ally and his chief rival in the regime, looks suspect to some: he was close to some of the militant Islamists in the early 1990s and made good use of them during the political crises and war of secession from 1992 to 1994. Some important figures who were militants in the early 1990s no longer are, as can be seen in the case of al-Fadhli. Conversely, some notables who have in recent years become militants were not so in the past, as illustrated by Sheikh Husayn Badr Eddine al-Huthi, the leader of a militant Islamic uprising in the north of Yemen who was killed in 2004 after a bloody three-month fight with government forces. Years earlier, al-Huthi had been a founder of the conservative al-Haq Party and a member of parliament.[65]

The Salih regime has often tried to square the circle—that is, to satisfy the United States at the same time as answering its supporters at home, as well as its secular and Islamist opponents and critics. When in doubt or caught in a dilemma, the regime has usually chosen to risk angering the United States rather than its domestic audiences. It has tried to do what the United States wants done, but in a way that is politically palatable at home. For example, it has vigorously pursued and jailed suspected Islamic militants and then, since 2003, run them through a re-education program—a "dialogue program"—after which most of them have been granted amnesty and often put on the military payroll in no-show positions. Several hundred detainees had been processed in this fashion by late 2004, much to the skepticism and alarm of the United States.[66] Another use of soft power has involved buying off the tribal sheikhs who previously sheltered suspected Islamists, thereby avoiding military operations that are costly in terms of money and lives—and political capital. Using these and more strenuous methods, the government in 2004 claimed to have dismantled 90 percent of Al Qaeda's cells and network in Yemen, an estimate generally greeted with skepticism.[67]

Many Yemenis have grievances against the United States, including those who support the effort against transnational revolutionary Islam. The tone and content of the U.S.'s announcement of its Israeli-like take-out of al-Harithi embarrassed and angered the government and many informed Yemenis. After all, al-Harithi was Yemeni and was killed by a rocket fired from an American drone deep in Yemen's sovereign airspace.

The detention of many Yemenis since 2001 or 2002 at the U.S. military prison in Guantanamo, Cuba, without charges, hearings, or access to attorneys, has been an affront to the Yemeni government and hard to explain to an angry public. Moreover, in 2003 and 2004, there were the arrests—sometimes by means regarded as illegal or otherwise inappropriate—of high-profile and highly esteemed Muslim leaders from Yemen.[68] There are also the widely publicized charges by the U.S. Treasury Department that Abd al-Majid al-Zandani, the well-known spiritual leader of the Islah party and head of al-Iman University, was involved in financing the recruitment and arming of terrorist groups—charges condemned at the highest levels in Yemen.[69]

The U.S. invasion and occupation of Iraq in 2003 has been a political nightmare for the Salih regime. The president and government have tried heroically but with difficulty to distinguish between the U.S. action in Iraq and the effort against transnational revolutionary Islam. In no uncertain terms, they have opposed the former and supported the latter. The regime's efforts have not been helped by the constant effort of the Bush administration to equate the two and to make Iraq the main battleground against militant Islam and its use of terror. Another problem has been the United States' halfhearted support for the new Afghan government in Kabul, in contrast to its continuing pursuit of bin Laden and the Taliban in the countryside. Finally, and of great concern to most Yemenis, there is the United States' apparent siding with Israel and the Sharon government against Palestinians, especially since 2001.

Nevertheless, relations between the United States and the Republic of Yemen in early 2005 were good and getting better. For the immediate future at least, U.S. military and economic aid is being exchanged for more Yemeni support and participation in the effort against transnational revolutionary Islam and terrorism.[70] In 2005, a stream of senior visitors arrived from CENTCOM, the Defense Department, and the State Department, usually with praise and a promise of new aid for Yemen. The supply of coastal gunboats and training for the coast guard by the U.S. in the spring of 2004 was accompanied by a promise of more of the same. It was also announced that with the enhanced port security, the United States would probably, for the first time since the USS *Cole* bombing, allow its warships to stop at Aden for refueling. The lifting of the United States' fourteen-year-old ban on the supply of new military equipment and spare parts to Yemen—for instance, for the latter's aging F-15 fighters—was announced in 2004. At the June 2004 meetings of the

G-8, President Salih was an honored guest; he spoke in support of the United States' call for a new initiative on development and democratization in the Middle East region.

Possible Future U.S. Policy toward Yemen—and Will It Matter?

What can the United States do to make the Republic of Yemen an even more stalwart ally in the effort against transnational revolutionary Islam and terror? What can it do to immunize Yemen against these phenomena? What can the United States do to prevent the chaos, civil war, or revolution that would make Yemen vulnerable to—and an easy prey of—revolutionary Islam? Not very much, it seems. Indeed, just cheering from the sidelines, if done too loudly, could be counterproductive.[71]

That said, Yemen is able to contribute a little more to the effort against transnational revolutionary Islam and terrorism. Similarly, the United States can do more—in the form of material assistance, guidance, and political sensitivity—to make it possible for the Salih regime to do more. For example, the United States could act in ways that are sensitive to and take into account Yemen's domestic politics and the delicate balancing act that the regime faces in trying to satisfy both its domestic constituencies and the United States.

The United States can and should increase its development aid to Yemen from the current modest level at least back to the levels of the 1980s. Such aid should focus on job-creation, poverty alleviation, and the provision of educational, medical, and other welfare services. It should be channeled through governmental agencies that are less prone to corruption, such as the Social Fund for Development.

Military assistance probably should be maintained at the current level or increased only slightly. Since the struggle against transnational revolutionary Islam is not going to be won on the battlefield in Yemen or anywhere else, the emphasis should not be on advanced weapons systems, airplanes, tanks, or artillery, but on such things as the capacity to secure borders and ports, interdict smuggling, and carry out security and intelligence operations. To the extent possible, the United States should insist that military and security assistance be channeled into the effort against bona fide terrorist groups and not be used more generally for domestic political repression. As the old cold war paradigm suggests, it would be easy for Yemen to use the "war against terrorism" as an excuse to repress the opposition, and for the United States to ignore, accept, or even justify this general crackdown. This urge would be counterproductive and must be resisted.[72]

Using whatever leverage it has, the United States should discreetly urge, cajole, and even pressure the Yemeni government to implement in a timely fashion the remaining parts of the IMF/World Bank structural reform package. The focus should be the fight against corruption and the reform of the civil service and the judiciary. The goal should be to make Yemen safer and more attractive for the foreign and Yemeni investment that will create jobs, economic opportunity, and a more promising future for most of the population. The United States can help to finance generously these reforms and can urge other donors to be more forthcoming and demanding regarding them. The United States should also partner with the IMF and the World Bank in sponsoring and ensuring the success of donor pledging sessions.

The political reconstitution of the regime itself is probably required if major socioeconomic reforms are to go forward in a timely fashion. If reconstitution is required, the United States should discreetly urge it and apply a modicum of pressure on the Yemeni leadership. Yemen will not tolerate much U.S. involvement in this area, however; anything smacking of meddling or interfering in Yemen's politics will be counterproductive.[73]

More fundamentally, the attempt to engage Yemen more effectively in the effort against transnational revolutionary Islam would benefit from a redefinition of the effort. A better definition would both focus on the socioeconomic root causes of the phenomenon and shift the emphasis from the military ("war") to intelligence operations and police actions. It would be both easier and more productive for Yemenis to engage fully in such a reconfigured effort.

Conclusions

The Republic of Yemen has become over the past few years a strong ally of the United States in the effort against transnational revolutionary political Islam and terrorism; it does not, at present, constitute a bastion of terror. However, this may very well change—soon and quickly.

The record of the past decade, since 1995, suggests that the Yemeni regime and state lack the will and capacity to plan and implement the major socioeconomic reforms required to restore the country's viability and to meet the basic wants and needs of most of its people. The evidence is overwhelming. The economy, so dependent on the state, oil revenues, and outside donors, has created few jobs and little wealth, with the result that the alarming levels of unemployment, poverty, and malnutrition have remained as high as or grown higher than they were a decade ago. The middle class has been pauperized and has probably shrunk, and the gap between the rich few and the many poor has grown much wider and more visibly so. And finally, the education, health, and social service systems are worse than they were, qualitatively and quantitatively.

Unless political reforms are quickly adopted, Yemen will be in serious political trouble. Indeed, based on the record of performance over the past decade, and especially the past few years, the fragile Yemeni state is already failing—and it risks becoming a fully failed state. Unable to deliver on the wants and needs of most of the people, its support and legitimacy are declining.

If the state does fail, then the country could slide into anarchy or civil war. Under these circumstances, Yemen could become an arena in which transnational revolutionary Islam becomes a serious contender for power. At the very least, a Yemen in or near anarchy or civil war could not be expected to be a stalwart ally of the United States in the effort against transnational revolutionary Islam and terrorism. In mid-2005, unlike in the early 1990s, the United States, based on this new shared interest, had close, friendly ties with a Yemeni regime that was still firmly at the helm of what could quickly become a sinking ship.

Whether or not the Republic of Yemen effects needed political and socio-economic reforms is overwhelmingly a domestic political concern, and there is but little that the United States can do to influence these crucial matters. It can, with sensitivity, urge the regime to pursue such reforms, it can provide more needed economic and security assistance, and can urge other countries and international bodies to do the same. As important, the United States can—perhaps must—both redefine the effort against transnational revolutionary Islam and substantially revise other key policies toward the region in ways that would resonate positively with the Yemenis. In any case, relegated for the most part to the sidelines, the United States should be deeply concerned that an unreformed Yemen will be an increasingly unreliable partner in the effort against transnational revolutionary Islam—and may well become that movement's victim.

Notes

1. Regarding terminology, in this article, revolutionary political Islam is contrasted with reformist political Islam or nonpolitical Islam; and transnational (or global) revolutionary political Islam is contrasted with "national" or even regional political Islam. Further, the "W word"—as in *war*—is not used, nor the words *fight, crusade,* or *struggle* (jihad?) when referring to the U.S. effort against transnational revolutionary Islam and the terror that it uses. Repeated often enough, strong ill-chosen metaphors have a way of changing perceptions of reality and reality itself, with often disastrous results.

2. In this context, *will* has to do with motives, values, and beliefs, and *capacity* has to do with abilities or capabilities based on skills, organization, and other resources.

3. Robert I. Rotberg, "Failed States, Collapsed States, Weak States: Causes and Indicators,"

in Robert I. Rotberg (ed.), *State Failure and State Weakness in a Time of Terror* (Washington, D.C., 2003), 1–25.

4. This reconstitution is not to be confused with the "regime change" that is now so readily advocated in certain circles.

5. Traveling from Sanaa down to the port of al-Hudayda, one passes to the south of a gently sloping mountain that rises to over 12,000 feet, the highest point on the peninsula.

6. The area of Saudi Arabia is nearly five times that of Yemen, and Yemen is somewhat larger than California in area. The 2004 census recorded 19.6 million people. *Yemen Times* (April 19, 2005).

7. Larger but still modest reserves of gas await major development.

8. Names notwithstanding, South Yemen was mostly to the east and even partly to the north of North Yemen. The capital of South Yemen, Aden, was almost due south of the capital of the north, Sanaa, and explains these popular, unofficial names.

9. The Yemeni imamate, dating back a millennium, was basically a theocracy headed by an imam charged with protecting and fostering the Islamic nature of the country. This mission was taken very seriously by the imams in the first half of the twentieth century.

10. See Robert D. Burrowes, *The Politics of Development: The Yemen Arab Republic, 1962–1986* (Boulder, 1987).

11. The population of the old North Yemen is about four times that of the old South Yemen, despite the fact that the area of the latter is about 50 percent greater than that of the former.

12. A longtime theme of the Salih regime, democratization has dominated political discourse at least since the run-up to the Emerging Democracies Conference hosted so successfully by Yemen in Sanaa in 1999. In late 2004, some months after President Salih's cameo appearance at the G-8 meetings, the Republic of Yemen joined with Turkey and Italy to administer a new program for the purpose of fostering discussion on political change, the Democratic Assistance Dialogue. The United States has promoted President Salih in this role. Joel Brinkley, "U.S. Slows Bid to Advance Democracy in Arab World," *New York Times* (December 5, 2004); Joel Brinkley, "Arab and Western Ministers Voice Different Priorities," *New York Times* (December 12, 2004).

13. Having been talking its talk for some time, Yemenis are beginning to walk the walk of democracy. Doing so is important, however, because it increases greatly the likelihood that someday soon Yemeni politicians and citizens will demand "real" democracy. In part, this chapter asks whether it is likely that Yemen will have the time or the setting for further democratic transition—whether democracy will deepen and broaden, and become more legitimate, in the near future.

14. The author was a monitor for the 1997 and 2003 elections. Administration and execution appeared to be better in the latter than in the former, but whether the 2003 elections were freer and fairer than those in 1997 is hard to say.

15. Arguably, the most important parliamentary elections were those of 1993, because the Republic of Yemen's legislature before and after those elections was a focus of attention and, accordingly, of some influence. Signs of a new assertiveness by the parliament and parliamentarians were evident in 2004 in regard to the government's role in an oil scandal. The standoff between a large part of the parliament and the prime minister persisted for several months.

16. This was an unnecessary, self-inflicted embarrassment for the Salih regime, coming as

it did only a few months after the successful, well-publicized Emerging Democracies Confer-ence. There was a credible opposition candidate from the Yemeni Socialist Party (YSP), but he was disqualified from running on a technicality. Had he done so, and despite an assured Salih victory, the Yemeni presidential elections would have provided a nice contrast to the referen-dum in Egypt that, at about the same time, endorsed Hosni Mubarak for yet another term with the usual 99 percent or so of the vote.

17. Unless it is repealed, the two-term limit in the constitution will prevent President Salih from running for the presidency in 2013.

18. Most dramatic was the escalating confrontation in 2004 and 2005 between the regime and the Yemeni Journalists Syndicate over the criminal prosecution of journalists and the suspension of publications.

19. During the 1980s, what could be described as an affirmative action program favored businessmen from the north over their then-dominant colleagues from Taizz and the rest of the southern uplands of North Yemen. The ruling group at the center began "commanding the periphery, top-down, through an elaborate system of patronage. The state became a family business. Around the family there developed . . . a military-commercial complex. . . . High-ranking army officers and a few great merchant families all had their hands in each other's pockets. Between them they had the state in their control." Paul Dresch, "The Tribal Factor in the Yemen Crisis," in Jamal al-Suwaidi (ed.), *The Yemeni War of 1994: Causes and Consequences* (Abu Dhabi, 1995), 33–55.

20. The unification process, and power sharing with the YSP during the transition period, interrupted and challenged this trend briefly from 1990 until 1994.

21. The Ministry of Education blazed the trail and set the standard in this regard in the sec-ond half of the 1970s. High officials in the ministry enriched themselves to the point that donors threatened to end their aid.

22. Joshua Charap and Christian Harm, "Institutionalized Corruption and the Klepto-cratic State," in George T. Abed and Sanjeev Gupta (eds.), *Governance, Corruption and Economic Performance* (Washington, D.C., 2002), 135–158.

23. Today, the big exception that proves the rule would seem to be the Social Development Fund, the relatively new government agency that runs "social safety net" projects and seems dedicated to its mission and free from corruption. In its dedication, honesty, and efficiency, one is reminded of the old Central Planning Organization—the CPO—under Abd al-Karim al-Iryani, its founding head, during the mid-1970s.

24. It should be noted that many public servants, some very high and some very low, have chosen not to participate in this system, or not to participate in it very much. In addition, many public servants are simply not in offices or posts through which much money flows; in today's Yemen, as in real estate, there are three keys to monetary success: location, location, and location.

25. Perhaps the word *silently* is not appropriate since the "succession issue" and the issue of nepotism—from the presidency on down to a wide range of lesser posts—became big themes in the press in 2004.

26. In 2004, Transparency International included Yemen on its list of the thirteen oil-producing countries most plagued by corruption. *New York Times* (October 21, 2004).

27. Max Weber, "Politics as a Vocation," in H. H. Gerth and C. Wright Mills (eds.), *From Max Weber: Essays in Sociology* (New York, 1958), 77–84. During the twentieth century, the Hamid al-Din imamate did adopt some of the elements of statecraft of the "modern" occu-

piers of Yemen; in previous centuries, the Yemen imamate had been even further from Weber's classic state.

28. For these modernists and their ideas, see Robert D. Burrowes, "The Famous Forty and Their Companions: North Yemen's First-Generation Modernists and Educational Emigrants," *Middle East Journal*, LIX (2005), 81–97.

29. The presidencies of al-Hamdi and Salih were separated by that of Ahmad al-Ghashmi, who in mid-1978, only months after taking office, was also assassinated.

30. Hassan al-Zaidi, "Eid Scarred as Five Die in Mareb: Tribal Killings," *Yemen Times* (November 20, 2003), 1–2.

31. The situation in the PDRY and for its smaller population was different in the late 1980s. Like Cuba, it was heavily dependent on the Soviet Union, the resources of which were being stretched very thin. Moreover, the prior claims of large oil reserves northeast of Aden were proving hollow.

32. Among the Arab states, Kuwait had been second only to Saudi Arabia as a source of economic aid for Yemen.

33. The sad condition of university professors and their centers of learning was only slightly more dramatic than that of most government workers and their departments and agencies. One is reminded of the pathetic situation of Yemeni academic colleagues in houses or apartments far too small for growing families, in threadbare sport coats or suit jackets with torn pockets and collars, and in old cars that barely ran—and that barely stopped when the brakes were applied.

34. The upbeat view of most Yemeni and non-Yemeni observers is captured in a cover article in an economics weekly that proclaimed that Yemen had emerged from the doldrums of recent years and was now "the economic Cinderella of the Middle East." Robin Bray, "Yemen Comes Back from the Brink," *Middle East Economic Digest* (MEED), XLI (1997), 4.

35. For example, for political reasons, the IMF allowed reforms originally scheduled for late 1996 to be deferred until after the spring 1997 elections.

36. According to IMF figures, by late 1996 inflation had already fallen to about 9 percent on an annualized basis, from almost 48 percent at the beginning of the year.

37. The riyal stabilized at about YR 125–130 to the dollar, a marked contrast to 1995, when it had fluctuated wildly on the free market, going as high as YR 80 and as low as YR 160.

38. In 1997, the cut in subsidies caused the price of petrol, kerosene, wheat, and flour to rise sharply. In mid-1998, the diesel fuel subsidy was abruptly cut.

39. Among these other efforts, the creation of the Aden free zone and container port was Yemen's most high-profile project. After many delays, the project took a major step forward in 1997, when a Singapore corporation became the operator and owner of 49 percent of the project; dredging soon began. The port was completed in 2000 after numerous delays. While the modernization of the Aden oil refinery continued to suffer delays, efforts proceeded to build a privately financed refinery on the Red Sea coast in the north. The mainstay of the economy, the oil industry reported modest new discoveries and increases in production; production stood at about 400,000 barrels per day at the end of 1997.

40. The abrupt cut in the diesel fuel subsidy at this time triggered demonstrations and riots throughout the country. These actions were dealt with forcefully by the authorities, and there were many fatalities.

41. Oil prices rebounded in 1999, leading to a good macro-economic profile for 2000; the higher oil revenues made it possible to combine some increased social spending with a lower deficit.

42. A family survey reported in early 2000 that over the past five years of reforms there had been a big increase in poverty and a widening of the income gap in Yemen. *Al-Hayat* (January 16, 2000).

43. *Yemen Times* (June 17, 2004), 1. In mid-September 2004, the World Bank again publicly criticized Yemen on reform and warned that further aid might not be forthcoming. Financial Times Information (September 17, 2004). This said, the bank did approve a $65 million loan to Yemen for basic education later that month. M2 Presswire (September 24, 2004). However, during a visit in mid-February 2005, World Bank president James D. Wolfensohn publicly told Yemen that the bank was sick and tired of Yemen's excuses for failing to keep its promises of reform, that further World Bank aid to Yemen was in jeopardy, and that, in any case, Yemen was in a very serious and worsening crisis. He said that Yemen had one of the largest World Bank project portfolios and one of the worst performance records.

44. Interview with James Rawley, *Yemen Times* (June 21, 2004), 1.

45. These facilities were supposed to take advantage of location and go head-to-head with Jabal Ali in Dubai and facilities then being built in Salala in Oman.

46. In addition, both the underemployed and the holders of multiple marginal jobs are numerous.

47. In the mid-1980s and again in the late 1990s, the world price of oil plunged from the heights to just below $10 a barrel.

48. The author last resided in Yemen for nine months from the beginning of October 2003 through June 2004 and again from mid-January to mid-March 2005. The assessment of social, economic, and political conditions in late 2004 is based on what he learned during this period.

49. A recent report judged that as of 2002, "Yemen is not a failed or failing state but it is a fragile one." After cautioning that "the carefully constructed edifice of the Yemeni state—a work still in progress—may yet come apart," it concludes that "signs of potential instability are offset by significant positive political developments. . . . A nascent democracy . . . , its government has shown a general commitment to developing the instruments of a modern state. . . ." If this estimate were largely valid at the time, then the situation in Yemen seems to have changed dramatically for the worse over the past three years. International Crisis Group (ICG), "Yemen: Coping with Terrorism and Violence in a Fragile State" (January 8, 2003), i–ii.

50. Legitimacy in Yemen is *instrumental*—that is, the political system is regarded as legitimate by the people under it to the degree that it gets the job that they want done and meets their perceived needs. By contrast, *consummatory* legitimacy characterizes a political system that is perceived by those under it to be intrinsically morally right and proper, for what it is rather than for what it delivers. With consummatory legitimacy, a political system has a cushion and can afford to be ineffective for a period of time; with instrumental legitimacy, there is no cushion and current performance counts most. The former tends to be more stable and durable than the latter. See David Apter, *The Politics of Modernization* (Chicago, 1965), 236–237, 266.

51. In this regard, some observers have been reassured because the Salih regime has proven in the past to be very adaptive and the Yemeni people can and will stoically bear great hardships. Yet, such malleability has its limits, even in Yemen.

52. If the Lebanese civil war had started in the world of 2000 instead of 1975, transnational revolutionary political Islam would almost surely have been a major force with which to reckon in Lebanon and in its neighborhood.

53. In the mid-1970s, sincere young men would say, and with some disbelief: "You know about Islam, and you're not Muslim. How can that be?"

54. To a remarkable degree, the shared experience of the struggle in Afghanistan in the 1980s and thereafter was for the Islamic world the equivalent of the Spanish Civil War in the 1930s for the secular socialist world. It radicalized and homogenized various local and particularistic strands of fundamentalist Islam and fostered the emergence of a militant transnational or global movement—an Islamic version of the Socialist International.

55. By contrast, Thomas Scotes, U.S. ambassador to the YAR in the mid-1970s, argued unsuccessfully with his superiors at the State Department that the interests of the United States would be best advanced if it served as an interlocutor between the overbearing Saudi regime and the popular al-Hamdi regime in Yemen. He thought that this posture would both give the latter a bit of room in which to breathe and best serve U.S. as well as Saudi interests in the long run.

56. Strategic talk at this time was of a new Soviet initiative, using local surrogates along an "arc of revolution" stretching from Afghanistan and Iran to the Yemens and then on to the Horn of Africa and Angola.

57. To get an idea of how much and for what reasons the salience of Yemen and the Horn of Africa has changed since 1990 in U.S. foreign policy circles, see Robert D. Burrowes, "The Other Side of the Red Sea and a Little More: The Horn of Africa and the Two Yemens," in David A. Korn, Steven R. Dorr, and Neysa M. Slater (eds.), *The Horn of Africa and Arabia* (Washington, D.C., 1990), 63–74.

58. The Goldmur Hotel bombing in 1992 slipped under the radar screen; it involved no U.S. deaths, occurred during a U.S. presidential transition, and was related to the fiasco in Somalia. The bombings in Saudi Arabia in 1995 and 1996, which did involve the death of U.S. military personnel and attracted close U.S. attention, were attributed for the most part to Hezbollah and Iran.

59. Also in 1998, the bombings of the U.S. embassies in Kenya and Tanzania raised questions about Yemen for some. But it was the fatal hostage taking by the Aden-Abyan Islamic Army that focused attention on the country. This incident also led to rounds of undiplomatic mudslinging between the Yemeni government and that of Britain, from where most of the dozen or so tourists came. The Yemenis won the final round when it was revealed that the whole bizarre sequence started with the arrest near Aden of several British citizens with arms and explosives and that the tourists had been kidnapped at the behest of Abu Hamza al-Masri, the father of one of the arrested British citizens and a militant Muslim cleric in London.

60. The linkage of Osama bin Laden—and transnational revolutionary Islam and terrorism—to Yemen was reinforced by the constant reference to the fact that his ancestral home was Yemen, a country he may never have visited.

61. Improved relations between the United States and the Republic of Yemen are increasingly and almost exclusively focused on the effort against transnational revolutionary Islam and terror. It is eerily reminiscent of the single-mindedness of U.S. thinking and relations during the cold war, as well as the way other countries took advantage of this obsession.

62. Many Yemenis were aware that not much more than a year after the USS *Cole* bombing, and shortly after 9/11 and the U.S. assault on Al Qaeda and the Taliban in Afghanistan, a question being asked in the Bush administration and elsewhere was: who is next? Although Iraq soon won the honors, Yemen and Somalia were high on some lists. Rumor also had it that bin Laden and Al Qaeda were planning to relocate to Yemen from Afghanistan, adding to the likelihood that Yemen might be targeted by the United States.

63. The arrest in late 2003 of Muhammad Hamdi al-Ahdal, allegedly one of the most senior leaders of Al Qaeda in Yemen, was one of the most notable cases. *Yemen Observer*

(December 6, 2003). The regime has also sponsored a "dialogue" and rehabilitation program for suspected militants in custody. It has even tried preventive persuasion, hiring an itinerant poet to travel in tribal areas and make the case against the sheltering of suspected terrorists. *Yemen Observer* (May 8, 2004), 1; *Seattle Times* (October 21, 2004), 13.

64. The head of the FBI team was very insensitive, acting in Yemen, a sovereign nation-state, as if he were leading a federal investigation of a civil rights case in the state of Alabama.

65. Al-Huthi's brother is currently a member of parliament. By early 2005, it was clear that the al-Huthi episode was a major event and possibly a turning point in the recent political history of Yemen. It both polarized Yemeni politics and narrowed the political base of President Salih and his colleagues. While leaders of most political persuasions shared this view, they differed as to whether it boded well or ill for reform and the future of Yemen.

66. President Salih requested the much-publicized program in 1992, and it has been led and promoted by Hamoud al-Hitar, a charismatic Supreme Court judge. Al-Hitar has demonstrated and explained Yemen's dialogue approach, billed as a better alternative to jail terms, in Britain and elsewhere. *Yemen Observer* (May 8, 2004).

67. See the *Yemen Observer* (April 10, 2004), 1; *Yemen Times* (April 22, 2004), 1.

68. The case most condemned by informed Yemenis is that of Muhammad Ali Hassan al-Moayad, a well-known cleric. Al-Moayad was lured by the FBI from Yemen to Frankfurt in 2003, arrested by German authorities, and then extradited to the U.S., where he faces trial on charges that he was an important intermediary in the financing of terrorist activities. Muhammad Alanssi, the Yemeni who played the key role in the sting operation against al-Moayad, set himself on fire in front of the White House in mid-November in protest against the FBI's ingratitude for his services. *New York Times* (November 27, 2004), 1, 14.

69. See the *Yemen Observer* (March 6, 2004).

70. The revived USAID program in Yemen since 9/11 is explicitly justified in terms of contributing to the "war against terror" and to this end is focusing on projects designed to raise household incomes and nutritional levels of the poor in five Yemeni governorates in the north and east. Interview with Kyle Foster, development specialist, Sanaa, February 2005.

71. Similarly, there is only a little that the IMF, World Bank, United Nations agencies, and the rest of the donor community can do to affect what is primarily a sensitive domestic political matter.

72. International and Yemeni human rights groups are already criticizing the Republic of Yemen for its harsh treatment of alleged Islamic militants and for its using this effort as an excuse to crack down on opponents in general.

73. It is tempting to say that, along with urging Salih and enlightened colleagues to purge the regime of those linked to Islamic militants, the United States should urge them to remove those who are standing in the way of needed political and socioeconomic reforms. Again, this is a very sensitive political issue. Indeed, in 2004 the U.S. ambassador was accused by opposition elements of meddling in Yemen's domestic politics.

8

Kenya
The Struggle against Terrorism

Johnnie Carson

In combating the regional threat posed by international terrorism, no other country in East Africa or the greater Horn of Africa is more important to the United States than Kenya. Although the United States currently has combat troops stationed at Camp Lemonier in Djibouti and has developed increasingly close ties with the armed forces of Ethiopia and Uganda, Kenya remains a core partner and ally in tracking down Al Qaeda–affiliated terrorists in East Africa and preventing any future anti-Western terrorist attacks in Kenya and the region.

However, Kenya's stagnating economy, its continued high level of corruption, and the marginalization of its largely coastal Islamic community continue to make it one of the principal recruiting grounds for local terrorist sympathizers and supporters. Kenya also remains a prime target of terrorism. Abundant hotels and tourist facilities as well as the presence of a large number of foreign diplomatic missions, a major United Nations complex, and a wide range of Western-owned businesses continue to provide Kenyan and international terrorists with a variety of reasonably accessible soft but high-value targets.

Although Kenya has not produced any independent or indigenous terrorist organizations, at least one, and perhaps two, Al Qaeda–affiliated cells have operated in Kenya for over a decade. More than a half dozen Kenyan nationals and their family members have been implicated in high-profile Al Qaeda terrorist attacks, and three of Al Qaeda's senior leaders in East Africa and the greater Horn of Africa have traveled in and out of Kenya on a regular basis, generating genuine concern that Kenya could be the site of future attacks inspired by the group.

Because of its strong pro-Western policies and the impact that it has already suffered from the two most devastating terrorist attacks in sub-Saharan Africa, Kenya is not likely to back away from the United States in the fight against international terrorism and political extremism. Nevertheless, the United States will have to remain vigilant against future terrorist attacks on U.S., Western, and Israeli interests in Kenya and invest heavily in working with Kenya to upgrade Kenya's counterterrorist efforts.

More important, Kenyan officials will have to improve the economic, social, and political opportunities for the country's largely neglected Muslim population, as well as being far more diligent in protecting its porous land and sea borders and monitoring the activities of Saudi Arabian charities and an active Saudi embassy in Nairobi. The United States will also have to recognize that the battle to defeat terrorism in Kenya, East Africa, and the greater Horn of Africa is not a struggle to be waged or led by the military alone but requires a much broader effort, involving additional development resources and greater diplomatic engagement, coupled with enhanced bilateral and multilateral intelligence, police, and military cooperation.

Kenya's Critical Role in the Region

Kenya is the regional economic powerhouse of the greater Horn of Africa; it is also the most stable and reliable democracy in the area. The role it plays in the fight against terrorism in eastern Africa and the Horn is crucial in helping to reduce and eliminate terrorist threats and assisting broader U.S. and Western antiterrorism efforts in both regions. Although substantially smaller in size than its three northern neighbors (the Sudan, Ethiopia, and Somalia) and smaller in population than the Sudan, Ethiopia, and neighboring Tanzania, Kenya is the economic, transportation, and financial hub of an area that covers East Africa, the greater Horn of Africa, and the Great Lakes region.

Although Kenya's economy has been in the doldrums for the last decade, it is the largest and most diversified in the region, and the largest non-oil- and non-mineral-based economy in sub-Saharan Africa. Broadly diversified across a number of sectors, it is based on agriculture, tourism, small-scale manufacturing, transportation, and banking. Agriculturally, Kenya stands out as one of the world's leading producers of tea, coffee, and vegetables and ranks as the largest exporter of cut flowers to Europe. Kenya's tourist sector is sophisticated and highly developed, making it one of the premier destinations for European and American travelers. Each year, tens of thousands of tourists visit the country's beaches and national parks, earning the country substantial amounts of foreign exchange.

Kenya's regional economic importance rests squarely on its substantial transportation infrastructure. The country's transportation network is the best by far in the greater Horn of Africa and serves as an essential economic artery for more than six states. Mombasa, Kenya's primary port, is the fourth largest on the east coast of Africa, and not only supplies Kenya's hinterland but acts as the principal port for goods going to Uganda, Rwanda, Burundi, and the eastern Congo. In addition, Mombasa serves as a secondary harbor for goods flowing into the southern regions of the Sudan, Somalia, and Ethiopia and into the northwestern part of Tanzania.

Equally important is the country's national airline. Kenya Airways, the third largest commercial carrier in sub-Saharan Africa and one of Africa's safest and most profitable, links Nairobi with most of the continent, Western Europe, and the Middle East. Kenya's capital also serves as home to the largest number of international companies and banks in the region and hosts one of the United Nations' four regional headquarters—the only one outside the United States or Western Europe. No other country in East Africa or the Horn rises to Kenya's regional economic stature.

Relations with the United States

Kenya has always valued its political and economic relationship with the United States. Its important relationship with Britain, its former colonial sovereign, is discussed below. Fundamentally pro-Western in political orientation since its independence in 1963, Kenya (unlike its neighbors) has maintained a cordial and unbroken diplomatic relationship with the United States for over forty years. During this period, Kenya has gradually emerged as America's most consistent, reliable, and helpful partner in the region.[1]

Although Kenyan-U.S. relations have suffered a few rough patches intermittently throughout the late 1980s and 1990s, largely over issues of corruption, episodic violations of human rights, and the country's slow return to multiparty democracy, the two countries have always found a way to work together on a variety of regional and international issues. Kenya's first two presidents, Jomo Kenyatta and Daniel arap Moi, clearly viewed themselves as close friends and allies of Washington and London, and sought whenever possible to strengthen those ties and to accommodate the political and international interests of the United States and Britain. In contrast to its three northern neighbors in the Horn of Africa, all of whom flirted with Afro-socialism or with Marxist-inspired systems of governance, Kenya eschewed left-wing and communist-oriented policies and opened its doors to Western companies and financial institutions. Throughout the most intense period of cold war competition, Kenya remained solidly allied to the United States and Britain at the UN and in other international fora. In response, the United States rewarded Kenya by making it one of the largest African recipients of foreign assistance and by sending it hundreds of U.S. Peace Corps volunteers.

Following the overthrow of Emperor Haile Selassie and the emergence of a hard-line Marxist regime in neighboring Ethiopia in the 1970s, Kenya's regional importance, as well as its relationship with the United States, expanded significantly. One manifestation was the growth of the official American presence in Kenya. Over the past two decades, the U.S. embassy in Kenya has become the largest in sub-Saharan Africa and the second largest in Africa. The embassy's size and prominent location at one of Nairobi's busiest downtown intersections also made it an attractive target for terrorists.

Like Kenya itself, the U.S. embassy in Nairobi has also taken on regional importance. In addition to managing relations with Kenya, the embassy has had a major role in monitoring developments in the Sudan, supporting the Kenyan-led North-South peace process, and coordinating U.S. developmental assistance to southern Sudan. The embassy has also had primary responsibility for coordinating policy on Somalia and following the episodic peace negotiations among Somalia's various political factions.

Security Cooperation with the United States

As the U.S. embassy has grown in size and Kenya has taken on more regional significance, the number of U.S. military personnel in Kenya has increased and U.S.-Kenyan security collaboration has expanded. From a relatively small presence in the 1960s and 1970s, the office of the U.S. defense attaché has grown to include military representation from the U.S. Army, Navy, and Air Force.

The Defense Department has two other large operations in Kenya: the Kenya-U.S. Liaison Office (KUSLO), which handles military assistance and training programs, and the Walter Reed U.S. Army Medical Research Unit, which conducts scientific research in tropical and infectious diseases. Both of these operations have expanded over the years, with KUSLO taking on increased responsibility for programming the additional antiterrorism assistance that Kenya has received from the United States since 9/11. The Army Medical Research Unit, with offices in Nairobi and Kisumu, is attempting to find cures for a variety of infectious diseases that American forces have encountered in recent military campaigns in Kuwait, Afghanistan, and Iraq.

As the U.S.-Kenyan military relationship has matured, the Kenyan military has received larger amounts of U.S. military assistance to purchase equipment for its army, and a growing number of Kenyan officers have benefited from training opportunities in the United States under the International Military Education and Training program (IMET). Military exercises in Kenya have also increased. While the focus has been on medical and veterinary exercises that help local communities, in recent years the U.S. Marine Corps has conducted a number of live-fire exercises in northeastern Kenya. Kenyan military units have frequently participated in these training exercises and have gained valuable experience operating alongside their American counterparts.

Although more guarded and less visible to the public, the intelligence cooperation between Kenya and the United States has also increased significantly. Positive changes in Kenya's domestic politics, especially in the areas of democratization and human rights, have contributed to this improvement. As the Kenyan intelligence service has increasingly turned away from ensuring regime survival and presidential protection, it has been able to devote more of its time to defending against national security threats, tracking down potential terrorists, and preventing future terrorist attacks. Collaboration between the Kenyan and U.S. intelligence services, as well as the FBI, has been instrumental in identifying and capturing some of the perpetrators of the 1998 attack against the American embassy in Nairobi and the 2002 bombing of the Paradise Hotel in Mombasa.

But much of what the United States has been able to accomplish in the security field was considered politically and publicly acceptable as a result of the long-standing military relationship between Kenya and Britain.

Security Cooperation with Great Britain

Since independence, Kenya has maintained extremely close ties to the British military, and in many ways the existence of that excellent and ongoing association paved the way for the emergence of the U.S.-Kenyan military relationship. The extended and highly visible British military presence has also made the presence of foreign troops more acceptable among political leaders and the general public.

The British military has been extremely active in Kenya for many years. After independence in 1963, Kenyan officials reaffirmed an agreement permitting British troops to train in Kenya. Under the existing protocol, three British infantry battalions and one engineering unit spend six to eight weeks a year in northern Kenya, conducting training and live-fire exercise at Archers Post and Dol Doi.[2] To support this mission and the movement of troops, the British maintain a permanent military and training assistance group at their embassy in Nairobi and a small office at Nairobi's main international airport. In addition, British naval vessels make routine calls at Mombasa, a practice that dates back many years. Although British and Kenyan troops do not train together, camaraderie between British and Kenyan officers is excellent. Most Kenyans—on both political and military levels—continue to believe that their relationship with the British military is positive.

The U.S.-Kenyan Access Agreement

The mechanism that has given the U.S.-Kenyan relationship its greatest political and military significance is the nearly quarter-of-a-century-old military Access Agreement.[3] Originally negotiated in 1981 as an adjunct security element to America's greater Middle East policy, the Access Agreement has provided the United States with a major platform and strategically important bridgehead for carrying out a wide range of both bilateral and multilateral humanitarian and relief operations throughout East Africa, the Horn of Africa, and parts of the Great Lakes region.[4] In fact, over the past twenty-five years, every major American-led rescue and relief operation in the region has involved direct access to and use of Kenya's principal transportation hubs.

The Access Agreement permits the United States to use—on short notice and with very few bureaucratic and political obstacles—Kenya's main seaport at Mombasa as well as the country's principal international airports in Nairobi and Mombasa. Under the agreement, the United States has also been able to maintain on a permanent basis a small warehouse and office facility on the grounds of the airport in Mombasa. This facility has been used frequently over the years for both long- and short-term military exercises and full-scale relief and humanitarian operations.

The Access Agreement with Kenya has permitted the United States to use Kenyan facilities in Mombasa and Nairobi to respond to over a half dozen humanitarian crises in the Great Lakes and the Horn of Africa. The first major use of the agreement came in 1988, when the United States and other members of the international community used air and port facilities in Mombasa and Nairobi as the main transshipment hub for dispatching huge quantities of relief supplies to drought- and famine-ravaged Somalia. Between 1988 and 1993, under Operations Provide Hope and Restore Hope, U.S. forces made almost daily use of Kenyan facilities in Mombasa to ship food, medical supplies, and relief materials into southern Somalia and Mogadishu, Somalia's capital. When the security situation in Somalia deteriorated sharply and U.S. and UN peacekeepers came under continuing attack by various Somali warlords, the United States used Kenya as a rear base to help supply and then ultimately to extract all American forces and UN peacekeepers.

Following the outbreak of the Rwandan genocide in April and May 1994, American military units used Kenyan facilities to undertake the largest relief operation ever carried out in Central Africa. Responding quickly and affirmatively from August to November 1994, American forces transshipped hundreds of tons of humanitarian assistance through the airport in Nairobi and the harbor in Mombasa to tens of thousands of Hutu and Tutsi refugees in eastern Congo and western Tanzania, preventing additional losses of life among the homeless and starving.

The United States has also been instrumental in persuading Kenya to allow the international community to use its territory to achieve multilateral humanitarian objectives. Operating outside the parameters of the Kenyan-U.S. Access Agreement but with strong initial American encouragement, Kenya has served as the principal base for Operation Lifeline Sudan. Established in 1989 to provide emergency food aid to drought-ravaged southern Sudan, the UN-run but American-inspired and -funded relief program has fed hundreds of thousands of displaced persons in that war-torn part of the country. Operating out of Lokichoggio, a small airfield in the northwestern corner of Kenya, dozens of relief planes fly food, medical supplies, and international relief workers into remote and inaccessible parts of southern Sudan on a daily basis.

Political Cooperation with the United States on Regional Issues

Kenya and the United States have also cooperated closely to find negotiated solutions to a range of serious regional conflicts. With active U.S. encouragement, as well as strong financial and diplomatic backing, Kenya acted as the principal regional mediator in the effort to find a lasting solution to the twenty-two-year-old conflict in the Sudan between the government of President

Omar Hassan al-Bashir and the Southern People's Liberation Movement (SPLM), led by John Garang. In a much more difficult and complex context, Kenyan officials led the regional effort to restore peace to Somalia and to persuade the country's competing warlords to sign a comprehensive peace agreement and form a new government. In many ways, Kenya's close political, military, and intelligence connections with the United States have provided a firm foundation for the strong cooperative relationship that has emerged in dealing with major acts of terrorism in Kenya and with regional terrorist issues.

Terrorism Strikes Nairobi and Mombasa

More than any other country in sub-Saharan Africa, Kenya has felt the devastating effects of international terrorist attacks. On the morning of August 7, 1998, two Al Qaeda terrorists drove a small bomb-laden panel truck to the rear entrance of the American embassy in Nairobi. In the subsequent blast, the rear half of the embassy was extensively damaged and an adjacent building was completely destroyed. Two hundred and fourteen people were killed (including forty-four American and Kenyan personnel in the embassy building). Over 5,000 people were injured and wounded, mostly Kenyans on the streets and in neighboring buildings. Although most of the individuals involved in the planning of the Nairobi attack managed to flee, Mohamed Rashed al-Owahili, one of the two Al Qaeda suicide bombers in the truck, decided at the last moment not to take his own life but fled the scene and was subsequently apprehended by Kenyan police officers.

Just over four years later, on November 22, 2002, Al Qaeda terrorists struck Kenya again. In a sophisticated and well-orchestrated attack, several terrorists drove an explosive-filled land cruiser into the lobby of the Paradise Hotel, an Israeli-owned beach resort in a small village just north of Mombasa. The attack coincided with the arrival of a large group of Israeli tourists who had just flown in on a charter flight. The blast killed sixteen Israeli and Kenyan citizens. However, the number of casualties would have been much higher had the blast occurred a few minutes earlier. Because a large number of the arriving tourists chose to go into the hotel restaurant to eat breakfast, many of the Israelis avoided death or serious injury.

At the same time as the bombing was taking place at the Paradise Hotel, two terrorists standing in different locations fired shoulder-launched surface-to-air missiles at an Israeli charter flight that was returning to Tel Aviv from Mombasa airport with Israeli tourists from the Paradise Hotel. One rocket

missed the airplane completely but the second skidded off the fuselage, causing no injuries or damage to the aircraft. The attackers were able to escape in
a waiting vehicle, but evidence collected at the scene revealed that the two
attacks (on the plane and the Paradise Hotel) were carefully choreographed to
take place at the same time—a strategy that Al Qaeda has frequently employed
in past international attacks.

While many of Kenya's top political leaders reacted slowly to the notion that
an Al Qaeda cell might exist in their country or that Kenyan citizens might be
actively engaged in supporting terrorists, the two terrorist attacks in Nairobi
and Mombasa have resulted in even closer collaboration between the U.S. and
Kenya, especially in the military and intelligence areas. Following the 1998
attack on the American embassy, Kenyan officials cooperated fully in the investigation of the bombing. Kenyan police and intelligence officers welcomed
their American counterparts and actively assisted FBI investigators in tracking down leads in Mombasa and Nairobi and questioning dozens of potential
witnesses and suspects. The investigation was helped in its early stages by the
capture of al-Owahili, who had been in the truck that carried the bomb to the
rear of the embassy. Although many of the individuals involved in planning
and organizing the attack had fled the country, a number of suspects were
arrested overseas as they disembarked from planes that had left Kenya on the
morning of or the night before the blast. Mohamed Sadek Odeh, who was
arrested in Pakistan and swiftly returned to Kenya, and al-Owahili, who was
apprehended by Kenyan police, were promptly turned over to FBI and intelligence officials at the American embassy in Nairobi.[5] Because of the close
cooperation between U.S. and Kenyan authorities, the Kenyan government
did not seek to detain Sadek Odeh and al-Owahili or put them on trial in
Kenya. Acting with virtually no legal precedent or formalities, Kenyan officials
waived all local legal and extradition procedures and released the suspects
directly into U.S. custody. Fearful that Kenya might be subject to future terrorist reprisals, Kenyan officials agreed to turn the suspected terrorists over to
American authorities to prevent Kenya from becoming involved in what would
be a long, complex, and sensitive judicial procedure.

Surprisingly, no Kenyan citizens were arrested, convicted, or deported for
being involved in the embassy bombing, although a number of investigators
believed strongly that the bombing could not have taken place without some
type of local assistance. Most of the suspicion centered on a small group of
individuals in Mombasa's Muslim community, where some of the terrorist
suspects had established themselves before the bombing and where the small
panel truck that carried the embassy bomb had been modified in a local auto

repair shop. It was not until after the second major bombing that American and Kenyan investigators were able to confirm the existence of at least one Al Qaeda cell in Kenya and the full extent of the interlocking connection between Al Qaeda terrorists and a number of Kenyan families.

The successful and destructive attack on the Paradise Hotel shattered any doubt about Al Qaeda's presence and operating capabilities in Kenya. Although not nearly as devastating as the 1998 embassy attack, Kenyan, Israeli, and American officials responded quickly and within a matter of days were able to determine—from interviews with witnesses and evidence around the bombing site and at the Mombasa airport—that Al Qaeda operatives were responsible for the Mombasa blast and that the perpetrators had used the same modus operandi in planning the Mombasa and Nairobi attacks. Methodically, they had used the same materials, purchased locally, to construct their car bombs and then had followed the same routine in renting houses in upscale neighborhoods to make the bombs, rendezvous with the non-Kenyan suicide bombers, and coordinate and launch their simultaneous attacks.

But in the case of the Mombasa attacks, the terrorists were sloppy and perhaps overconfident. American and Israeli investigators, collaborating with Kenyan authorities, discovered a technical trail leading back to a small group of Kenyans who had been linked peripherally—through marriage, family, and an Islamic school—to some of the individuals suspected of being associated and involved with the 1998 embassy bombing. Although suspicions about some of these individuals had remained high, none had been arrested or indicted because of the absence of clear incriminating evidence. As American and Kenyan investigators in Mombasa continued their work, it became increasingly clear that links existed between the Nairobi and Mombasa bombings and between the foreign suicide bombers and a small group of local Muslims. Investigators were able to retrieve the two projectiles that were fired at the Israeli charter plane and to determine that the missiles came from a batch that had been stolen in the Middle East, several of which had been used in Saudi Arabia and Yemen. Investigators speculated that the missiles had been moved from Saudi Arabia to Yemen and then transported, undetected, across the Red Sea by dhow directly to northern Kenya, or to southern Somalia and then overland to Kenya.

Pursuing Terrorists in Kenya

Kenyan and American authorities publicly acknowledged that they were actively looking for three Africans in connection with the 1998 embassy attack and the 2002 hotel bombing: Fazul Abdullah Muhammed, Saleh Ali Saleh Nabhan, and Sheikh Ahmed Salim Swedan. Two of the three are Kenyan citizens and the third is a Comoran married to a Kenyan woman. All were directly linked to one of the two attacks and have been repeatedly identified by U.S. officials as the leading Al Qaeda operatives in East Africa.

Fazul Abdullah Muhammed, who has lived intermittently in Kenya for many years, is believed to be the leader of the group and is reputed to be one of the key strategists of the 1998 embassy bombing. Saleh Ali Saleh Nabhan, a Kenyan-born citizen, was one of the key operators in the 2002 Mombasa attacks. Nabhan reportedly rented the house where the bomb was built and purchased the vehicle that was used by the suicide bombers to blow up the Paradise Hotel. And Sheikh Ahmed Salim Swedan, also a Kenyan citizen, is wanted for his involvement in the embassy bombing, having bought and retrofitted the small panel truck that carried the bomb.

Although a great deal is now known about Al Qaeda's key leaders in Kenya, domestic politics and a host of systemic problems and bureaucratic shortcomings have slowed and sometimes derailed the fight against terrorist operations in Kenya and the region. Although many government officials have been extraordinarily supportive and helpful, others have not. President Daniel arap Moi sensed immediately the dangers that global terrorism posed to the Western community as well as to moderate pro-Western countries like Kenya. During his last five years in office, Moi endorsed and encouraged the close cooperation that developed between the U.S. and Kenyan security services, especially in the intelligence arena. In a very dramatic manifestation of his views following the 9/11 attacks in the United States, President Moi took to the streets of Nairobi and walked in a parade to protest bin Laden's actions and to express his sympathy for the victims of the Al Qaeda attacks in New York and Washington.

Following Moi's departure from office in December 2002, Mwai Kibaki, Kenya's current president, and his two closest political confidants, Karitu Murungi (minister of justice) and Chris Murangaru (former minister of state for internal administration and security), also recognized the need to take action against the ongoing terrorist threat in Kenya and East Africa. They were supported in their judgments by the senior leaders of Kenya's intelligence services. However, a significant number of high-ranking politicians and long-time civil servants rejected the notion that Kenya had a domestic terrorism problem and that the government's weak administration had contributed to it. Fearful of a backlash from Kenya's Islamic community, some politicians simply rebuffed the idea that any Kenyans were involved in terrorism. Others were concerned that acknowledging that Kenya had a home-grown terrorism problem would undermine the country's image and reputation and would devastate the country's international tourist industry. Among them were Kalonzo Musyoka, then Kenya's foreign minister, and Ambassador Francis Mutharia, Kenya's most powerful civil servant and the president's cabinet secretary.

Progress was also stifled by widespread corruption, inefficiency, and sometimes sheer incompetence throughout various levels of Kenya's bureaucracy, especially in the police force and in the customs and immigration services. Following the attack on the American embassy, investigators discovered that lax immigration procedures had allowed a least one terrorist to obtain fraudulent Kenyan travel documents and to remain in the country for more than two years.

Much more seriously, Kenyan police officers had Fazul Abdullah Muhammed in their custody on two different occasions, but let him get away. In July 2002, five months before he masterminded the destruction of the Paradise Hotel in Mombasa, Fazul was actually arrested and taken into custody in Mombasa for attempting to make a purchase with a stolen credit card. Despite the fact that his picture was in wide circulation because of his role in the 1998 bombing, he reportedly managed to escape one day later, when several police officers took him back to his house to retrieve stolen goods.[6] Twelve months later, Fazul escaped from police custody for a second time. In August 2003, police in Mombasa tracked down and arrested two Al Qaeda suspects wanted in connection with the hotel bombing. In the process of transporting them to the police station, one of the men exploded a concealed hand grenade, and in the ensuing confusion the second suspect, generally thought to be Fazul, escaped.[7]

It is widely believed that during his first arrest, Fazul succeeded in bribing low-level Kenyan police officers into setting him free, and that during his second arrest, improper police procedures and sheer incompetence (not thoroughly searching the two suspects) led to his escape. Sloppy police procedures also may have allowed Saleh Ali Saleh Nabhan to escape on at least one occasion.

Kenya's judicial authorities have not performed much better than the police in the war on terrorism. The attorney general's office, the government department most responsible for bringing suspects to trial, has not acted with great speed or purpose. Nor have the senior state prosecutors demonstrated any great legal skill in prosecuting the Kenyans arrested for allegedly aiding and abetting Al Qaeda operatives or for participating in the criminal conspiracies that produced the attacks in Nairobi and Mombasa. In June 2005, after over two years of preparations and judicial proceedings, Kenyan judges in two separate cases acquitted seven Kenyan nationals suspected of having planned, supported, and participated in the November 2002 destruction of the Paradise Hotel and the attempt to shoot down the Israeli airplane in Mombasa. The failure of the police to apprehend leading terrorist suspects and the failure of the courts to convict their accomplices will not improve Kenya's antiterrorist reputation among Western governments or serve as a serious deterrent to Kenyan nationals engaged in terrorist-related activities.

The Roots of Terrorist Support in Kenya

There is at least one Al Qaeda cell in the Mombasa region, and perhaps two. Al Qaeda leaders operating in Kenya have been able to rely on the support and sympathy of a small group of individuals in Kenya's Islamic community. Their ability to organize and operate clandestinely for months and years at a time demonstrates how deeply Al Qaeda's operatives are allied with some parts of Kenya's Muslim population.

Kenya's Muslim community constitutes only about 10 percent of its population, roughly 3 million people, but it is highly concentrated in the northeastern part of the country (among Kenyans of Somali origin) and along the Indian Ocean coast (among Kenyans of Arab origin and of African-Arab origin). Despite the widely accepted idea that Somalia and Somali groups in East Africa have been a source of terrorism, there is no proof that anyone in Kenya's Somali population has been directly involved in any Al Qaeda–related terrorist operations in Kenya. However, the same is not true of Muslims from Kenya's coastal community.

Most of the Muslims living along Kenya's coast have deep cultural, historical, religious, and linguistic ties to Saudi Arabia and the Gulf States. They are descended from Omani and Yemeni Arabs who sailed their dhows across the Indian Ocean from the Saudi Arabian peninsula to trade with Africans on the mainland. Some of those early Arab traders eventually settled and established cities and towns along Kenya's Indian Ocean coastline. After hundreds of years of intermarriage and Islamic proselytizing among indigenous Africans living along the coast, large numbers of Africans, some of mixed Arab and African ancestry known as Swahili, also became devout Muslims, adopting modified Arab dress, culture, and religious traditions. The ease of transportation across the Red Sea and Indian Ocean also helped to keep their religious, cultural, and linguistic ties with Yemen, Oman, and Saudi Arabia strong. Until Kenya's independence, the predominately Muslim-populated coastal zone was regarded as a British protectorate (not a colony) and was governed separately and differently from the rest of what today is modern Kenya. As a result, many people along the coast viewed themselves differently from the rest of the Kenya; some coastal families of Arab descent maintained stronger ties with the Saudi Arabian peninsula than with Kenya's largely African interior.

During the years prior to Kenya's independence and for nearly a decade afterward, the coast prospered economically. Revenues and jobs from a growing tourist industry, the Mombasa harbor, and a rapidly expanding transport network put Mombasa on the financial map and created a vibrant and successful economic environment. However, over the past thirty years the situation has changed significantly. A major influx of Africans from western Kenya has seriously undercut employment opportunities for coastal residents, especially on the docks and in low-paying jobs in the tourist and transportation sectors. In addition, the consolidation of political power in Nairobi under Presidents Kenyatta and Moi resulted in a substantial reorientation of the government's political and spending priorities. As a result, the political influence and economic prosperity of the coastal Muslim community declined sharply.

Today, Kenya's Muslim community holds both economic and political grievances against the government in Nairobi, composed largely of ethnic Africans, for not providing the coastal peoples with their fair share of the country's social services and financial benefits. Muslim leaders assert that Mombasa and the coast, which include only 10 percent of Kenya's population, account for as much as 25 to 30 percent of Kenya's wealth and economic productivity. Yet, most Muslims along the coast say that they have fallen further and further behind economically since Kenya's independence. They complain that the revenue generated from beach tourism and the port of Mombasa have subsidized the growth and development of other parts of the country.

As a result, relative to the rest of Kenya, living conditions all along the coast have declined and health care and educational attainments have fallen steeply among coastal Muslims since the late 1960s. Coastal Muslims also claim that they have been cut out of much of the labor market and that all of the best jobs in the tourist industry and the transportation sector have gone to Kenyans of African ancestry—not those of Arab and Muslim heritage from along the coast. Muslim grievances have intensified over the last two decades, as the Kenyan economy has contracted and competition for jobs has become more acute.

Most of the political and economic grievances of the coastal community have been championed by senior religious leaders, not by the region's political and parliamentary representatives. Throughout most of the 1980s and

1990s, the Muslim community was poorly served by its political leadership. Many of the region's most senior Muslim political leaders were members of the then-ruling party, the Kenyan African National Union (KANU). Some were close associates of former president Moi. After decades in power, they had grown increasingly corrupt and out of touch with the Islamic communities that they represented. No one fit this picture better than Sharrif Nassir, a close and aging colleague of Moi and the most powerful political leader on the coast. During his last decade in office, Nassir did little or nothing for the district he represented or for the larger Muslim community that composed his Mombasa constituency. In a vain attempt to get better representation for the coast and the Muslim constituency along the coast and the northeast, Muslim leaders established the Islamic Party of Kenya. Fearing that the party would divide Kenyans and generate sectarian political strife, Moi moved swiftly in 1992 to outlaw political parties based solely on religious grounds. Although the banning of Kenya's Islamic Party did not generate any sustained outcry, it probably further embittered a more fundamentalist segment of the Muslim community that saw the move as a way to maintain KANU's national political dominance as well as to suppress the Muslim community.

As opportunities and hope have dried up along the coast, many Muslims have turned toward Islam and the east—for jobs, education, and religious support. Young men, especially those with some knowledge of Arabic, have gone off to the Middle East to find employment and economic opportunity. Others have traveled there to seek academic scholarships and further secular education. Others have gone abroad for religious and cultural studies. Disgruntled as most of them were when they left, a very small number became radicalized and returned to preach and stoke the anger of others at home. Where Kenyan governmental organizations have faltered, Muslim charitable organizations, mostly from Saudi Arabia and the Gulf States, have stepped up their activities and increased their funding for clinics, hospitals, and Arabic-language religious schools in both rural and urban communities along the coast. The Saudi Arabian embassy in Nairobi has also been actively helping to improve social and economic conditions by supporting the construction of schools and mosques and assisting Kenya's major Islamic leaders and their organizations. Within this broad mix of activities, a small number of Kenyan Muslims have come under the influence of radical Islamic thinking, with radical imams preaching a stricter adherence to Islam, a greater disdain for Western culture, and a strong abhorrence of the United States as an anti-Islamic state. The emergence of Al Qaeda in Kenya is an outgrowth of the alienation and radicalization of a small number of Kenyan Muslims.

Kenyan and U.S. Responses to Increased Al Qaeda Activity

Despite the close collaboration between Kenyan and American intelligence, law enforcement, and security officials after the Mombasa bombing, officials in Washington and Nairobi had different perceptions about the continuing nature of the terrorist threat and the necessary response to combat it. Terrorist experts in Washington thought that another attack in Kenya was imminent and that the Kenyan government was moving too slowly in upgrading the country's security and detaining Kenyans suspected of supporting terrorist activities. On the other side, many senior and mid-level Kenyan officials accused the United States of exaggerating the threat and portrayed their country as a victim of international terrorism. Many blamed the terrorist problem on outsiders, especially Somali: the absence of any central authority, the presence of organized warlords, the growth of politicized Islamic organizations like Al Itihad Al Islamiya, and the proliferation of thousands of small arms, combined with Kenya's long porous northern border, were enough to indict Somalia and its people. As a result, Kenyan officials were extremely reluctant to acknowledge that any Kenyan citizens were directly and actively involved in carrying out terrorist activities in their own country.

Even though there was growing evidence that a small number of individuals in the Muslim communities in Mombasa, Malindi, and Lamu were probably aiding and abetting terrorists, senior government officials were extremely concerned about further alienating the coastal community and arousing anger and resentment against the government and KANU in the Islamic community. As additional evidence surfaced about individuals who might have aided the terrorists involved in the Paradise Hotel blast and the embassy bombing, the United States increased its pressure on the government of Kenya to arrest and prosecute them. The U.S. ambassador appeared on local television and wrote several articles explaining the threat that international terrorism posed to the safety and well-being of Kenya's citizens as well as to the country's economy and international image.[8] The embassy urged some nonessential U.S. personnel to leave the country and the United States released travel advisories warning Americans to postpone unnecessary visits to Kenya.

As concerns about security mounted, Kenya was dismayed by the White House's decision to postpone President Bush's trip to Africa in early 2003. His itinerary had originally included a prominent stop in Nairobi to applaud Kenya's extraordinarily successful national elections in late 2002 and to push along the North-South peace talks for Sudan. When the president's trip was finally rescheduled, the White House dropped the Kenyan stop entirely (and substituted Uganda). Kenyan officials were bitter and visibly upset. Although the White House did not say so publicly, the primary reason for canceling the stop was fear that Al Qaeda terrorists in East Africa, who had still not been apprehended, might seek to use shoulder-launched surface-to-air missiles against an official U.S. plane, just as they had against the Israeli plane in 2002.

During this same period, the Kenyan government, with significant financial and technical assistance from the governments of the United States and Britain, stepped up its security at the main airport in Nairobi. It appointed a new airport security chief, installed new passenger and baggage screening equipment, and established roving military patrols in and around the airport, as well as along the final landing and take-off approaches. In 2003, the government temporarily suspended all flights into and out of Somalia from Wilson airport, a secondary aerodrome in downtown Nairobi that had been the source of ongoing security concerns because of its proximity to the temporary site of the American embassy.

Stung by American and British criticism that it did not have effective legislation in place to apprehend and arrest terrorists in an expeditious manner, the government hurriedly prepared a new antiterrorism bill and submitted it to parliament. The legislation was widely criticized by Kenya's Muslim community and also by many opposition politicians, who claimed that it would abridge the civil liberties of the country's citizens, roll back the clock on recent democratic gains, and lead to new human rights abuses by the government. As domestic pressure mounted against the legislation, the government quietly withdrew it.

After persistent prodding, the Kenyan authorities have finally recognized and responded to the terrorist threat. They have upgraded their airport security, improved their immigration and screening procedures—especially for citizens from high-risk countries—established better coordination among their police, military, and intelligence services, and dedicated more resources to scrutinizing those Kenyan citizens who might pose a terrorist threat. They have also tried to gather more accurate information on the number of madrassas and Qur'anic schools operating in the country and the number of Muslim organizations funded from overseas that are at work in Kenya.

The United States and Britain have also been actively working with the Kenyan authorities to improve antiterrorist efforts. In 2003, the United States established a $100 million East Africa Counterterrorism Initiative (EACTI). Approximately $35 million of that amount has been allocated to Kenya to improve coastal, border, and airport security. The Combined Joint Task Force–Horn of Africa based in Djibouti has also been actively engaged in helping to improve the capabilities of the Kenyan military along Kenya's northern borders with Ethiopia and Somalia—which have been penetrated by insurgents and bandits from both of these neighbors. Much more should be done.

Conclusions and Policy Recommendations

U.S. money and assistance and Kenya's increased concern about and attention to international terrorism will substantially advance the war against terrorism in Kenya and the region. However, none of these actions will end the threat or eliminate the potential for another catastrophic terrorist attack. In order to reduce the threat of terrorism in Kenya, officials in Nairobi must recognize that effectively dealing with terrorism requires a coordinated security response from the police, military, and intelligence services, as well as a comprehensive social, economic, and political response that focuses on Kenya's Muslim population. Kenyan officials must continue to improve national security procedures and dramatically overhaul elements of the internal security apparatus. Kenya's police force, its customs and immigration services, and its border patrol and coastal protection units are professionally weak, poorly managed, and underfunded. As a result of poor pay and low professional standards, many policemen and immigration officials remain susceptible to corruption by criminal as well as terrorist elements. Some American and Kenyan investigators believe that Fazul Abdullah Muhammed, Al Qaeda's most senior leader in East Africa, would be in custody today were it not for the incompetence and corruption in the Kenyan police force.

Kenyan political leaders and senior government officials must also recognize and address the social, economic, and political causes that generate support as well as sympathy for terrorist causes. Government officials and political leaders must reduce the social marginalization of the country's approximately 3 million Muslims. Until Kenya is able to spend more on the development of the coast, expand political and economic opportunities in the country's coastal communities, and reduce or redress the growing anger of a new generation of Muslims, the hot, humid breeding grounds of East African terror will continue to fester in Kenya.

The United States has a clear strategic interest in helping Kenya to deal with these issues and should pursue and fund a set of bilateral and regional policies that advance our mutual objectives. On the bilateral side, the United States should:

—Substantially increase its overall development assistance allocation to Kenya in recognition of that country's critical importance to the region, its current and past friendship with the United States, and its current cooperation in the fight against terrorism.

—Increase and direct more economic, public health, and educational assistance to the largely Muslim communities along the coast and in the northeastern region of Kenya. In doing so, it should put a special emphasis on allocating more funds to education and scholarships for girls, the expansion of rural health care clinics, and the extension of microfinance and micro-enterprise programs.

—Reestablish a permanent American diplomatic presence in Mombasa by reopening the former American consulate general with capacity to carry out a full range of diplomatic activities. Above all else, the consulate should focus on expanding American outreach to the Muslim community. It should also coordinate and support U.S. military activity along the coast.

—Develop and help finance an ongoing program to help the Kenyan government to improve its border and coastal security; strengthen its passport and immigration system, especially at its main airports; and improve its counterterrorism programs.

—Encourage the government to strengthen its judicial and legal systems and to enact effective legislation that will make it easer for the justice ministry to arrest and successfully prosecute individuals involved in or actively supporting terrorist activities.

—Expand the counterterrorism and intelligence training of Kenyan counterterrorism officials in the United States and develop mechanisms for expanding bilateral collaboration and cooperation on counterterrorism, intelligence, immigration, and port security issues.

The United States must also recognize that enhancing Kenya's security and counterterrorism posture cannot be considered separately from the instability and insecurity that prevails in Somalia and along Kenya's other lightly patrolled northern borders, especially those with Ethiopia and the Sudan. In order to improve Kenya's overall security and to promote greater regional stability, the United States should:

—Develop a more comprehensive policy toward Somalia that will advance peace and reunification in that country, drawing on Kenya's leadership in the Intergovernmental Authority on Development (IGAD).

—Create a specialized and effective mechanism or subregional organization that can coordinate closely and on a real time basis on transnational issues, especially terrorism, arms trafficking, money laundering, and the movement of suspicious individuals across borders and throughout the region.

—Put more diplomatic and political pressure on Ethiopia and Saudi Arabia to help to resolve internecine conflicts in Somalia.

—Establish a mechanism to provide more visible funding for development assistance in Somalia, especially in the areas of education and health care, even before diplomatic relations with a government in Mogadishu are formally resumed. The United States should also revive the plan of establishing a Somali-language radio station in Kenya that would broadcast news and information to Somalia.

No one of these recommendations by itself will affect the outcome of the security situation in Kenya, but a number of them taken together will help strengthen Kenya's antiterrorism posture and its will to remain one of the United States' best and most reliable partners in the fight against terrorism in East Africa and the greater Horn of Africa.

Notes

1. Kenya is the only large country in East Africa and the greater Horn of Africa that has never broken diplomatic ties or had a major or prolonged diplomatic rift with the United States. Political upheavals in Uganda (during Idi Amin's era), Ethiopia (during Mengistu's rule), Somalia (after Siad Barre's demise), and the Sudan (under Bashir and Turabi) have all resulted in the recall of U.S. ambassadors or the closure of U.S. embassies. Political differences with Tanzania resulted in the withdrawal of the Peace Corps during President Julius Nyerere's reign.

2. British troops have been training in Kenya since 1945, and Kenya remains one of Britain's most important warm weather live-fire training locations.

3. For over two decades, the agreement was the only one of its kind in existence between the United States and a sub-Saharan African country. In 2003, a Status of Forces Agreement was successfully negotiated with Djibouti as a part of America's effort to increase its post-9/11 presence in the Horn of Africa, to monitor developments in Somalia and Yemen, and to prevent the spread of international terrorism.

4. John Peterson, *Defending Arabia* (London, 1986), 118; Joel D. Barkan, "Kenya after Moi," *Foreign Affairs*, LXXXIII (2004), 87–100.

5. Mohamed Sadek Odeh and Mohamed Rashed Daoud al-Owahili were indicted in the U.S. District Court for the Southern District of New York on November 4, 1998, with Osama bin Laden, Mohammad Atef (bin Laden's military deputy), Wadhi El Hage (a naturalized American citizen and bin Laden's former secretary), and Fazul Abdullah Muhammed. Wadhi El Hage helped establish the Al Qaeda cell in Kenya and was the principal planner for the August 7 bombings in East Africa. U.S. Department of State, "Patterns of Global Terrorism Report 2003" (Washington, D.C., 2004).

6. Andrew England, "Terror Suspect Evades, Outwits Kenyan Police," Associated Press (June 24, 2004).

7. "Terrorist Linked to al-Qaeda," South Africa Press Association AP (August 4, 2003).

8. Carson, "What We Can Do to Fight and Defeat Terrorism," *Daily Nation* (Nairobi) (June 1, 2003).

Contributors

Robert D. Burrowes taught at New York University (1961–1972), the American University of Beirut (1973–1975), Hunter College, CUNY (1985–1988), and the University of Washington (1991–2003). He has resided, conducted political research, and done other work in the Yemen Arab Republic and in the united Republic of Yemen for many years, most recently from October 2003 through June 2004 and from January to March 2005. Burrowes is the author of dozens of articles and papers on contemporary Yemeni politics and two books, *The Yemen Arab Republic: The Politics of Development, 1962–1986* (Boulder, 1987); and *The Historical Dictionary of Yemen* (Lanham, 1995).

Timothy Carney is now a consultant in the private sector, after spending thirty-two years as a U.S. Foreign Service officer. He was the last U.S. ambassador accredited to the Sudan, having departed in November 1997. Carney and his wife will conclude a three-year book project with a British photographer and his wife to photograph all of the Sudan. Carney has served in various modern peacekeeping missions, including Iraq in 2003, Cambodia in 1992–1993, and Somalia in 1993–1994.

JOHNNIE CARSON joined the National Defense University as senior vice president in August 2003 upon his return from the Republic of Kenya, where he served as U.S. ambassador from August 1999 to July 2003. Prior to the assignment to Kenya, he served as principal deputy assistant secretary for the Bureau of African Affairs at the Department of State. He is a minister-counselor in the Senior Foreign Service. Since joining in 1969, Carson served as U.S. ambassador to the Republic of Zimbabwe and to the Republic of Uganda, and served in the U.S. embassies in Nigeria, Mozambique, Portugal, and Botswana. At the Department of State he held the position of desk officer for Angola, Mozambique, and Namibia in the Bureau of Intelligence and Research. Carson served as staff director for the Africa Subcommittee of the U.S. House of Representatives and as staff officer in the Staff Secretariat in the Office of the Secretary of State. Before joining the Foreign Service, Carson was a Peace Corps volunteer in Tanzania.

DAN CONNELL is a lecturer in journalism and African politics at Simmons College. His reports and commentary on the Horn of Africa have been carried by the BBC, the Voice of America, AP, Reuters, the *Boston Globe*, the *Guardian*, *Le Monde*, *Foreign Affairs*, and the *Nation*, among other media in North America and Europe, and he has consulted for numerous aid agencies and human rights organizations. A two-time MacArthur Foundation grantee, he is the author of six books, including *Against All Odds: A Chronicle of the Eritrean Revolution* (Trenton, 1997); *Rethinking Revolution* (Trenton, 2002); and *Collected Articles on the Eritrean Revolution* (Trenton, 2003, 2004). Connell founded and directed the Boston-based development agency Grassroots International. Shortly after 9/11, he founded the Gloucester-based Cape Ann Forum, which he continues to chair.

KENNETH J. MENKHAUS is professor of political science at Davidson College and a specialist on the Horn of Africa. He held a Fulbright research grant in southern Somalia in 1988–1989. He returned to Somalia in 1991 to work with the Red Cross on famine relief. In 1993–1994 he served as special political advisor in the UN Operation in Somalia; and in 1994–1995 he was visiting civilian professor at the U.S. Army Peacekeeping Institute. In 2002 he was the recipient of a U.S. Institute of Peace grant to study protracted conflict in the Horn of Africa. He is author of over two dozen articles and monographs on Somalia, including *Somalia: State Collapse and the Threat of Terrorism* (London, 2004).

ROBERT I. ROTBERG is president of the World Peace Foundation and director of the Program on Intrastate Conflict and Conflict Resolution in the Kennedy School of Government, Harvard University. He was professor of political science and history at MIT; academic vice president at Tufts University; and president of Lafayette College. He is the author and editor of numerous books and articles on U.S. foreign policy, Africa, Asia, and the Caribbean, most recently *Crafting the New Nigeria: Confronting the Challenges* (Boulder, 2004); *When States Fail: Causes and Consequences* (Princeton, 2004); *State Failure and State Weakness in a Time of Terror* (Washington, D.C., 2003); *Ending Autocracy, Enabling Democracy: The Tribulations of Southern Africa 1960–2000* (Washington, D.C., 2002); *Peacekeeping and Peace Enforcement in Africa: Methods of Conflict Prevention* (Washington, D.C., 2001); *Truth v. Justice: The Morality of Truth Commissions* (Princeton, 2000).

LANGE SCHERMERHORN's Foreign Service career included assignments in the Department of State, Sri Lanka, Vietnam, Iran, the United Kingdom, Belgium, and lastly as ambassador to the Republic of Djibouti (1998–2000). She served as the political advisor to CJTF-HOA from October 2003 to June 2004. She also wrote "Threats and Responses: Djibouti: Fulcrum of the Horn," United States Institute of Peace (Washington, D.C., 2004).

DAVID H. SHINN was a career Foreign Service officer for thirty-seven years before becoming an adjunct professor in the Elliott School of International Affairs at George Washington University. While with the State Department, he served in seven countries in Africa and one in the Middle East. He was ambassador to Burkina Faso (1987–1990) and Ethiopia (1996–1999). His Horn of Africa experience also includes positions as desk officer for Somalia and Djibouti and assistant desk officer for Ethiopia (1969–1971), deputy chief of mission in Khartoum in the Sudan (1983–1986), State Department coordinator for Somalia during the U.S.-UN intervention in 1993, and director of East African and Horn of African Affairs (1993–1996). He co-authored *A Historical Dictionary of Ethiopia* (Lanham, 2004) and has written numerous articles concerning the Horn of Africa.

INDEX